BEFORE
THE
FIRST
SHOTS
ARE FIRED

BEFORE THE FIRST SHOTS ARE FIRED

How America Can Win or Lose Off the Battlefield

GENERAL TONY ZINNI

AND

TONY KOLTZ

palgrave
macmillan

First published in 2014 by PALGRAVE MACMILLAN® in the United
States—a division of St. Martin's Press LLC, 175 Fifth Avenue, New York, NY
10010.

Where this book is distributed in the UK, Europe and the rest of the world,
this is by Palgrave Macmillan, a division of Macmillan Publishers Limited,
registered in England, company number 785998, of Houndmills, Basingstoke,
Hampshire RG21 6XS.

Palgrave Macmillan is the global academic imprint of the above companies and
has companies and representatives throughout the world.

Palgrave® and Macmillan® are registered trademarks in the United States, the
United Kingdom, Europe and other countries.

ISBN: 978-1-137-27938-5

Library of Congress Cataloging-in-Publication Data is available from the
Library of Congress.

A catalogue record of the book is available from the British Library.

Design by Letra Libre, Inc.

First edition: September 2014

10 9 8 7 6 5 4 3 2 1

Printed in the United States of America.

CONTENTS

PREFACE

SEVERAL YEARS AGO I SET OUT TO WRITE A BOOK about the differences between the conflicts we find ourselves embroiled in today and the conflicts of the past. But as my research and thinking progressed, I began to reflect more and more on actions that happened away from the battlefield and how significantly these actions affected success or failure on the battlefield, especially those that were taken, or not taken, before we put our troops in harm's way. That seemed to me to be a far more important story, and far more helpful to understanding how we should deal with military commitments today.

When I joined the United States Marine Corps as an eighteen-year-old in 1961, I would have told you that wars are always decided entirely on the battlefield. That's where the generals win or lose. I retired in 2000 after four decades of service and multiple experiences in wars and military interventions. By then I had come to realize that there is more to it than that. Political decisions, intelligence estimates, strategies (or their absence), and many other non-battlefield components influenced outcomes to a far greater degree than that eighteen-year-old new Marine could have ever imagined. These off the battlefield components have become increasingly significant as each new intervention is attempted in today's complex world.

Few Americans realize how many essential pieces have to fall into place before Johnny goes marching off to war, or how much these pieces drive success or failure after he deploys "over there." If we have a top-notch team of decision makers, strategists, and analysts in Washington, Johnny's or Jane's chances of success on the battlefield are exponentially enhanced.

There have been times in the past when we've had that team and times when we didn't.

"War is too important a matter to leave to soldiers," said French premier Georges Clemenceau—an idea often rephrased as "War is too important to be left to generals." Truth is, I've never met a general who wants a war to be left to him alone. When our nation sends military forces into action, every general I have known wants his civilian political masters as committed, involved, and accountable as he himself must be.

Too often, that is not the case. And too often, I have seen severe disconnects between civilian and military leaders. There is a war battlespace and a "Washington battlespace," as former Defense Secretary Robert Gates calls it.[1] These battlespaces are not in sync; they are separate and distinct. This split—I would call it a chasm—lies behind all the failures Gates saw in the bumbling management of two wars and other twenty-first-century crises. Instead of direction and leadership, we have political infighting, personal frictions, political generals who lost their warfighting ethos while serving in the capital, and greater anxiety over political blowback than battlefield success.

The split is growing and must be fixed.

To fix it, we need to analyze our past military experiences, especially our most recent ones, and learn from them.

Tony Zinni

ONE

HOW THE HELL DID
WE GET HERE?

Never, never, never believe any war will be smooth and easy, or that anyone who embarks on the strange voyage can measure the tides and hurricanes he will encounter. The statesman who yields to war fever must realize that once the signal is given, he is no longer the master of policy but the slave of unforeseeable and uncontrollable events.

Sir Winston Churchill

Everything in war is simple, but the simplest thing is difficult. The difficulties accumulate and end by producing a kind of friction that is inconceivable unless one has experienced war.

Carl von Clausewitz

OVER THE LAST FIVE DECADES, I HAVE PERSONALLY taken part in commitments of our military to a variety of missions inside and outside our country, ranging from war to humanitarian assistance, and I've witnessed many more. I have followed these commitments from their initial spark or trigger, through the planning and execution, and to the final assessment after it was all over. I have seen these experiences from every possible perspective, from the battlefield to decision briefs inside the Oval Office. More than anything else, I've been impressed in each of these actions by the tremendous dedication, adaptability, and resourcefulness of our troops on the ground. They take the mission to heart and give their all to succeed. They have never let us down.

And yet, after our military actions have ended, I've too often been left with worrisome questions. Why do we now find ourselves fighting so many wars that end without a clear victory? In recent times the end state of American wars and military interventions hardly ever looks anything like their original goals. Too often there is a disconnect between decision and conclusion. I'm sure President Kennedy did not foresee the consequences when he decided to greatly increase the number of advisors into Vietnam in the early 1960s, nor did President Johnson when he began sending in US ground forces there, nor did President Bush when he ordered the toppling of the Taliban in Afghanistan and the invasion of Iraq. Time and again, I have come away from a military commitment with a nagging sense that our involvement started with a clean slate, as though earlier ones have been forgotten or ignored. We seem to start essentially from scratch each time we consider launching another military action. Didn't we learn from the last one, or the one before that? Do wars and conflicts have to be like the film *Groundhog Day,* with each one doomed to repeat earlier mistakes?

And ultimately, how do we get into these conflicts in the first place?

The course and end state of every war may be unknowable in every detail, but the general process of military commitment follows a clearly repeating pattern, with similar stages. We can extract lessons from this pattern that will help us understand the actions we need to take, or to avoid, when the next foreign crisis appears.

Although we have been struggling for decades to define our role and purpose in an ever more confused and confusing world, one thing is certain. The world is much more interdependent and interlocked than it was when the Iron Curtain came crashing down. That means American interests and security, as well as the global leadership we have taken up and that the rest of the world expects of us, will continue to require our military to be involved in missions around the globe. Still, we have to be realistic. Our resources and abilities are limited; we can't do it all. Carefully choosing our commitments and courses of involvement and clarifying our objectives at the outset are more crucial today than ever before.

Americans often imagine that when we're hit with a troubling event that may require a military response, the president and his chief advisors make a quick but thorough study of the options; he forms a clear-eyed decision; the armed forces are launched; and the crisis is on the way to resolution. In reality, military responses normally take a twisted path, from the triggering event to conclusion to long-term impact. Virtually every recent American military operation follows a disconnected, sometimes convoluted, series of actions that lead to outcomes we never foresaw or intended.

"How the hell did we get here?" is the question we are left with when the smoke clears. And, inevitably, the answers we get from the men and women who lead us into these commitments are laced with excuses. "We can never know how things will turn out," they tell us with a bewildered shrug. "It's the nature of war to be unpredictable." Or they say, "The burden of all our responsibilities and the crisis response timing made clear planning and actions impossible." Or, "Every war is different."

These are copouts.

VIETNAM—NOT OUR FATHER'S WAR

In August 1970 I went back to Vietnam for my second tour of duty there. American troops had been fully committed to the war since the 1965 decision by President Johnson to send ground forces to the conflict. The initial advise, support, and train phase of the war ended with that decision, and for the next five years America clearly owned the war. But five years of brutal fighting never produced the results the generals had predicted. With each incremental increase of troop strength that was requested, and then granted by the Johnson administration, the anticipated victory slipped further from our grasp. Richard Nixon in 1968 had campaigned on a promise to end the war. Now, with the Nixon administration fully in place, we were systematically withdrawing. How would this end? That was a question many of us who had fought in the Vietnam War were asking. We already knew the answer to the other basic questions about how and why we had gotten into it—a slowly escalating and winding path that spanned four presidential administrations since that of Dwight D. Eisenhower's in the 1950s.

By 1970 I had been on active duty for five years. During those five years, the Vietnam War had become the most critical and consuming part of my life.

During my previous tour in 1967, I was a young lieutenant serving as an infantry advisor to the battle-hardened Vietnamese Marines. The experience opened my eyes to perspectives available to few Americans. We wore their uniforms, spoke their language, ate their food, lived in their villages, fought in every part of their beautiful country—rugged high-lands, steaming jungles, coastal plains, delta swamps—and encountered few other Americans. I lived through a different kind of war from the one experienced by US troops who saw Vietnam from inside our own units. I made a very different connection to the culture and the people. I began to see the war through their eyes.

For the people of Vietnam, the war would continue to be what it had always been—seemingly endless and pointless violence, springing out of the ambitions of colonial powers, oriental empires, and clashing ideologies. The nation had not known true peace since before the Japanese invasion (1940) during World War II. After Japan's surrender in 1945, the French returned to reclaim their colonial possession. The Vietnamese resisted, and the French Indochina War followed. When that conflict ended in French defeat in 1954, the nation was divided into the Communist North and nominally democratic South. War broke out again, and the people were tossed back into the cauldron of violence. Generations had never experi-enced lasting peace; the people were exhausted.

In my months living and fighting with the Vietnamese Marines, I made dozens of close Vietnamese friends and got to know their society and culture from the inside. I felt for them. They deserved better than the seemingly never-ending bloodshed they were caught up in. I hoped the South would prevail and they would find that elusive lasting peace. But

I left that tour unsure whether our approach to this war would get them there. I wanted to believe that their sacrifices, and ours, would bring the kind of victory we sought. But I questioned whether our chosen course would achieve it.

We got into the war to stop the communists from tumbling the "dominoes," the small nations of Southeast Asia under threat of Red domination. We went at this mission with tremendous passion and commitment. We would bring peace, democracy, and freedom to these poor, beleaguered people. Eventually and unfortunately, we allowed ourselves to believe we would achieve these goals by battlefield attrition. We would shoot our way to victory. Sure, we mouthed the words of pacification and seeking to win hearts and minds. We even set up myriad organizations and programs to be measured from every which way to show we were winning this part of the fight. In reality, however, the priority for the United States was winning it all on the battlefield.

Our magnificent troops lived up to their end of the bargain. Despite the withering of support from the folks back home, our troops gave every last measure of effort. But the American victories on the battlefield clearly weren't enough to win the war. We fought through the same hills, villages, and rice paddies over and over again.

My experiences on the ground in Vietnam taught me a lesson that has resonated ever more fully with time. The war we were fighting could only be won or lost in the hearts of the people of Vietnam. This wasn't just a slogan; it was a reality. "We need something to die for," an elderly woman in a rural rice paddy village told me back then. She understood firsthand the clear contest of wills that lay at the heart of the war. The enemy was directly focused on the prize, the people. You only had to read the words of Mao Tse-tung to understand this: "The richest source of power to wage war lies in the masses of the people. The guerrilla must move among the people as a fish swims in the sea." He and Ho Chi Minh knew what the insurgents needed from the people—fear, apathy, or support. Any of these would do. To counter the insurgents, we needed people's courage, commitment, and rejection of the enemy.

These truths were confirmed in conversations I had with captured Vietcong and North Vietnamese army fighters and villagers who supported them, in captured documents translated by Vietnamese Marine officers, and even in mail we took from a carrier we ambushed while he was making deliveries in a region we patrolled. These sources showed how the intense indoctrination that enemy combatants and supporters had been put through had convinced them of the rightness of their cause and the inevitability of their victory. They had a laser-like focus on winning over the people or coercing them into submission.

The true battle—for the souls of the people—was a difficult one for the United States to win. We were outsiders; the cultural differences that separated us and the Vietnamese people were great. We have never fully understood what it takes to win conflicts like these, with stakes like these. We've never understood that when we intervene, we own it. In the eyes of the Vietnamese people, the rotating generals taking over their government by coup after coup in Saigon belonged to us, just as the corrupt government in Afghanistan does now. We've never entirely grasped that no matter how low-cost these interventions seem when we start out, they end up costing far more in casualties, treasure, troop commitments, and prestige than we anticipated. No one, least of all our political leaders, expected Iraq and Afghanistan to become trillion-dollar wars.

This doesn't mean that conflicts like those in Vietnam or Afghanistan are unwinnable, or that the people will always cross over to the homegrown insurgent. I believe we could have prevailed in Vietnam if the people had had a government in Saigon they could fight for, a government they could believe in, that was there to meet their needs. Insurgencies have failed in the past when their leaders misjudged the people. The most revered guerrilla leader of the last century, Che Guevara, whose bearded, piercing image is on the T-shirts of wannabe radicals and guerrillas all over the world, failed catastrophically in Bolivia. After a string of minor successes, his revolution failed to ignite the hearts and souls of the people. He ended up wounded, emaciated, captured, and executed. "The peasants do not give us any help, and they are turning into informers," he lamented just before his death.

In Vietnam, victory wasn't all about firepower. Our leaders did not understand this. In their previous experiences if you defeated the opposing military on the battlefield then everything else would fall into place. To them this was a logical, sequential process. But the conflict in Vietnam was a simultaneous war, not a sequential one. You had to fight and build—or rebuild—a society at the same time. To paraphrase a senior general, Lewis W. "Lew" Walt, the commander of US Marines in Vietnam in the mid-60s, this was a strange war with a strange strategy. It wasn't his clean World War II experience in which you knew who the enemy was.

In between tours, I taught counterinsurgency theory—the importance of understanding the culture, the unique tactics, and the characteristics of this form of conflict—to young US Marine officers headed for Vietnam.

In 1970, I was back in-country as a captain commanding a US Marine infantry company in the north.

By then the unpopularity of the war back home had led to the opening stages of the US withdrawal. The new strategic bumper sticker was "Vietnamization"—the label given to President Nixon's policy aimed at extracting American forces from the conflict and turning the war over to a fully prepared and supported South Vietnam. At least, that was the sales pitch. Quietly, many involved in conducting the war felt, and privately grumbled, that Vietnamization was just a maneuver to gain a decent interval while we got out in an orderly fashion. Then we would hope for the best for our South Vietnamese friends. I knew the South Vietnamese forces could hold their own after we left as long as we provided training and support, but I doubted we had the will to continue to provide all they would need to stave off the inevitable onslaughts from the North Vietnamese Army.

Our political leaders wanted out. The will of the American people was shaken by the casualties, cost, duration, and lack of a definitive end.

From my perspective, at the time of my second tour of duty, we had never addressed two great barriers to a successful end. The enemy had a secure base of operations in North Vietnam, and the government we supported in the South was corrupt and out of touch with the people's aspirations and needs. Even to a junior officer like me, it was clear that as long as the enemy had a sanctuary where he could regroup, recover, and refit, and as long as the people didn't have a responsible, credible, and honest government to respect and fight for, the struggle could not have a clear, positive ending. Years later, I saw a similar situation in Afghanistan with the Taliban's safe haven in Pakistan and a corrupt government in Kabul. "Blindly following COIN [counterinsurgency] doctrine," wrote Karl W. Eikenberry, the former US ambassador to Afghanistan and a retired general who had commanded the Coalition forces there, "led the US military to fixate on defeating the insurgency while giving short shrift to Afghan politics."[1] He could have been writing about Vietnam forty years earlier.

The brave young Vietnamese Marine officers I fought next to shared this view. They were frustrated by the leadership in Saigon and the protected sanctuary of the North. They needed our help to get powerful outside forces (North Vietnam, China, and Russia) off their backs and our influence to change their government. They did not need us to push them aside and lead a charge headlong into remote villages. As one Vietnamese battalion commander told me in frustration after a US unit twice ignored his offer to lead an operation, "You do my job once and I will thank you. You do it twice and you have the job."

If you travel to Vietnam today, the Vietnamese people now call the war "The American War." If we wanted to prevail in that war, it couldn't be our war. The villages had to be won by the South Vietnamese government and military, and those villagers had to want them to win. We cannot arrogantly write the doctrine and totally take over the mission to transform a society, then push the mission off on a poorly prepared local force when we tire of it.

When I taught counterinsurgency theory between Vietnam tours, I taught a doctrine derived from studies of past insurgencies. Prevailing in these conflicts, the doctrine stated, required three conditions: you must effectively fight the guerrillas; you must protect the people, vital resources, and infrastructure; and you must improve the environment (change the conditions and deal with issues that fueled the insurgency and gained support for the insurgents). All of it made sense, but for me the last task was the most important, and it was the one where we were failing. We would not succeed if we wanted to win this war more than the majority of the Vietnamese people themselves did.

How would the war end? I kept asking myself. I had no clear answer.

My battalion commander at the time of my second tour of duty, Lieutenant Colonel Bernard E. "Mick" Trainor, was a brilliant, highly respected officer (he later rose to the grade of lieutenant general and became a noted journalist and author after he retired). He wasn't just a skilled tactical commander; he had a remarkably clear understanding of the strategic and political levels of the war. Junior officers like me respected Trainor for both qualities. As I was struggling to sort out in my mind where this thing was going, I knew that if anybody could give me intelligent and insightful answers, it would be Colonel Trainor.

An opening came one memorable evening during operations in the Que Son Mountains west of Danang. We had stopped on a high mountaintop after monitored enemy radio transmissions had led us to suspect that enemy forces were operating in the valley below. It was a crisp, clear, starlit night, the middle of monsoon season in these northern provinces. Colonel Trainor and I sat together on a large boulder overlooking the valley while I briefed him on my company's defensive positions and our planned night ambushes. It seemed like a good moment. So I fired away.

After gathering his thoughts, he answered.

Given the current course of events in Vietnam and our own country, he explained, a clear and definitive victory in the short term was not in the cards. Although the South Vietnamese could hold the major population areas as far ahead as he could see, the fight for the countryside would continue to be chronic and ongoing. After we left, the North would surely come in force . . . probably not immediately, but some years after our departure. Could the forces of the South hold? That, in his view, would depend on our continued support, the continued improvement of the South's military capabilities, and support from their war-weary populace.

He reconfirmed what I'd sensed for a long time: We were winding down a war that we never really understood. Our generals and political leaders, their careers forged in the crucible of World War II and Korea, saw the conflict in conventional military terms. Though they had attempted to understand and respond to communist-inspired insurgencies, they continued to believe that this war could be won primarily on the battlefield. The hearts-and-minds business took a backseat to combat operations. After all, that was real soldiering.

Meanwhile, a rising number of critics, such as Bernard Fall, John Paul Vann, and Lieutenant Colonel William Corson, were voicing thoughtful and credible concerns. All of them had experienced the war on the ground; they had the mud of Vietnam on their boots. Fall, a French journalist who had covered the French Indochina War and had later patrolled with the US Marines (he was eventually killed by a land mine while on a Marine patrol), had sharp questions about how we were conducting operations. After years spent deep in the countryside advising the Vietnamese, Vann became an outspoken but respected critic of our pacification programs (he also lost his life in Vietnam in a helicopter crash). Corson, who had served on the American commander General William Westmoreland's staff, wrote a scathing account of the "corruption, mismanagement, and self-deception" he had witnessed in the Saigon headquarters of the Military Assistance Command Vietnam (MACV). As the war progressed, critics like these drew increasingly serious attention.

I had seen in my previous tour how the enemy was focused on the people. We in the American military were not. With a few notable exceptions, our leaders never really understood the Vietnamese people, or even tried to.

That night, I couldn't sleep. I lay on my poncho gazing at the stars, wondering what would become of my Vietnamese friends, and asking myself how we had made so many misjudgments in this confusing war.

In 1972, as Mick Trainor predicted, the North did come southward in force—the famous Easter Offensive. That time the South Vietnamese military turned them back. I was proud of how well they fought. The North Vietnamese Army came again in 1975; but by then we had drastically cut our support for the South (the United States withdrew all our forces in 1973). Along with the lack of resources that resulted, their leadership made critical operational mistakes and they came apart in the face of the massive onslaught.

I was a staff officer at our Marine headquarters in Washington when word came that Saigon had fallen. We watched on TV as the Peoples' Army of North Vietnam (PAVN) tanks rolled into the city and their troops pulled down the iconic statue in the city center honoring the Vietnamese Marines; we witnessed the humiliating evacuation of our embassy . . . Vietnamese frantically trying to break into the embassy grounds to escape the invading NVA, helicopters taking off from the embassy roof, people clinging to the skids. It was like helplessly watching a dear friend die in agony after a long, drawn-out illness. I left work early that day. I couldn't clear the deep depression and grief out of my mind for a long time.

But grief eventually led to reflection. I heard our generals talking about putting Vietnam behind us. "We're coming out of the jungles," they were saying. After all, we had a Cold War threat that still loomed; we had a pressing need to rebuild our military to meet that challenge and shuck off the negative effects of a decade of war.

That was all true. Yet I had a nagging sense that we should also take a clear, sober look back at what we had just gone through. There were lessons to be learned. Sure, maybe the wounds then were too fresh. But at some point we had to do it.

EXCUSES, EXCUSES, EXCUSES

"Those who cannot learn from history," says a line attributed to the philosopher George Santayana, "are doomed to repeat it." The line is overused, but remains relevant. We keep failing to heed its message. My generation learned bitter lessons in strange wars and interventions, beginning with Vietnam. We swore never to repeat the mistakes and failures we had witnessed in those conflicts, if and when we rose to high command. Unfortunately, time passed, our ranks dwindled, and a new generation of military leaders took charge who did not have Vietnam burned into their souls. They forgot (or never learned) the lessons of Vietnam. They forgot that politics and policy must be aligned with the strategy, and the strategy must be aligned with the operational design on the ground. And that operational design must be aligned with the actions of the troops all the way down to the lowest tactical level. When these get out of whack, we are headed for disaster. This is the most important lesson we should have learned. All these elements must be well thought out and aligned.

Time moved on. New crises came. New wars and interventions. And, again, they didn't turn out as we expected.

Sure, as Churchill and Clausewitz wisely pointed out, we never achieve in war everything we plan for, and only a fool will predict the outcome with any detailed certainty. Military conflicts, by their very nature, are hard to manage. Too many variables and unknowns can confound planners and leaders as they struggle with decisions and actions during conflicts. And add to this the fog and friction of war, which amplifies the confusion and unpredictability.

Regrettably, however, the fog and friction also provide leaders with a far too convenient cover-up for their own failed choices and actions—the "stuff happens" excuse famously made by former defense secretary Donald Rumsfeld early in the Iraq War.

But this is not the only excuse leaders fall back on.

As we launched into the Iraq War, critics were warning against repeating the mistakes and misjudgments of earlier conflicts like Vietnam. This is how then Secretary of Defense Rumsfeld answered those critics: "There's an old adage that this war is not like the last war. This war is not like the next war. This war is like this war. The point being that they're all different."

Yes, in some respects Rumsfeld was right. Each war or conflict has its own unique characteristics, its own context. Wars are by nature messy. The unexpected and the surprising are normal. A seamless match between outcome and original intentions is rare.

Yet the past does offer lessons that we should not ignore.

The "every war is different" rationale allows leaders to ignore the lessons of the past that can show the similarities and the traps and mistakes that should not be repeated.

And then there's the "weight of other burdens" excuse.

"One reason the Kennedy and Johnson administrations failed to take an orderly, rational approach to the basic questions underlying Vietnam," wrote Secretary of Defense Robert McNamara, who served in those administrations, "was the staggering variety and complexity of other issues we faced. Simply put, we faced a blizzard of problems, there were only twenty-four hours in a day, and we often did not have time to think straight."[2] The weight of other responsibilities conveniently becomes an additional rationale for mistakes and misjudgments.

In Iraq and Afghanistan we have seen too many mistakes that eerily remind us of Vietnam. And we also hear similar excuses.

AFGHANISTAN: WHAT GOES AROUND COMES AROUND

On a chilly afternoon early in December 2011, I was flying by Black Hawk helicopter from Kabul to the Khyber Pass on the volatile eastern border between Afghanistan and Pakistan, where I expected a firsthand view of security measures at the chaotic border crossing. But as I gazed down at villages, mountains, valleys, and military bases rolling by below me, my mind was far from border security. It was on a striking conversation I'd had with a National Guard brigadier general earlier that day over lunch at a mess hall in Kabul.

The flight to the Pass came in connection with an assessment of operations in Afghanistan that General James Mattis, the superb commander of the US Central Command (CENTCOM), had asked me to make. (I had made a similar assessment in 2008 in Iraq.) My travels took me all over Afghanistan. I visited dozens of US, Coalition, and Afghan units and commands, both large and small; I ate meals with Afghan units, and met with Afghan political and tribal leaders. Later, my report to General Mattis and to General John Allen, the commander in Afghanistan, covered the complete range of US programs, political and military operations, and state of training for Afghan forces in the country that I had observed.

Mattis and Allen, two brilliant officers I had known for years, had inherited a decade-long war and were doing everything in their power to straighten out the confusing quagmire they now owned. They had the unenviable task of winding down a war whose path had taken many turns that they had not chosen to take but whose consequences they had to deal with. Like General Raymond T. Odierno, the excellent commander in Iraq at whose request I had made my assessment there, they had had multiple tours of duty in these war zones and had learned a great deal from the trial and error approaches they had witnessed. They had learned to keep close contact with events down to the lowest levels and not to push preconceived ideas that events on the ground had shown to be unworkable. They had learned to change course and adapt—to readily alter operational plans and schemes to meet a changing or unexpected environment. And I'm sure they learned from the decade of botched handlings of these conflicts how constantly changing course adversely affects the end state. They wanted an ending we could be proud of.

"We have to end this war with honor," General Odierno said to me in a conversation about how magnificently our troops had performed in Iraq. (He knew this personally; his son had lost an arm in combat there.) I knew what he meant: we owed it to the fine men and women we had thrown into this cauldron. His words took me back to Vietnam.

The brigadier general in that mess hall in Kabul headed a small task force training Afghans in border security procedures—one of my many briefings from officers leading forces or programs of various sizes throughout the country. But our conversation took us far beyond the brigadier general's own duties and assignment; it lasted well beyond the scheduled time.

Though his was a very small organization that, by his own admission, played only a very small role in the war effort, he had an insightful and perceptive view of the war overall that impressed me. We discussed a broad spectrum of issues from the overall strategy to day-to-day operations . . . and, most interestingly, the US and Coalition policy that moved commanders in and out of the country with dismaying rapidity. Top commanders never stayed in one place long enough to give a firm, clear shape to their command or their operations. It was even worse in Vietnam as commanders rotated through command slots at all levels, with barely enough time to truly understand the complex nature of the environment they were in. At least in Afghanistan and Iraq we were now rotating entire units as opposed to individuals, as we had done in Vietnam. This created greater unit cohesion, yet we were still rotating individual commanders in and out of the top spots.

I had calculated before I arrived in Afghanistan that during ten years of operations in that country, our forces there had seen two presidents, three secretaries of defense, five chairmen of the joint chiefs, seven CENT-COM commanders, and ten commanders on the ground. (Since then we have added further replacements to this lineup.) Each new commander had a different operational approach. One would emphasize counterinsurgency; another would emphasize combat operations, or rules of engagement, or new areas of operations. Tactics changed. Guidance was altered. New operational directions shifted geographic orientations.

"Anyone who knows anything about the conduct of military operations," I told the brigadier, "realizes that this kind of turnover at the top of the chain of command generates changes, confusion, and turmoil in how things get done. Could you imagine changing out the Eisenhowers, Bradleys, Nimitzes, or Pattons like this? God save us from a constant parade of new commanders with good ideas."

He smiled, nodded, and then gave me his ground-level wisdom. "This has not been a ten-year war," he told me. "It's been ten one-year wars."

I couldn't have said it better.

He had summed up perfectly what my travels around Afghanistan had been teaching me (the same lessons I had witnessed in Iraq a few years earlier). Despite the efforts of strong, smart, highly-experienced commanders like Mattis, Allen, and Odierno, we were fighting these wars in ever-changing increments that had little continuity or coherence. We were making it up as we went along. Policies and strategies were constantly changing. Top leader styles were constantly changing. Battlefield tactics were constantly changing. At the whip end of all this were those sergeants and captains and ground troops doing the day-to-day fighting, tour after tour. For them, rules of engagement changed; new bright ideas came from new generals with new coteries of think tankers and eager, young, overeducated officers trying to make a name for themselves; and politicians, doing touch-and-goes on their battlefield, who came with political agendas. The price for confused direction is always paid for in the foxhole.

I was wrapped in that thought when the helicopter flew over Bagram Airfield with its massive buildup of supplies and equipment. The scene took me back to my tours in Vietnam. As an awestruck young lieutenant, I had flown over the sprawling logistics base at Long Bin, the largest such logistics base ever constructed in our military history. Here in Afghanistan, as before in Vietnam, acres and acres of containers and vehicles had accumulated. Déjà vu.

We always seem to take all of America to the battlefield. Bases with fast-food restaurants and ice cream machines, souvenir shops and rug merchants, massive gyms, and mess halls with multiple lines to suit every taste. What happened to the warrior ethos I learned and trained for as a young Marine? In today's wars, young soldiers go immediately from the horrors of battle to the base's miniature replica of a mall back in the States. When their tour ends, they jet home in hours. It's like getting beamed up to the Starship *Enterprise*. From the terrible horrors of war . . . flash, bang . . . and they're back home in a warm and welcoming kitchen. The effects of the shocking contrast are clear. Thousands of combat veterans are wrestling with the traumatic ends of the emotional spectrum they must cope with.

A few days before my conversation with the brigadier general, the commander of the logistics effort in Afghanistan and the general in charge of moving all that stuff back to peacetime bases had briefed me on the extensive challenges he faced.

Before I got to Afghanistan, I read reports that the cost of cleaning up, packing, and moving everything was expected to be nearly $6 billion. The scale of planning and executing these operations was monumental. During the three years we were scheduled to remain in the country, we had to close and clean up *each month* 20 bases, move 1,100 vehicles, pack and move out 767 containers, set up and run 140 wash points (all gear has to be cleaned and inspected before it can be sent home), and man and operate 37 inspection points (where inspectors check for cleanliness, operational condition, accountability, and so on).

Add to this the precarious routes everything had to traverse to get out of this landlocked country. One route went through Pakistan and the other through Central Asia. Security, political cooperation, and infrastructure conditions were serious challenges on the lines of withdrawal.

Washington warriors advocating a quicker withdrawal had no concept of what we had gotten into and what it would take to extract ourselves. Checking into these hotels is easy, but checking out is a very different matter. As our military commitments grind on over months and years, the buildups grow—often uncontrolled. We are not a cheap date. One service chief told me that the cost of maintaining a single Soldier or Marine in Afghanistan for one year was well over $1 million!

A *Washington Post*-ABC poll reports that today, thirteen years into the Afghan War, 66 percent of the American people believe the war was not worth fighting. When it began there was almost unanimous support. This should not come as a shock. Americans see how badly the war has been managed and how much it has cost.

HOW THE HELL DID WE GET HERE?

On September 14, 2001, three days after the shocking 9/11 attacks, President George W. Bush—standing on the ruins of the World Trade Center in New York—assured us that the perpetrators of the deadliest attack on our soil since Pearl Harbor would be brought to justice. On that day, through a bullhorn, he proclaimed to the cleanup crew, "I can hear you.

The rest of the world hears you. And the people who knocked these buildings down will hear from all of us soon."

Imagine someone who had slipped into a coma after hearing the president that day waking up a decade later. What would he or she make of our world?

How do we explain the escape of Al Qaeda leaders when we had them trapped, the long, almost ten-year search for Osama bin Laden, the removal of the Taliban government from power in Afghanistan (and the re-emergence of the Taliban), or our continued presence in that country thirteen years later? Could someone waking from a thirteen-year sleep follow the twisted, confusing course that climaxed with the invasion of Iraq? The weapons of mass destruction that weren't there? The alleged connection between Al Qaeda and Saddam Hussein that did not actually exist? Could he or she understand the president's "Mission Accomplished" proclamation years before we finally got ourselves unstuck from Iraq, and while we were still fighting in Afghanistan?

"Was the mission *ever* accomplished?" the sleeper might reasonably ask. "What was the mission? Nation building? . . . How the hell did we get here?"

Great questions!

The conflicts sparked by 9/11 have cost us almost $2 trillion and counting, all of that put on a credit card for the first time in our history (in the past funding was raised for operations as we conducted them). We have suffered tens of thousands of our magnificent troops killed, wounded, or traumatized by war. Iraqis, Afghans, Pakistanis, and others have suffered casualties in the hundreds of thousands. The Iraq War lasted from 2003 to 2011—longer than the American Revolution, the Civil War, or the first or second world wars. We launched the war in Afghanistan in October 2001, and it isn't over yet—the longest war in American history.

The decision to place military forces in harm's way is not casual. It is the most serious decision our president and Congress can make. All Americans—not least of all the many at risk of getting shot at—deserve answers to questions of if and when and why the United States goes to war.

Each war has its own unique character, but that doesn't mean consistent patterns don't emerge from one to another. A careful study of wars will reveal these patterns and help us to learn lessons we can apply to future conflicts. We know about battles won or lost, and we tend to assign responsibility for their outcomes to the generals who fought them; but what about the political decisions that can make or break a mission? How often do we assign accountability for those decisions?

One of Clausewitz's most famous observations is that war is "a true political instrument, a continuation of political activity by other means."

It is ironic that military leaders devote enormous time and effort to studying past conflicts to glean operational lessons and yet political leaders rarely make an effort to analyze and understand the political and strategic lessons. When they are faced with leading and managing conflicts, they do not have decades-long experience and education to prepare them for making the complex decisions. I once listened to a senior civilian Defense Department official as he addressed a group of young officers, glibly dismiss the detailed military planning process that he obviously did not understand and showed no interest in learning or understanding. All he needed, he told them, was a short "conversational discussion around the table" to understand the decisions that had to be made.

"That's the problem," I said to him.

"I knew *you* would say that," he responded. He was aware that I was a vocal critic of the lack of serious planning and strategic thinking at the senior civilian levels of our government. We have had too many dilettantes placed in these positions who do not have the depth of knowledge or experience to make sound military decisions or offer credible recommendations. The crew in the Rumsfeld Pentagon that drove a severely flawed strategic and operational direction in Iraq and Afghanistan is a prime example of that.

People like that glib Defense official don't put in the time and effort these complicated issues demand. Our system runs people through high political office with a frequency that does not allow much time to learn. There is no intuitive gift of superior decision making that comes with election or appointment to high political position. Many officials, from undersecretaries to ambassadors, are appointed to positions because of political loyalties and financial contributions rather than proven merit. Yet people in those positions have to make efforts to understand the details and complexity that the Pentagon official wasn't interested in, or we as a nation, and our troops, will get into trouble we didn't anticipate. You can't look at a military intervention in a shallow, cursory way. The traps lie buried many levels below, and only detailed study and planning reveals them.

It's almost as if our political leadership sees no relationship between their political responsibilities and their military responsibilities. They miss Clausewitz's most important point. Political leaders must be involved, in depth, in every large-scale military mission and must stay engaged throughout the conduct of the mission. They can't just make a "handoff" of responsibilities to the generals then blast them when things go wrong. War is a political act from start to finish. This requires a thorough understanding of the military, of military interventions, and of war that few political leaders possess or feel it is necessary to gain. This thorough understanding requires education and a study of past conflicts—from start to finish, and after—to gain the insights that should guide their decision making and direction.

Secretary Rumsfeld could have learned many lessons that Secretary McNamara learned the hard way and that those troops on the ground in Vietnam, Afghanistan, and Iraq learned in an even harder way.

An officer's education necessarily involves study of past wars, campaigns, and battles; yet learning facts and statistics is obviously not enough. The kind of understanding an officer needs comes from deep analysis—dissecting each battle, campaign, or war and drawing coherent lessons from each study with the help of experienced mentors, templates such as the Principles of War (the fundamental concepts normally applied for the successful conduct of military operations), and other frameworks for study and analysis. Was the objective clear? Was there true unity of command and purpose? How was the Principle of Maneuver or Mass appropriately employed or not employed? How was the strategy translated to the operational level and that level to the tactical level?

Of course, I am not saying that military officers don't make the kinds of mistakes that our senior civilian leaders make. Many of them, too, don't learn from their training and education, or choose to ignore it. But at least their career paths are guided by education and experiences designed to provide lessons on the best ways to conduct military operations. When the White House asked General Stanley McChrystal, the commander in Afghanistan, to provide the number of troops he required to succeed there, he gave a figure: forty thousand. The White House responded that he would only get reluctant approval for thirty thousand. Forty thousand was a number based on military judgment, planning, and assessments. You could certainly argue with that number from other military perspectives. But each perspective would then start from a common military basis. Thirty thousand was a political number. Based on what? How do you weigh the differences when you start from no common basis?

Abraham Lincoln invested a great deal of time studying the conduct of war. He recognized his limited knowledge and knew he needed to understand how generals translated (or failed to translate) his political directions into actions on the battlefield. Those elected, or politically appointed, who must make critical decisions in time of war or provide advice on its conduct must understand the effects of their decisions and recommendations. Understanding the consequences of political decisions begins with asking, "How the hell did we get here?"

For many years, in various conflicts, I have struggled to answer that question. I've studied the numerous situations in our history, and in my personal experience, where our leaders elected to employ military force toward achieving some political objective. From these studies a consistent pattern emerged, specific stages in the process that started from a triggering event and led to the lasting impact of our military actions. This pattern was present in every one of our military actions, and provided me with windows through which I could see where events and choices have taken right turns and, in my view, wrong turns. And, more important, I could draw lessons from what caused the right and wrong turns.

The road to war is often long and twisted. I came to understand that each stage in this process from trigger event to end state is critically important in itself. No less important is its relation to the other stages. If you get one step wrong, or fail to think it through, or to see that it is out of sync with the others, or if you take your eye off the progress, the entire effort can be thrown off course and possibly ruined. It is like a chain—only as strong as its weakest link. A bad strategy, for example, is not going to be saved by great operations and tactics. The Germans learned this in World War II. You can't simply shoot your way to victory and win it from the bottom up.

Any time this nation decides to go to war, we need to get all of it right—the analyses, decisions, policies, strategies, objectives, and leadership. We owe it to those who will do the sweating and bleeding to give them the same kind of commitment and dedication that they give on the battlefield.

After coming out of surgery to mend wounds suffered from three bullets in my side, I prowled the wards in the hospital in Danang searching for my fellow Marines who had been wounded with me on a hill in the Que Son Mountains. I found one of my lance corporals who had been shot in the leg and ankle, a big, athletic Marine who now faced repeated surgeries and, potentially, permanent damage. We talked for a while and then he looked up to me and asked, "Sir, what are we doing here?" I gave him the conventional answers about stopping the spread of communism and helping the Vietnamese keep their freedom. But I realized as we talked that his question was much more profound. It wasn't about what we were trying to accomplish. It was about how we were trying to do it. He was doing his part. Were those who designed the strategy and made the policies doing their part?

Before the first shot is fired, we must be sure everything we have analyzed, planned, and decided—every possible scenario we have tried to anticipate—puts that lance corporal in the best position to succeed. His battlefield should be shaped to give him every advantage before he steps onto it.

TWO

A DATE WHICH WILL LIVE IN INFAMY

Yesterday, December 7, 1941—a date which will live in infamy—the United States of America was suddenly and deliberately attacked by naval and air forces of the Empire of Japan.

President Franklin Roosevelt,
Address before Congress, December 8, 1941

"YOU AMERICANS," A MIDDLE EASTERN FRIEND SAID to me, "have a very warlike reputation."

Astonishing words that set me back on my heels. "No!" I bristled, "that's not true! We use military force only as a last resort. We are a nation of immigrants; most of them chose to come to our country in order to escape the chronic wars and conflicts back where they came from. Look at our Great Seal," I continued with a smile. "We put the laurel branches of peace in the right talon of the bald eagle, our nation's symbol, and the arrows of military might in the left talon to signal just that."

Returning my smile, he began to rattle off facts: American military interventions since World War II, warlike metaphors we use every day. "In your politics, you have campaigns, war chests, battleground states, attack ads. You declare 'war' on drugs, cancer, poverty, and illiteracy!"

After long debate, we agreed to disagree about Americans' warlike nature. But he made me think. I couldn't deny that out in the world we are not always perceived as we like to see ourselves. Our military might has been so dominant and frequently used that it has become for many around the world more of a symbol of who we are than the qualities that best identify us; such as our freedoms and civil liberties, our manner of self-governance, our rule of law, and our striving for social equality.

When I was the commander of the US Central Command (CENT-COM), I made a routine call on a senior official in the government of one of our allies in the Persian Gulf region to discuss security issues. I knew him well and respected his always sage advice. During our discussion, he stopped and reflected. "You know, General," he said, "when the people of this region think about Americans, do you know what image they have?" He paused, then continued: "A soldier in full combat gear. And when they think about others, like the Chinese," he added, "this is their image: investor, diplomat, humanitarian worker." His comment was not hostile or challenging. He meant it as constructive criticism. He was a friend of America who wanted us to change how we are perceived in his part of the world.

To that end, he encouraged me to conduct interviews with local media to, in his words, "put a human face on the US military." Because security requirements kept us locked down in remote desert bases, our military and the locals had little contact. Yet thanks to the propaganda of our adversaries and hostile coverage from some media outlets, locals were keenly aware that we were there, and we were presented, at times, with a negative image. Our numerous and increasingly frequent military actions in the region only heightened this perception.

I took him up on his offer to meet with the local media, and gave a series of interviews to Al Jazeera that did not totally change our image, but, based on the feedback, did make it a little more positive.

I think I understood how the locals felt. The United States had inherited the primary security mission for the Middle East when the European powers abandoned the region in the 1970s after screwing it up following World War I and the fall of the Ottoman Empire. We became the cop on the block; sometimes appreciated, sometimes not. Access to oil, keeping open critical trade routes, ensuring stability, deterring regional hegemons, protecting allies, defending against malign outside influence or invasion, and many other reasons kept us pinned there.

Nations that are far more dependent on the region's energy resources than we are have contributed little—or nothing—to the protection of this volatile region. Not one Chinese ship or soldier, for example, has been involved in that task. In the early 1970s we took on the primary role of maintaining security in the region, and we have kept the commitment through the tanker wars, Iranian threats and mischief, the Iran-Iraq War, Saddam's invasion of Kuwait, terrorist threats and attacks, and our interventions in Iraq and Afghanistan. When a threat manifested itself, we responded.

WHY DO WE ASSUME THESE RESPONSIBILITIES?

Why, in fact, has our military been actively engaged since World War II so often in so many parts of the world? Why have we gone to war so often?

Sometimes the answers are clear. Sometimes they are not.

On the day after the Japanese attack on the US bases at Pearl Harbor, my father listened to the radio broadcast of FDR's address to Congress asking for a declaration of war. My father, a World War I vet, understood why that was necessary and he fully supported it. So did the vast majority of Americans. The declaration of war was rendered by Congress within hours of Roosevelt's address.

Early in 2003, six decades later, we invaded Iraq. During the run-up to that war, I was anything but certain that it was necessary. Because the American people largely backed military action, it was difficult to question it. Emotions were running high after 9/11; Americans quickly bought into the case for war. Those of us advising against war in Iraq and stressing the importance of focusing on Al Qaeda in Afghanistan were not popular and were ignored by the administration. I believed that relegating Afghanistan to a secondary effort would come to haunt us. We were underestimating what was required to take on both missions; and destroying Al Qaeda should clearly have been mission number one.

On August 26, 2002—a year after the 9/11 terrorist attacks on America and thirty-five years after my first Vietnam tour—I was in Nashville, Tennessee, at the Veterans of Foreign Wars National Convention to receive the VFW's Eisenhower Award for Distinguished Service. Because I was sitting next to the lectern that day, I was an eyewitness to Vice President Dick Cheney's keynote address, the speech that launched the Bush administration's all-out effort to make the case for war against Iraq.

Backstage before his speech, the vice president gave no indication that he was about to make the case for war. We talked about my work as envoy to the Israeli-Palestinian peace talks earlier that year, an effort he had personally endorsed and supported on a visit to Israel during my mission there. He and I remained disappointed that serious efforts and great promise had failed to produce an agreement.

During my mission to Israel, word reached the Israeli leadership that the US was considering military action against Iraq—a course that deeply worried them. They expressed their concern in a private conversation with me and the vice president, who was in the region trying to drum up support for military action against Saddam. They explained that they were determined not to repeat the experiences of the Persian Gulf War (1991), when we pressured them to take no military actions in response to Iraq's scud missile attacks. They agreed then and suffered. I was in Israel during those attacks. I knew they would never again be pressured into not responding militarily. Meanwhile, with a second Intifada on their hands (the Palestinian uprising against Israeli occupation), the possibility of an internal and external conflict raging at the same time was not attractive to them.

The vice president's opening words in Nashville touched on the VFW's important place in our society, our veterans, and our current fight in Afghanistan. No surprises there. But then he made a sharp, sudden turn to the case for war with Iraq.

"Simply stated," Cheney declared, "there is no doubt that Saddam Hussein now has weapons of mass destruction. There is no doubt he is amassing them to use against our friends, against our allies, and against us."

I was shocked. I knew Cheney. I thought he was more grounded than that. Hadn't he seen the intelligence I had seen that confirmed there was no credible evidence of an ongoing WMD (weapons of mass destruction) program in Iraq at that time? His claims were simply untrue. When he was the secretary of defense in 1991, he supported restraint rather than pressing on to Baghdad after we crushed Saddam's army on the so-called highway of death. He was wise enough then to see the mess we would inherit if we occupied that country. As Colin Powell said in his Pottery Barn warning, "You break it, you own it."

Though I had heard rumblings in Washington that the Bush administration was being pushed by the so-called neocons (neoconservatives) toward invading Iraq, I didn't expect the administration to go down that path. I did not then see any strong reason why we should invade that country and inherit the costs and problems that two previous administrations had carefully avoided. That judgment still holds. We had already effectively contained Iraq. We had done it with fewer troops than report to work at the Pentagon each day; they rotated in and out of the region so there were no permanently assigned combat forces there. We had no US bases there, only those shared with the host countries. We put in place pre-positioned equipment in the region so that we could quickly fall in on our gear without a large standing force indefinitely committed there. All this had been accomplished under a UN resolution that provided international support, legitimacy, and contribution; and our allies in the region picked up most of the cost of the containment.

The neocons—extreme hawks when it comes to intervention in the Middle East—had been pressing for war with Iraq for a long time. During the Clinton presidency, they had urged the president toward a military confrontation with that country, but Clinton wisely stayed on the course of containment that his predecessor George H. W. Bush had set. I sincerely hoped that the George W. Bush administration would not change that course. The administration was filled with serious and experienced people like Secretary of State Colin Powell, who knew better than to embark on a war with Iraq while we were in the opening stages of a potentially long conflict with extremists in Afghanistan and elsewhere in the Middle East and Africa. That had to be our military priority. The Saddam Hussein regime was fully contained. They were only a threat within their own country, and only to a few of their own people, such as political enemies of Saddam.

Evidence for this judgment came from intelligence I'd received during my last years as commander of CENTCOM and later. After I retired from the Marine Corps, I was asked to participate in high-level intelligence studies of Iraq's WMD potential. Both sources—containing all the intelligence available at that time—convinced me and everyone else involved in the studies that no clear evidence existed for an ongoing WMD program in Iraq. The work of the UN inspectors had prevented an effective, ongoing program from being restarted and their accounting for past capabilities indicated that the possibility of hidden capabilities was highly unlikely. WMD should not have been our chief worry about that country. We should have been more worried about internal collapse of Saddam's regime, the ensuing chaos, and the likelihood that we would be drawn into it.

And then in Nashville I listened, astonished, to Vice President Cheney's absolute statements: " . . . *no doubt* that Saddam Hussein now has weapons of mass destruction . . . *no doubt* he is amassing them to use against our friends, against our allies, and against us."

When it was clear that the Bush administration was set on invading Iraq, shock turned into anger, and I made my concerns known.

Shortly before the invasion, I spent a day with a number of senior retired officials at CIA headquarters in Langley, Virginia, to receive a briefing about Iraq WMD capabilities. We were there as consultants on Iraq's potential WMD responses to the invasion. After the briefing, I threw a fit. "I can't believe we are going to war based on this garbage," I told the group. "Please tell me that you have better intelligence locked in some compartmented program I'm not read into."

The briefer gave no response. And some of the group seemed disturbed that I challenged the intelligence justification for invasion. They shuffled their papers or stared in annoyance at their laps. I turned then to a respected retired senior intelligence official who was working with us. "Am I crazy," I asked, "or is there no clear evidence of a WMD program in Iraq?"

"General, you're not crazy," he told me.

Yet, on March 20, 2003, we launched an invasion.

Before the invasion, after tense diplomatic wrangling, Secretary of State Colin Powell had gotten unanimous agreement on a United Nations Security Council resolution that sent weapons inspectors back into Iraq (they had been removed some months earlier). It was clear that Hans Blix, head of the UN Monitoring, Verification, and Inspection Commission, and Mohamed ElBaradei, head of the International Atomic Energy Agency, were, once again, aggressively inspecting and investigating inside Iraq. Many on their inspection teams were respected Americans. Though the Security Council resolution did not authorize the use of force, it was clear that the Bush administration wanted a war. It was also clear that they would not be able to obtain the sanction of a UN Security Council resolution authorizing the use of force, such as the first President Bush achieved prior to the first Gulf War, unless there was absolute proof of a WMD program. The inspectors found no evidence of an ongoing WMD program and reported their findings back to the UN. Since, as a result, there could be no UN Security Council approved military coalition authorized to use force, a "coalition of the willing," as President George W. Bush put it, would have to do—a coalition made up of those nations we could persuade, incentivize, or browbeat into joining our cause. Secretary Rumsfeld, in addressing the findings of the inspectors, indicated that we should go ahead and invade anyway since our troops were already deployed in the region and shouldn't spend the hot summer there in the desert!

They would spend ten summers sweltering and bleeding in Iraq.

The neocons, well ensconced in the Defense Department and the White House, were leading the onrush toward war. Their spokesmen were bragging that the conflict would be a "cakewalk" and that we would be greeted as liberators, with flowers in the streets—calling up images of Paris in August 1944. Deputy Secretary of Defense Paul Wolfowitz, a leading neocon, assured a congressional panel that the war would come with no cost. Revenues from Iraq's oil would foot the bill.

I knew these arrogant predictions were wrong. They drew my memory back to Vietnam, when the Gulf of Tonkin incident of 1964, a phony casus belli, was trumped up to launch us into war and gain the support of Congress and the American people . . . soon followed by Defense Secretary McNamara's confident assurances in 1966 that the war would be over by Christmas.

I was getting calls from senior CENTCOM officers charged with planning the operation. "We can't believe what we've been told to do." they were telling me. "Our instructions are to treat the mission as an easy liberation rather than the difficult, dangerous, and risky occupation that years of planning and intelligence had taught us to expect." And they continued: "Secretary Rumsfeld has pressured your successor (at CENTCOM) into changing the war plan requirement for four hundred thousand troops to one hundred and sixty thousand." A clear disaster in my mind. Taking out the regime could be accomplished easily, but the aftermath of internal chaos and the potential for malign elements to enter Iraq would be catastrophic if we did not have from the beginning the overwhelming force needed to control the population and borders. Rumsfeld did not understand what he was in for. The stupidity of believing their own bumper stickers, that "Shock and Awe" would cause all opposition to cower in fear and melt away, had firmly taken hold in Washington. They did not understand the mire they were stepping into. "We are forbidden to even use the 'O' word"—occupation—a superb planning officer, an expert on the region and especially Iraq, told me in frustration and despair. "Can you believe these guys, Sir?" No. I could not.

Why did we choose to go to war in Iraq? Some speculated that President Bush sought revenge for the Iraqi regime's April 1993 attempt to assassinate his father during a visit to Kuwait. Others saw the invasion as a strategic move to implant democracy in the heart of the Middle East— a change they expected would counter extremist movements and spread throughout the region. Others blamed pressure from Israel. . . . Hardly possible, based on my own recent daily personal contacts with Israeli political and military leadership. They had no appetite for a war then. Just the opposite, as they had warned Cheney. Besides, given Israel's superb intelligence capabilities in the region and their past record of preemptively taking out Iraqi and Syrian WMD capabilities in previous attacks, why wouldn't they have removed any existing WMD program elements on their own or raised the alarm to us?

Did any of these explanations justify our invasion and long occupation of Iraq? I doubted it. Why was it so easy to respond with military force and shortchange all other options? The inspectors were back in, we controlled the skies, and we had regional support for our ongoing containment operations. Logic should have led us to continue the containment, deal with Al Qaeda and Afghanistan, and then evaluate a course of action regarding Iraq.

Our own history should teach us that it's way too easy to get into a war. There are plenty of injustices in this world that need fixing and plenty of potential and real threats looming over us that it would be desirable to remove. Add to that our possession of the most powerful military on the planet and the strong temptations and pressures to use it, and you can see why pulling the trigger appears so inviting. There have been presidents, members of Congress, and generals who never met an intervention they didn't like. The hard lessons from past wars and interventions go unheeded, and time tends to erase any reluctance to do it again. The "Vietnam syndrome," the "Somalia syndrome," or the "Iraq syndrome" have a short shelf life.

WHY WE HAVE FOUGHT

The singularities that America has ascribed to itself throughout its history have produced two contradictory attitudes toward foreign policy. The first is that America serves its values best by perfecting democracy at home, thereby acting as a beacon for the rest of mankind; the second, that America's values impose on it an obligation to crusade for them around the world.

Henry Kissinger[1]

During the more than two hundred years of America's history, the nation has committed its military to action hundreds of times for all kinds of reasons, both inside and outside our borders: to secure our freedom and independence; to remove obstacles to westward expansion; to put down insurrections; to protect our borders; to act against pirates; to expand our territories; to unify the nation and remove the blight of slavery; to pacify Native Americans (or expel them from territories our settlers wanted); to promote trade and open markets for our industry and businesses; to stabilize small nearby nations (or replace unfriendly regimes with ones more friendly to our interests); to provide humanitarian support; to counter criminal activity; to oppose threatening ideologies; to protect American commercial interests overseas; to support our allies; and to respond to attacks on us. Surprisingly, the nation has gone to war as the Constitution requires, with a formal declaration by Congress, only five times: the War of 1812, the Mexican-American War, the Spanish-American War, World War I, and World War II.

Notice the arc—the historic progression. Earlier wars were fought at home or close to home. The only exceptions were actions to protect our maritime trade assets and access to overseas markets. Later wars were fought at ever greater distances from home. This reflects a big change in how America's leaders—and the American people—have viewed our role in the world.

America's founders were primarily inward- rather than outward-looking. Because of a lack of existential threats in those days, our Constitution stated that our government would "raise an army and maintain a navy." Because we were distrustful of standing armies, we relied on local militias and a call to arms when and if the need arose. But because we saw ourselves as a maritime nation, dependent on foreign trade and bordered by two mighty oceans, our naval power was always to be sustained. Projecting power beyond our own boundaries, except for territorial expansion within our own continent (justified, starting in the 1840s as Manifest Destiny), was unthinkable.

In his farewell address (1796), President George Washington warned the new nation to "steer clear of permanent alliances with any portion of the foreign world." Thomas Jefferson in his inaugural address (1801) added, "Peace, commerce, and honest friendship with all nations—entangling alliances with none." These warnings became our established, fundamental doctrine. The nation would live behind those two mighty oceans in isolation from the temptations and turmoil of the rest of the world. We would not link our fate with others that might draw us into the endless European wars.

Our role in the world was to be the shining example of what could be—the society that strove to perfect how it governs itself and how its citizens can live happily and freely. Our beacon would shine as a sign of hope for others and a model to follow. We would welcome anyone who sought freedom and self-determination; but we would not impose our way of life on others outside our borders.

ON APRIL 2, 1917, PRESIDENT WOODROW WILSON went before Congress to request a declaration of war against Germany. Two days later the Senate approved, and two days after that the House of Representatives concurred. Despite the president's 1916 campaign promise to keep us out of the war, for a number of reasons the confrontation was inevitable: Germany's unrestricted submarine warfare, its attempt to bring Mexico into the war against the US, and our ever-increasing aid and support for Britain and France during the two years leading up to the declaration. Wilson entered office in 1913 much as President Lyndon Johnson would later do, with a political agenda focused on domestic issues. Wilson often criticized President Theodore Roosevelt, one of his recent predecessors, for unwisely trying to project our nation more onto an international stage where, he felt, we did not belong. But, also like Lyndon Johnson, he soon found himself drawn away from his intended agenda and immersed in a foreign war.

The United States was no longer to be isolated from the temptations and turmoil of the rest of the world. America was experimenting with a new and radically different role—we were becoming crusaders. Our crusaders believed we should no longer stay home and shine our beacon outward. We should take our model to others who needed help. We owed it to the world to share our blessings and to use our power to right wrongs wherever we could . . . while at the same time American businessmen saw opportunities overseas for new markets and ready access to raw materials. Wilson's postwar trip to France for the peace talks at Versailles raised hopes. He was greeted by cheering throngs who viewed him as the savior who would bring freedom and change to the world.

But not all Americans were ready for that dramatic shift. After the war, the idealistic Wilson sought to reorder the world in our democratic model with his Fourteen Points and League of Nations, but his noble, crusading voice fell on a war-weary and isolationist Congress, led by Henry Cabot Lodge, that wanted no part in that vision, and the nation retreated back to the principles that had previously guided us. America was in those days heavily engaged in industrial development that was delivering ever-rising prosperity. That wasn't worth risking in potentially costly global involvements and commitments.

President Wilson's attempt to remake the world in America's image was the first significant test of the "beacon versus crusader" conflict. Wilson did not succeed, but his vision kept returning, and often prevailing. As America grew, so did our influence. The debate continues to rage today as we struggle to decide our role, if any, in conflict-ridden nations such as Libya, Syria, and Afghanistan and commitments to the security of nations that most Americans cannot find on a map. Are we the world's policeman? Does an obligation come with superpower status? Should we be global nation-builders and protectors? If so, under what circumstances?

TWO DECADES AFTER WILSON'S FAILED ATTEMPT TO change the world, we were engaged in another worldwide war. World War II is often referred to as the "Good War." We went to war for clear and just reasons; the trigger that launched it was an intolerable act of aggression; our enemies' totalitarian ideologies and savage practices were a dire threat to all humankind; we mobilized our entire society for the war effort; our people valiantly supported it; and our goal of unconditional surrender was unequivocal.

After the war, we did not exact retribution. Rather, we reached out to our enemies and rebuilt their societies. And the United States emerged from the war as the greatest power the world had ever seen. America was respected and admired. All the free world counted on us. All the rest feared us. The Greatest Generation (as it would later be called) had delivered.

We were now full-blown crusaders.

THE CRUSADERS

In the decades that followed, the United States led the formation of an alliance of free nations, the North Atlantic Treaty Organization (NATO), to stand against another threatening ideology—communism—embodied most powerfully in still other totalitarian nations, the USSR and Red China. To counter that threat, we developed the most powerful military in the world, and, for the first time in our history, maintained all military components on a large scale, even in peacetime. These actions successfully deterred and contained the Soviet Union, while somehow avoiding the looming threat of mutual assured destruction (MAD) through the nuclear arms race. The great powers maintained enough nuclear weapons and the means to deliver them to char our planet into a cinder many times over. With a clash of titans unthinkable, our Cold War foes elected to undermine our power and influence through communist-inspired insurgencies in the poor, weak, unstable, and vulnerable nations of the world. We eagerly took on that challenge. It was a zero-sum game. Either a nation was with us or with them. Presidents Truman, Eisenhower, Kennedy, Johnson, and Nixon proclaimed doctrines that drew sharp lines that the United States would not allow the communists to cross. Their doctrines defined how, where, and why we would respond with force and support.

And they left us with military commitments that our forefathers could never have imagined possible. We fought limited wars, counterinsurgencies, and "police actions" in Korea, Vietnam, and elsewhere. We supported armed struggles resisting communist takeover from Central America to Europe to Afghanistan to Southeast Asia. Clandestine operations helped overthrow communist or left-leaning governments in Iran and Central America.

Unfortunately, these dirty little limited wars and military interventions turned out to be hard to manage. Our model was the "Good War," and we expected these new wars to play out according to that unambiguous model. They did not. They were messy, hard to define, and harder to sell, requiring tactics that in some cases seemed less than honorable—and not really true to American values. We supported dictators, we toppled governments, and we used clandestine methods to protect our interests and achieve our ends.

Then, to everyone's surprise and delight, in 1991 the Soviet Union was dissolved, and with it the Soviet Empire.

Leaders from all sides—including Soviet president Mikhail Gorbachev and George H. W. Bush—promised a New World Order, the atomic scientists readjusted backward the Doomsday Clock, and everybody looked forward to a "peace dividend." It did not come.

In the nearly three decades from the end of World War II to 1973, when the United States ended the draft and created a volunteer military, the Congressional Research Service has documented nineteen military deployments of various kinds throughout the world, from combat to humanitarian aid. In the four decades after 1973, there have been 144 foreign military deployments.

In this period, new terms have been coined to describe these new ambiguous missions. Low intensity conflict (LIC), military operations other than war (MOOTW), unconventional warfare (UW), counterinsurgency operations (COIN), counter terrorism operations (CT), and stability and reconstruction operations. In my assessments in Iraq and Afghanistan, I was amazed by the number of nonmilitary tasks our troops had taken on. American forces were involved in agricultural development, running museums and recreational facilities, conflict resolution negotiations, governmental anticorruption enforcement, infrastructure improvement, and many other non-traditional tasks. We are not only now "entangled," we are globally all in!

We do it all with the best of intentions.

On December 5, 1992, President George H. W. Bush decided to send 28,000 troops to Somalia to, in his words, "save thousands of innocents," a purely humanitarian mission that had broad support from Congress, the American people, and most of the world. The decision was made forty-seven days before President Bush left office—a highly unusual commitment near the end of a lame duck administration, since there was no imminent threat to US interests or people.

The *New York Times* reported that day that administration officials "expressed hope that the United States could begin to hand off some of the country to the existing United Nations peacekeeping operation before Mr. Clinton is inaugurated on January 20, but it was clear that the new President would inherit an ongoing military operation." General Colin Powell, then the Chairman of the Joint Chiefs of Staff, hoped to "see our way clear of this operation in a few months."

A few weeks before the inauguration of President Bill Clinton, President Bush came to visit the forces he had committed to Somalia. I was the director of operations for the operation, dubbed Operation Restore Hope. By then we had effectively accomplished our original mission to secure the area of southern Somalia so that humanitarian supplies and services could be safely provided and distributed by the outgunned UN force and nongovernmental organizations (NGOs) working in the contested areas. It was our understanding that our mission would be a short-duration imposition of force designed to provide a jump start to a more muscular, revamped UN military mission that would take the hand-off from us in a month or so. However, discussions with the special representative of the UN Secretary General in Somalia made it clear to us that neither he nor the secretary general, Boutros Boutros-Ghali, held any such understanding. They would not, in Boutros-Ghali's words, accept a "poisoned apple." To update that Colin Powell Pottery Barn Principle, "you *touch* it, you own it."

We felt, however, that surely the president had some clear understanding with the UN and President Bush would clear this all up on his visit. Surely this could not be an open-ended commitment, could it?

After briefings that our commander, Lieutenant General Robert B. "Bob" Johnston, and I gave the president, Bob asked the president whether there was an agreement with the UN on a turnover. President Bush turned to National Security Advisor Brent Scowcroft and White House Communications Director Marlin Fitzwater, who had accompanied him, to ask if they knew of any agreement or understanding with the UN. They pondered, stared at one another with puzzled faces, and shook their heads. They knew of none. Bob and I looked at each other in disbelief. Once again, we had checked in, but we were not checking out anytime soon.

The hand-off to the UN did not occur for seven more months, and then only after the UN's demand for a significant commitment of US forces to the follow-on operation was agreed on. In effect, the US ended up committed for over a year and a half. We left in 1994, but returned in 1995 to protect the withdrawal of UN forces. The casualties in the operation would far exceed what was anticipated for a humanitarian mission, and the loss of nineteen special operations troops on October 3–4, 1993, in a fight with one of the warlords, resulted in the resignation of the secretary of defense, Les Aspin, and the termination of the US commitment six months later. In 1995 I commanded the task force sent to protect the UN withdrawal.

I was deeply involved in Somalia during all this time—as the director of operations for the initial mission; then as a presidential representative, along with Ambassador Bob Oakley, sent to negotiate a cease-fire and gain release of a wounded US prisoner; and finally as commander of the task force protecting the withdrawal. We went into Somalia for all the right reasons. A compassionate president and public saw the horrific images on CNN and acted out of that compassion. But the disaster that followed made us leery of future commitments. It led to President Clinton's failure to act during the genocide in Rwanda and Burundi . . . his biggest regret as president, he said later. The Somalia experience paralyzed our ability to act.

"ISMS" AND OTHER TRIGGERS

Looking back over the centuries since our nation's founding, from time to time alien and evil concepts of governance or ideology have hovered over us, challenging us and directly or indirectly threatening our chosen way of life. Or, anyhow, they have been so perceived or portrayed by our leaders and people. They are the "isms": colonialism, imperialism, fascism, communism, and now terrorism. These are the bogeymen, the frightening potential existential threats that have often driven us to prepare and respond militarily. Some of our responses have been justified, such as after the Pearl Harbor attack that justified war against Japan and the 9/11 attacks justifying intervention in Afghanistan to root out Al Qaeda. Other responses have had less justification—or none at all—such as the invasion of Iraq, with its false connection to WMD and to the 9/11 terrorist attacks.

Of course, not all decisions to use military force have been connected to threats from "isms." But more often than not, "isms" have provided the overarching context used to justify our military reaction to triggering events. But that may be changing.

Every military intervention begins with an event that can't be ignored, a real or perceived threat, a red line crossed, an interest at risk, an ally threatened, a humanitarian tragedy, or some other cause or reason that in the opinion of our political leadership may require the use of force. Not all triggers or causes will be obvious, especially the ones we will probably run into in coming years. Environmental issues, water and resource scarcity, consequences from cyberattacks, mass migrations, ethnic, religious, and sectarian conflicts, and a host of other emerging causes may generate a reason to commit our military.

Today we have red lines drawn over chemical weapons in Syria, the development of nuclear weapons in Iran, and the potential threat to Eastern European members of NATO by Russia's aggressive actions in Ukraine. We sit poised to respond to an unpredictable dictator in North Korea. A metastasizing Al Qaeda can trigger a response to a terrorist attack almost anywhere in the world. Military units are at the ready to reinforce threatened embassies or to intercept pirates operating off the east and west coasts of Africa. Typhoons, hurricanes, tsunamis, earthquakes, and a host of other natural disasters continue to require rapid military emergency assistance as recently occurred in the Philippines, Pakistan, and Japan. Territorial claims and disputes by China, Japan, and the Philippines threaten to escalate into serious confrontations that can draw us in, depending on treaty obligations. These, and many more situations, are like spilled gasoline waiting for a match to ignite them and force the need to respond.

THREE

KNOWNS AND UNKNOWNS

There are known knowns; there are things we know we know. We also know there are known unknowns; that is to say, we know there are some things we do not know. But there are also unknown unknowns—the ones we don't know we don't know.

Donald Rumsfeld, Secretary of Defense, February 12, 2002

TELEVISION VIEWERS AROUND THE WORLD WATCHED with horror the ghastly images on TV—men, women, and children choking, vomiting, and dying in a Damascus neighborhood. Afterward, we expected the strong response from President Obama that he had threatened would follow a use of chemical weapons on civilians by Bashar al-Assad's regime. There were reports that the president had set in motion plans for what would be a devastating air and missile attack.

The president had drawn a redline on the Assad regime's use of chemical weapons. A clear violation meant he had to act militarily. The deaths and injuries in the Damascus neighborhood were caused by a chemical attack. No one doubted that.

Assad denied responsibility, and the Russians backed him up; they accused opposition fighters. UN inspectors were slow to reach the scene and were prohibited by their operating rules from identifying a guilty party. All very confusing to a president under tremendous pressure to act. He needed his intelligence team to clearly determine what happened and who did it. And he needed it now.

EVERY SUDDEN OR EMERGING CRISIS SPURS AN IM-mediate call from political and military leaders to intelligence providers: "Get over to the White House quickly!" Their input is the first step in the understanding needed to make an informed decision.[1] It begins the analysis part of the process.

Intelligence experts are charged with gathering data and turning it into useful information. They also must use their expertise to translate that information into an understanding of the situation and the environment faced by decision makers. Wise leadership ensures that everyone begins on the same sheet of music. President Obama, well aware of the Iraq WMD fiasco, certainly did not want to act and then find out that Assad was not actually behind the chemical attack.

INTELLIGENCE

The first step in good decision making is to clearly define the problem. Our intelligence agencies are charged with providing that unvarnished clarity and depth of understanding to our senior leaders. To be trusted and to ensure that decisions are made on the basis of factual and objective analysis, those providing intelligence to our senior leadership must be unbiased and avoid giving the boss what they think he wants to hear.

Secretary Rumsfeld's cryptic statement about knowns and unknowns came in response to questions at a Defense Department news briefing in mid-February 2002 about the inability of our intelligence agencies to find evidence that Iraq was providing WMD to terrorists. The statement is puzzling for reasons beyond its obviously tortured syntax. Why so many "unknowns"? A vast array of intelligence assets had focused on Iraq for over a decade. What was the basis for the absolute certainty that Saddam possessed WMD? Did the intelligence community fall into the trap of making assumptions not based on fact, or were they giving the senior administration officials what they wanted to hear?

Meanwhile, a lot of voices were screaming for action.

DECISION MAKERS NEED INFORMATION—THE MORE solid the better, and the more timely the better. Planning operations requires ample lead time, if possible. And, of course, some decisions have to be made today. In those situations, information that comes in tomorrow is useless. Equally useless is information that does not aid decision making. Leaders require what is known as "actionable intelligence"—timely and useful to aiding decision making.

An astonishing number of government and nongovernmental agencies, departments, and organizations are engaged in providing our nation's leaders with solid, timely intelligence: 1,271 government organizations and 1,931 private companies in 10,000 locations in the US. According to estimates, our annual intelligence budget is over $80 billion—a huge investment in minimizing unknowns. These agencies and companies work in areas such as human intelligence (HUMINT), signals intelligence (SIGINT), imagery intelligence (IMINT), open source intelligence (OSINT), and other "INTs." They collect information from spies and informants through eavesdropping, imagery, and nonclassified sources. The recent Edward Snowden affair has revealed the enormous extent of our collection efforts—especially through the National Security Agency—and has led to widespread questioning by members of Congress, reporters, and the general public of the legality of some collection practices.

The nearly 1,300 government and 2,000 nongovernmental organizations do not all report directly to our top national leaders. That's the job of the sixteen major US government agencies that form what's called the intelligence community. These agencies include the Central Intelligence Agency, the National Security Agency, the Defense Intelligence Agency, and others with specific information collection functions defined by law. The Community, under the Director of National Intelligence, is charged

with collecting, analyzing, and communicating intelligence to senior political, military, economic, and diplomatic leaders.

Daily briefings by our intelligence organizations keep the president
and senior administration, military, and congressional leaders up to date
on emerging threats, problems, or issues. These organizations also provide
initial information when a crisis or potential casus belli arises; and they
analyze and report on what might happen . . . or, better yet, on what's likely
to happen. Far from easy to do.

Even with all this capability and investment in intelligence gathering
and analysis, problems fall out of the blue.

Our intelligence services' record in predicting and forecasting has
been, at best, mixed. There have been clear successes, such as the detection of the Soviet missiles in Cuba in 1962 and the tracking of Osama Bin
Laden more recently.

There have also been big failures.

Just before the 2003 invasion of Iraq, then CIA chief George Tenet
announced that Saddam had WMD; it was a certainty, a "slam dunk," he
is said to have told the president. But no WMD were found in Iraq. We
missed predictions of nuclear tests, as in Pakistan and North Korea. We
did not foresee revolts, as in Iran in 1979 and more recently in Tunisia,
and government overthrows, as in Egypt. And we failed to predict military
invasions, as when Iraq invaded Kuwait in 1990.

And prescient warnings have gone unheeded.

In December 1998, while I was commander of CENTCOM (US Central Command), we were ordered to conduct air and missile attacks on
Iraq, an operation called Operation Desert Fox. The attacks immediately
followed the withdrawal of UN weapons inspectors, whose Iraqi minders
were preventing from effectively ensuring that the WMD program was
dismantled and its revival blocked. The aim of Desert Fox was to severely
punish Saddam for forcing the inspectors out of Iraq.

Because we struck without the usual buildup of additional forces that
the Iraqi leadership expected—which would have allowed them time to
prepare for an attack—we caught them by surprise. All targets were hit

with exceptional effect, and with results that were far more devastating to the Iraqi regime than we expected. The four days of attacks were a stunning success, but one that left troubling consequences.

In the months before Desert Fox, our intelligence agencies had never ceased to maintain that Iraq continued to possess WMD capabilities (after all, Iraq had earlier used chemical weapons against the Iranians in the Iran-Iraq War and against their own citizens); and I had dutifully reported that for the record in my annual hearings before congressional committees.

During the run-up to the attack, I got a call from General Hugh Shelton, the Chairman of the Joint Chiefs of Staff, with a question relayed from the White House: "How far could military strikes set back Saddam's WMD programs?"

"I'll get back to you after we do our target analysis," I told him.

I fully expected a target list from the intelligence agencies with clearly known WMD facilities. I got nothing resembling that. All the targets *could* be used to support a WMD program—dual-use chemical and pharmaceutical plants that could be converted to making chemical weapons, already permitted missile facilities, military forces that had previously protected WMD programs, high-tech equipment that could be used to support a WMD program, and Saddam's intelligence headquarters, which had been involved in past WMD programs. But where were the absolutely, positively, for-sure targets that had produced the strong assessments I had been given that a WMD program still existed?

There were no such definitive targets.

Given the targets we received, I told General Shelton before the attack that we could set things back two years. By that I meant it would take two years to reconstruct or reacquire what we had destroyed. My assessment seemed to get translated by administration officials and spokesmen to claim that Saddam's WMD "program" would be set back two years. "Wait," I thought. "I'm not so sure." The seed of doubt about the presence of an ongoing program was planted in my mind.

Meanwhile, Desert Fox had brought me new and unexpected worries.

Friendly foreign embassies in Baghdad were telling our government officials that the strikes had severely shaken the regime. The defiant rhetoric that usually followed our attacks was absent; the leadership appeared confused and demoralized. Leaders in Kuwait and Jordan, Iraq's neighbors, were concerned that a potential implosion in Iraq would send refugees pouring over their borders. "Do you have a plan if Iraq collapses from within?" a military leader from the region warned me. "We hear rumors of a possible coup attempt in Baghdad if the bombings continue."

It was a great question: we had no plan to deal with an internal collapse of the Saddam regime, which had ruled Iraq since 1979. And, second, our existing war plan contained no provisions to handle the myriad reconstruction and stability issues we would face no matter how the regime fell, by our hand or someone else's.

My CENTCOM intelligence crew put together a quick, cursory outline of what we might face in the aftermath of a regime collapse. It revealed a potential mess: extremists pouring across the border, anti-regime groups slaughtering government officials, ethnic and religious groups with long hatreds for each other committing violent acts, and looting and criminal activities potentially erupting. Saddam's Ba'ath party, which ruled with an iron fist, was made up of, primarily, Sunni Muslims, but the nation's majority were Shi'ite Muslims; tensions and fighting had grown between them over many years and a Shia insurgency, supported by Iran, was ongoing in Iraq's southern provinces. The Kurds in the northern provinces were protected from Saddam's wrath ever since the Gulf War when they had revolted, had been ruthlessly attacked by Saddam, and then had been brought under our protection by the no-fly and no-drive zones we imposed. We needed, I realized, an in-depth analysis of all we would face in this confused environment and then a plan to deal with it.

My staff recommended a war game conducted by a major defense contractor, Booz Allen Hamilton, and I agreed. We called the game "Desert Crossing." War games force you to react to predicted or possible situations. They test your decision making and bring out the shortfalls in planning and allocation of resources necessary to meet challenges. Integrating intelligence with operational decision making in an open, unscripted "game" (free play, no predetermined scenarios and actions) creates an undiluted view of the operational environment we could face and an honest assessment of what we would need in order to deal with it.

Because I knew many of the problems we would face were not military ones, I wanted to invite senior officials from the Department of State, Department of Defense, National Security Council, Central Intelligence Agency, and other government agencies. The Joint Staff and Department of Defense okayed that.

The Booz Allen Hamilton folks made clear to me that it could not be "my game." If I wanted honest answers, I had to be a player, not a driver of the game. In other words, I couldn't sit above the game as an observer. I had to be engaged in the game, make decisions, and deal with the consequences.

For three days in June 1999, we made game "moves" at the Booz Allen Hamilton facility near Washington, DC, against conditions we might face. We were given situations or challenges that our intelligence people thought we would encounter, and then we had to decide on a course of action to resolve the problem. After each move, our action was assessed by experts from the different agencies. What would we do if religious sects began fighting with each other? How do we handle malign forces crossing the Iranian or Syrian borders? Who takes care of massive movements of refugees or displaced persons? What if the Kurds decide to create their own independent state? How do we handle massive looting or revenge attacks?

The findings were astonishing. Though we could easily win a battlefield victory over the regime's armed forces and remove the regime itself in less than three weeks, it was clear we did not understand the source of far greater problems—the likely messy post-Saddam environment in Iraq.

Since stabilizing and reconstructing societies do not require military operations as much as they call for civilian programs, my next goal was to get an interagency effort underway from those who supposedly knew how to build political, economic, and social institutions in order to plan these programs. The suggestion fell on deaf ears. The detailed planning culture of the military did not reach other agencies of government. I have long felt that, unlike the military, the other government agencies we would need on the ground to rebuild a society lacked the resources, planning ability, and operations capacity to take on missions such as nation-building. This was one more instance of that striking absence. My only remaining option was to take on the planning at CENTCOM. We could at least develop an understanding of the environment, the capabilities required, and the tasks that needed to be accomplished if we ever were to intervene in Iraq or if the regime collapsed for some other reason. The planning was still ongoing when I retired in 2000.

Later, in the run-up to the 2003 invasion, I was hearing ridiculously rosy assessments about what we would face in Iraq and what we would need in order to successfully stabilize the country after we tossed out the Saddam Hussein regime. Hoping to shine a light on what we could really expect, I called the CENTCOM deputy commander. "Look at Desert Crossing," I told him. "You'll find lots of useful insights there."

"Desert Crossing? What's that?" he answered.

The lessons, assessments, and recommendations of Desert Crossing had either been forgotten or deliberately ignored. They did not fit the Pentagon's rosy assumptions. I wondered what had become of the intelligence community that in their preparation for the game had so accurately predicted what would later happen in Iraq.

The lesson I drew from all this (and I hope that leaders senior to me also drew): intelligence is only as good as the questions we ask and the way we task the intelligence community. Looking at only the defeat of the regime and its military forces was too limited a view. We were clearly going into Iraq to totally transform it, yet we did not understand what the totality of that mission required and what threatened its success. When we directed the intelligence community to provide a picture of what we would face in taking down the regime and its military forces, they gave it to us. Yet, when the decision to invade was made, our leaders discounted the importance of the morning-after threats and issues, and the earlier insights from our intelligence agencies had been shelved or never asked for. To sell this invasion, the administration had to make it look clean, short, and easy.

Cherry-picking intelligence, choosing not to ask honest questions, reaching conclusions before making an exhaustive and open analysis of the situation, or twisting and manipulating intelligence can lead to the disasters we have seen all too often in our history. More recently, in Iraq, Afghanistan, Libya, and elsewhere in the Middle East, we've seen the price we pay for shallow thinking and analysis. We missed the Arab Spring and still don't fully understand who is in the streets in Cairo, Benghazi, and Damascus. Are they freedom fighters, disenchanted youth, extremists, or all of the above, or some other element we hadn't detected? Whom do we support or not support?

CONTEXT

"We're a superpower," said Ryan Crocker, US Ambassador to Afghanistan from 2011 to 2012, and one of the finest diplomats our Foreign Service has ever produced. "We don't fight on our territory, but that means you are in somebody else's stadium, playing by somebody else's ground rules, and you have to understand the environment, the history, the politics of the country you wish to intervene in."[2]

Detailed information about what we are up against is only the beginning of the understanding needed for sound analysis, assessment, and decision making. After getting the best cut from the intelligence community, the next step is to look at options, policy implications, consequences, and other issues that influence a decision. You also need "context." Everything takes place in a complex, interconnected environment shaped by history, culture, economics, religious beliefs and practices, and much more. Understanding what you see, extract, and analyze is useless unless it is viewed through the prism of its entire context. Why is the enemy doing that? Why aren't the people responding to our efforts? Why was our well-meaning action seen as an insult?

George Tenet, the director of Central Intelligence during my tenure as CENTCOM commander, called me one day to ask if he could come to my headquarters in Tampa to "get some briefings."

"You're certainly welcome," I told him, "especially since I'm very appreciative of your superb support for our command. But," I asked him, "what am I going to brief you on, George? You see all the intelligence and have the best analysts in the world to assess it."

"Yes," he replied, "I see all that, but I also need the context to put it into. I want to see your part of the world as you see it day in and day out. I want the context around all that I see. What do I need to know to give me that?"

I meditated on that question before he visited and considered how I had tried to achieve insights into the region I was responsible for during my long immersion in it.

When George came to Tampa, I recommended books to read, places to visit, and people to talk to. I talked about influences on the cultural and political environment, such as leaders' personalities, Islam, the desert, the colonial period in the region's history, and the local customs that I had worked to understand. These were the same lessons I learned as a young lieutenant in Vietnam. Look at everything through the prism of the culture. The resulting insights allowed me to effectively interpret events and make better decisions. It was an ongoing learning experience for me. I certainly did not consider myself an expert on the culture and region, but I continually strove to understand the environment and what shaped it.

Over the years, senators such as Chuck Hagel, John Warner, and Ted Kennedy, and congressmen like Jack Murtha and Walter Jones from time to time asked me and others whose views they respected to meet with them to give views on a whole host of issues—"to run the trap lines," as I called it. These meetings, over lunch or in a casual setting, provided context that went beyond what they could glean from the numerous levels of information they already had access to. They invited me to a session not only when a specific event or issue arose, but more frequently to simply update my views and observations or to inform their own thinking. They wanted a variety of views. They also wanted depth. It was easy to make the case for taking out Saddam when the rationale was freedom and democracy versus an evil, authoritarian regime, but, as some Arab friends told me, it was also about Persians versus Arabs and Shia versus Sunni. Understanding the implications, connections, and consequences at all levels is what those members of Congress sought. Unfortunately they were rare exceptions.

Do we really understand what's going on in Egypt, or in Pakistan, or within the Syrian opposition? Sectarian divides run along tribal or religious lines and exist under the surface of what may appear to be straightforward opposition to an authoritarian or corrupt regime. If we naively take a side thinking that a conflict is simply about freedom fighters versus an evil dictator, we can find ourselves enmeshed in a religious or ethnic conflict whose ending may not result in freedom for anybody involved. What we think is an insurgency may actually be a civil war or a tribal war, and who we think may be carrying the day in the streets in the midst of a revolution may not be who ends up in power. The Russian Revolution should have taught us that lesson.

We have a tendency to characterize groups in monolithic terms that ignore the many overlapping subgroupings that may exist underneath a nominal label. In Iran, a political protest group called the Green Movement sprang up after the 2009 election. President Mahmoud Ahmadinejad was the official victor, but the results were widely believed to be fraudulent. Large-scale demonstrations, organized by the Green Movement, followed, with tens of thousands of participants. The demonstrations, initially peaceful, turned violent, with arrests of opposition leaders coming soon after. The movement was brutally crushed by the regime. Curious to know more about the movement, I asked an intelligence officer who had kept close watch over the demonstrations to fill me in. I had initially thought it was a coordinated, tightly focused political organization. The intel officer told me otherwise. The movement was a disparate assemblage of dissidents opposed to the government for all kinds of conflicting reasons. There was little coordination among them other than whatever it took to get people out on the streets.

Subgroups can be at odds with each other while still sharing the goal of challenging their government. And sometimes, differences with each other outweigh differences with the government. The enemy of my enemy may be my enemy.

Back before we overthrew the Saddam Hussein regime, I was often asked whether Iraq's Shia Arabs would side with Sunni-led Iraq in a conflict with Iran, or would their religious affinity with Shia-dominant Iran lead them to support that country. Which was stronger—religion or ethnicity? My answer was always, "It depends." In the Iran-Iraq War ethnicity trumped religious affinity, and Iraqi Shias stood with their own country. After our invasion of Iraq, they have more often than not tilted toward Iran and have allowed Iran to gain significant influence in the post-Saddam, Shia-dominant Iraq.

In Vietnam there was often violent friction between Catholics and Buddhists. In Somalia clan and sub-clan rivalries underpinned warlord loyalties. If you don't account for cultural issues that complicate decision making, you can add to already existing strife, inadvertently take sides when you hope to maintain neutrality, or make unintended enemies.

STYLE

How do presidents, their advisors, and other leaders in an administration handle the analysis that allows them to make critical decisions to commit our military to action?

Styles of handling intelligence, assessment, and decision making vary from administration to administration. Each president's and advisor's background and experience, the process they inherit or choose to put in place, the way information is presented to them, and many other factors influence a decision. Lincoln chose a "team of rivals" in his cabinet to give him an outspoken variety of opposing views. Eisenhower wanted strong, strategically brilliant advisors outside his cabinet to give him open debate on issues.

We would like to think that whatever the structure a presidential administration uses, its decision making is driven by a logical process with deep analytical thinking by the best, brightest, most experienced, and unbiased advisors, but in reality the process can be a scramble.

Bob Woodward describes how the president and his advisors developed their response to the 9/11 attacks. "Bush was concerned," he wrote, "that the war cabinet had not had sufficient time to really debate and evaluate their course of action, consider the options and plans. The NSC meetings were too rushed and short, sometimes lasting sixty to ninety minutes, sometimes much less. His time was being chopped into small pieces to accommodate the demands of both his private and public roles in the crisis."[3] The Bush administration had to quickly respond to Al Qaeda's 9/11 attacks. Americans wanted action, and Al Qaeda had to feel our might before they became even more emboldened. The administration, however, also threw the Iraq invasion on the table. This created a complicated combination of actions that needed more deliberate planning and analysis. Iraq, unfortunately, was mixed together with the urgency of Al Qaeda, and in the end both efforts suffered.

Rushing to decisions rarely pays off in good decisions, whereas establishing a process and structure before a crisis occurs often does yield sound decisions.

President Dwight Eisenhower came to the presidency from the strong planning culture of the military. "Plans are nothing, planning is everything," he once said, famously. He understood that planning meant thinking deeply and thoroughly, anticipating potential setbacks. Planning meant constantly acquiring more insights. It was not simply a means to produce a plan. Plans rarely survived the first shot, but planning was an investment in understanding the total situation. Eisenhower, supreme commander of the Allied Expeditionary Force for Operation Overlord (better known as D-Day, the invasion of France in 1944), was used to directing large and diverse staffs toward a decision, and he consequently put more structure and process in place than presidents with less high-level executive experience.

His presidency is known for thorough analysis and careful decision making. Like all great military commanders, he wanted to use all the time available to fully understand the implications of a decision. And, like most great military commanders, he had no love for war; but he knew how to fight.

Shortly after taking office in 1953, Eisenhower and his secretary of state, John Foster Dulles, met in the White House Solarium to discuss the growing threat from the Soviet Union. After the meeting, Eisenhower concluded that he needed advice and guidance on countering the threat from the best, most experienced experts—brilliant strategic thinkers like George Kennan, General James McCormack Jr., and a number of hand-picked senior military officers. A team was formed. The task became known as the Solarium Project.

The president wanted from this team deep, thoughtful analysis, diverse opinions, and open, spirited debate. He attended meetings and listened to discussions, but refrained from interjecting his own views. The Solarium group developed the strategy of containment and deterrence that served the nation well until the collapse of the Soviet Union decades later.

In 1917 President Woodrow Wilson created a group called The Inquiry to help him prepare for the postwar peace negotiations. Because he was an academic (a former president of Princeton), Wilson chose for the group 150 academics, many of whom accompanied him to France at the end of World War I for the peace talks at Versailles. The materials the group prepared aided the president in developing his innovative and radical ideas for a new postwar order.

There is no set way by which a president must structure how he or she obtains advice. Truman created the National Security Council in 1947. It remains the element in the president's staff whose formal function is to provide strategic security advice and direction. Some presidents depended on that structure as their primary source of security guidance; others have used the entire cabinet for that, while others have chosen less formal sources, such as trusted individuals or small, select ad hoc groups to lean on for advice. Eisenhower's approach was the select group. George W. Bush was primarily influenced by Cheney and Rumsfeld.

President Obama's policy decisions have been almost exclusively influenced by a small group of White House advisors—far less experienced, by all accounts, than Eisenhower's Solarium Group, yet far more closely involved in operations. Senior members of Cabinet agencies complain that they are not involved in critical decisions. Former Secretary of Defense Robert Gates writes that the Obama White House and national security staff "took micromanagement and operational meddling to a new level." Gates continues, "His White House was by far the most centralized and controlling in national security of any I had seen since Richard Nixon and Henry Kissinger ruled the roost."[4]

Obama's micromanaging style and his advisors' inexperience and operational involvement have led at best to confusion and at worst to hostile dissension. The president has often seemed out of sync with senior cabinet leaders like Secretary of State John Kerry. During the Syrian chemical weapons crisis, the president and Kerry put out different messages. Kerry took the lead and gave numerous press conferences, but his message was not coordinated with statements out of the White House. Kerry seemed surprised when the president decided to back off from the threat to use military force and to go to Congress for approval; and the White House seemed surprised when Kerry commented that destroying his chemical weapons would give Assad a way out—a comment that the Russians leaped on, and which led to the deal we are now trying to implement. An administration that looks confused or whose positions and messages are uncoordinated could be outmaneuvered in future negotiations or go in from a perceived position of weakness.

CONSEQUENCES

Unleashing hell brings with it many consequences. If all goes as planned, and it never does, every action will lead directly to the success of the mission and no stray effect will occur. All presidents desire a nice clean course of action.

In some cases the course of action may be clear. You are attacked and you must strike back. Consequences will emerge, and you have to deal with them. But the immediate crisis determines your actions.

More often, however, your course of action is murkier. Your actions will have consequences, but what consequences? The many possible second- and third-order effects of an action will complicate the decision. Do you destroy enemy industrial targets now to force them to capitulate? What if you need those assets during reconstruction to stabilize and rebuild the society?

Iran develops a weaponized nuclear capability. The president decides to preemptively strike Iran. Iran strikes back by closing the Strait of Hormuz and bombing Kuwaiti and Saudi oil fields and shipping terminals, choking off the flow of oil and natural gas from the Persian Gulf region. The price of oil and natural gas soars, and remains high for months. The world economy dives.

How does the dive affect us? The globalized economy will surely be badly hit.

Looking beyond the immediate retaliation, we see that a military action may have severe economic consequences.

A systems approach is necessary to understand the full impact of a decision to use force. Everything can be linked like the gears of a watch. Tinker with one gear and you may freeze the others, or drive them wildly out of sync. There can be political, economic, diplomatic, humanitarian, and other repercussions to such a military decision, so the thinking and assessment must be comprehensive in order to avoid unforeseen consequences, and to prepare for those that are foreseen.

Syria presents an example of extremely complex problems for the Obama administration that defy simple responses. The divided opposition forces, religious and ethnic divisions, and complicated loyalties must be understood when choosing sides or providing support. Russian backing of the Assad regime adds to the complexity and blocks our ability to get things done through the UN, where Russia holds a seat, with veto power, on the Security Council. The mediation efforts in Geneva are tricky. *Who* exactly represents the opposition? Many groups claim to. Might a final agreement leave Assad in power? The role of Iran and neighboring factions like Hezbollah in the country further muddies the situation. Other issues—the humanitarian crisis, the worsening effects on bordering countries such as Jordan, Lebanon, Turkey, and Israel, along with the removal and destruction of chemical weapons, and the disagreement within our own government over which actions to take—stir yet more mud into this vexing problem.

Every action the Obama administration has taken—drawing a redline, agreeing to a Russian-proposed agreement to remove and destroy Syrian chemical weapons, taking or not taking military action (air strikes, no-fly zones), arming or not arming the opposition, and negotiating with the Assad regime—has drawn fire from politicians, allies, and adversaries. This is a wicked problem, and there is no simple, clear, or sure path to a successful resolution.

CURIOSITY

A president's job is extremely complex. He must know a lot about a lot of things—from politics to international relations to economics to the environment to energy issues to military matters. He does not possess, however, as popes are said to have, an inherent, infallible proclamation capability that comes with the office. In addition to being well advised, a president needs to be able to learn.

Some years ago, David Gergen, a senior political advisor in both Republican and Democratic administrations, was discussing on CNN how presidents engage with difficult decisions such as the use of force. Some presidents are deeply involved and actively engaged, he pointed out. Others are more passive and disengaged. Which president is more effective? It's obvious. A president needs innate curiosity.

Imagine a president who is not passionately engaged with the questions it's his job to answer, a president who thinks that decision making is simply a matter of choosing options that have been thoroughly vetted by his staffs, weighed, and presented. All he has to do is select one of the recommendations. George W. Bush called himself "the decider." But there is a difference between simply making decisions and truly knowing and understanding the risks and consequences of a decision. That knowledge comes only from deep involvement and natural curiosity.

I have briefed a number of presidents and senior political leaders. Some of them pushed me to explain details; others just skimmed the surface of issues.

Some presidents and their advisors are content with the bare minimum of information—a few PowerPoint slides with a set number of discussion points. Amazing! How can the biggest decisions be reduced to a handful of PowerPoint bullets? I find that shocking. Yet, unless leaders are deeply endowed with the interest and curiosity that David Gergen spoke of, a flashy presentation can easily outweigh substance. Does the arrogance that sometimes infects senior leaders convince them of a God-given, intuitive ability to make sage decisions without a genuine depth of understanding of what they are getting us into?

President Jimmy Carter was accused of boring too far down into the details. President George W. Bush was accused of lack of interest in the details. President Clinton more often than not got the details about right.

Before a briefing to Clinton on an air and missile strike into Iraq, I was warned by his minders not to give him a lot of detail. That was all fine in principle, but the operation was so complex, and the flow of the operation was so critical to understanding it, I felt he needed details on timelines and decision points. He could not have gotten the decision right without this information. I decided to give him the detailed brief. There were sighs as I rolled out on the table in front of him a master air attack plan (a large matrix diagram of actions, events, and timelines), but he welcomed the details, studied the plan with care, quickly grasped its complexity, and focused immediately on where and when he had to make critical decisions. Exactly what I needed to get across. Afterward, he played it all back to me to make sure he had it right. He clearly did. And then he asked, "What else do you need from me?"

Responses like his are the best responses a general can hear from a president. Clinton understood the operation and the importance of his timely decisions. He also knew his decisions didn't just require his "OK, do it," and he could then stand back and watch. He had to follow events and be prepared for the other critical decisions he had to make as the operation played out.

PERSONALITIES

All through our history, there have been advisors who were able to create a special bond with a president through their depth of knowledge and experience, strength of conviction, like-mindedness, forceful personality, reputation, stature, or other strong qualities. These individuals have the president's confidence. They have influence that others wish for. Some may have formal government positions; others, such as heads of prestigious think tanks, may not. Sometimes leaders from allied nations have significant clout with our leadership. Certainly Ronald Reagan and George H. W. Bush listened carefully to Prime Minister Margaret Thatcher, and Bill Clinton's respect for Tony Blair was well known. I met Margaret Thatcher on several occasions; it was obvious to me how the "Iron Lady"—a forceful and determined person with deep convictions—could be a strong source of influence.

It is normally not hard to tell which key presidential advisors have a dominant voice; it isn't dependent on their official position. During the buildup to the Iraq War there is no doubt that Vice President Dick Cheney and Secretary of Defense Donald Rumsfeld were George W. Bush's closest advisors. Secretary of State Colin Powell's cautions did not sync with Bush's chosen course of action. George Marshall as army chief of staff during World War II, definitely had FDR's ear, as did national security advisors Henry Kissinger with Nixon, George Shultz with Reagan, and

Zbigniew Brzezinski with Carter. Even someone with no official status or position can have the president's ear, as Colonel Edward M. House did with Woodrow Wilson.

During the process of assessing and analyzing options, powerful voices can sway interpretations of information and the course of decisions. Some advisors can come with preconceived notions or agendas about how things should play out. If they are influential, as the neocons have sometimes been, or if there are not thought-out alternatives, discussions, and debates, they may carry the day.

Who has the President's ear? This is always the stuff of Washington insider gossip.

OPTIONS

A wise old diplomat once told me that the president's spectrum of options ranges from a strong letter of protest to a ten-kiloton nuclear airburst. The choice of which option to execute in a particular situation depends on how much leverage we have, the cost relative to the outcome, the consequences of our action, the limits of our power in the situation, likely international public opinion, or the domestic acceptability of the action.

Having multiple options on the table broadens the discussion and helps work through the consequences and outcomes. Some coercive options short of the use of force, such as diplomatic or economic sanctions, can be effective. International pressure is another alternative that may be brought to bear through the United Nations or regional organizations. Foreign or military aid can be withheld. No-fly zones or no-drive zones, such as those imposed on Iraq, can be an effective use of limited military force. Military actions such as the air and missile strikes that we conducted against Saddam, or the mining of Haiphong Harbor in North Vietnam, are also options using limited but graduated force.

Military options have a great range. Though putting boots on the ground is always the most difficult decision, other, more high-tech options like missiles and drones are not necessarily an easier or better choice, and may turn out to be just as controversial. Choosing to preempt a growing threat will also likely turn out to be contentious unless the threat is clear and imminent. The Bush Doctrine of the right to strike preemptively is based on the right to self-defense; but if the threat turns out to be nonexistent, as it did when no WMD were discovered in Iraq, then credibility is lost, both internationally and domestically.

President Obama faces several challenges, such as the civil war in Syria, the tensions in Ukraine and Russia's military incursion into Crimea, the threat that Iran will develop nuclear weapons, and the drone war in Pakistan and Yemen. He has been pressured to intervene in Syria. But how? With humanitarian aid to the fractious, many-headed opposition? How will that facilitate the overthrow of Assad? Arm them? Whom would we be arming—friends of ours or enemies? With what kind of arms? Impose no-fly zones? That does not stop the ground fighting and may give sanctuary to elements that we don't want to support. None of our options points to an outcome we can live with. And there is every likelihood that any action Obama takes will fail to leave us with steadfast allies inside Syria once the civil war in that country has been resolved.

This is not to say that we are or should have been helpless.

At the outset, borders should have been monitored and closed to malign forces, such as those from Iran and Hezbollah, whose entry into the fray confused the composition of the opposition forces. Cooperation and support for humanitarian aid and refugee management could have been better structured in neighbors like Jordan and Turkey. Direct support for the opposition forces with arms and equipment should have been established early in the conflict. (Now it may be too late, given the confusing and often hostile makeup of opposition forces.) Support for redlines among allies should have been determined before we were embarrassed by events such as the negative vote in the British Parliament on punishing the Syrians for their chemical attacks. And more should have been done to develop a coordinated regional or international approach to the Syrian problem (perhaps under NATO). But our allies in NATO and elsewhere have not rushed to volunteer for action in Syria.

"There are plenty of so-called allies who are happy to hold our coat," a senior Pentagon official told me during a discussion of options for Syria— a statement that holds true for many other challenging issues. Rarely is another nation willing to share the risks, burdens, costs, casualties, and responsibilities that we get saddled with. The US is expected to lead and provide the greatest force. Our powerful global position and the scale of our military strength makes that understandable, but allies should, at least, share the commitment and the responsibility for the aftermath.

LEVERAGE

Before a decision is made, it's important to analyze what leverage we have to influence a situation. Diplomatic, economic, or military leverage may exist from support or aid programs in place, agreements in effect, or dependencies that exist. These give us bargaining chips we may not realize we have.

In the early 1980s, I was working on a study to improve our military strategy to face a possible Warsaw Pact invasion of Western Europe. This work led me to interview a Soviet defector, an ex-intelligence officer. I kept after him to give me Soviet military vulnerabilities—a weakness in their doctrine, tactics, training, or equipment that we might exploit. After listening to all this, he leaned back and smiled. "You're after the wrong things," he told me. "You feed the Soviet military," he added. Russia had suffered serious agricultural failures. We had been sending them grain shipments. This was a good deal for our farmers, but not everybody was happy that we were helping the Soviets out. Why were we feeding our enemy? What I then realized is that we had created a leverage point. Their military, according to this defector, had become dependent on our grain. This might in fact be a far greater vulnerability than the strictly military weakness I was seeking.

Today we debate military aid to the Egyptian military. Should it be canceled, suspended, or maintained? The Egyptian military have been acting in troublesome ways since the Arab Spring uprisings of 2011. They have forcibly removed an admittedly dysfunctional elected government, but there is concern in Washington that they may be reinstalling military rule and that in their efforts to prevent radical Islamists from taking power they are ending for now the possibility of a democratically elected government. Some American leaders contend that squeezing aid will force the Egyptian military to move toward open elections. On the other hand, we can lose a great deal of leverage with Egypt if we reduce or cancel military aid. Will canceling aid threaten their important support for the Israeli-Egyptian peace agreement, access to the region through critical air and sea routes, commitment of their military to join us in regional missions, and other benefits? Very possibly. Do the losses outweigh the gains? Very likely. It's not an easy decision.

LESSONS FROM THE PAST

Thoughtful and reflective guidance for decision makers on whether or not to use military force often comes from past leaders with extensive military resumes, leaders like Colin Powell and the late Caspar Weinberger, two highly experienced national security experts.

In 1984, in the aftermath of the bombing of the US Marine barracks in Beirut and the withdrawal of our troops from Lebanon, Secretary of Defense Caspar Weinberger laid out criteria for committing forces to a conflict. In a speech delivered at the National Press Club in Washington in October of that year, he outlined what later became known as the Weinberger Doctrine. The speech, entitled "The Uses of Power," laid out six criteria:

1. The United States should not commit forces unless the vital national interests of the United States or its allies are involved.
2. American troops should only be committed wholeheartedly and with the clear intention of winning.

3. US combat troops should be committed with clearly defined political and military objectives and with the capacity to accomplish those objectives.

4. The relationship between the objectives and the size and composition of the forces should be continuously reassessed and adjusted if necessary.

5. Troops should not be committed to battle without a reasonable assurance of support of public opinion and of Congress.

6. The commitment of US troops should only be considered as a last resort.

In 1990, in the run-up to the Persian Gulf War, General Colin Powell, at that time the chairman of the Joint Chiefs of Staff, posed eight questions that should be answered before US military forces were committed to action:

1. Is a vital national interest involved?
2. Do we have a clear, attainable objective?
3. Have the risks and costs been fully and frankly analyzed?
4. Have all other nonviolent policy means been fully exhausted?
5. Is there a plausible exit strategy to avoid endless entanglement?
6. Have the consequences of our action been fully considered?
7. Is the action supported by the American people?
8. Do we have broad, genuine international support?

Although the Weinberger and Powell doctrines offer useful guidelines, they don't cover every possible case. They apply best to existential threats, such as to the nation's very existence or to a vital national interest. But they shine less light on the murkier, more confusing challenges we often face in today's ever-changing, ever more complex world, where interests and values grow ever more varied.

In 1999, during my time as commander of CENTCOM, Secretary of State Madeleine Albright invited me to join a small group for dinner at the

State Department. High-ranking State Department officials and other senior military leaders were also in attendance, including the recently retired chairman of the Joint Chiefs of Staff, John Shalikashvili.

After we sat down, the secretary of state explained her purpose in inviting us. The Balkan crisis was worsening, and the Clinton administration had been wrestling with the choices.

"How do you commit the military to missions with limited objectives, limited political will, and limited resources?" She concluded. A stunning question. There is no clear answer to it and we had none that evening. It relates to America's role in the world and how that is accepted by the American people and the international community. We understand how to fight the "Good War," but other kinds of conflicts have always been difficult for us.

My tour at the US European Command from 1990 to 1992 had made me familiar with the Balkans and its problems. I watched the old Yugoslavia break apart after the death of the communist strongman, Marshal Josip Broz Tito. I was aware that the fragmenting of the Balkans and the return to ancient ethnic and religious feuding could spread over to the highly fragile states just emerging from Soviet control. I likewise knew that although the current crisis was serious for the region and tragic for those caught up in it, none of our own vital national interests were directly at risk. And because we had recently gone through the Somalia experience and our military was severely stretched with commitments in the Middle East, Korea, and elsewhere, I knew there wasn't much stomach for another military intervention. On the other hand, we had obligations to our NATO alliance that were being tested in this crisis. Furthermore, no one was convinced the violence would stay confined to the Balkans—a region infamous as the powder keg that ignited World War I—or how the problems there might affect the rest of Europe and the newly emerging eastern European states, the former Soviet republics, and a transitioning Russia. This kind of conflict was not what NATO was created for, but this threat seemed to some NATO members like a logical post–Cold War mission for the transitioning alliance. Though intervention was a difficult sell if you applied the Weinberger and Powell doctrines, we were about to come into the conflict to protect the Bosnians from Serbian aggression.

General Wesley Clark, the Supreme Allied Commander Europe (SACEUR) at the time, summed up the Albright dilemma: "Operation Allied Force was a modern war—limited, carefully constrained in geography, scope, weaponry, and effects. Every measure of escalation was excruciatingly weighed. Diplomatic intercourse with neutral countries, with those opposed to NATO's actions, and even with the actual adversary continued during and around the conflict. Confidence-building measures and other conflict prevention initiatives derived from the Cold War were brought into play. The highest possible technology was in use, but only in carefully restrained ways. There was extraordinary concern for military losses, on all sides. Even accidental damage to civilian property was carefully considered. And 'victory' was carefully defined."[5]

Except for the controversial bombing campaign in Serbia that General Clark conducted under extremely frustrating limitations, we were able to walk the minefield of the Balkans with relatively minimal military commitment. The bombing campaign was designed to coerce Serbia into ceasing its ethnic cleansing actions and ending its support for the Kosovo Liberation Army conducting attacks against Muslims. Though the campaign was successful and the ethnic cleansing ended, the duration of the bombing, the collateral damage, and the anxieties of European allies led to questions about this strategy. Even the US Congress began to challenge the president as the 70-plus days of bombing exceeded his authority under the War Powers Act, which required that he come to Congress for approval of continuing any military action beyond 60 days.

The Balkans experience was a precursor to the complex conflicts we would become immersed in at the dawn of the twenty-first century. Murky missions, reluctant allies, weak domestic support, unclear end states, and unacceptable costs would characterize these new interventions. Decision making has not become easier, but there are still things we can learn from past experience.

In his book *In Retrospect*, written decades after the Vietnam War, former secretary of defense Robert McNamara reflected on how the two administrations he had served had contributed to, as he put it, "our disaster in Vietnam."[6]

He listed eleven failures in judgment. Among them: Our leaders had misjudged the capabilities of the enemy, the political forces in South Vietnam, the motivation of the North Vietnamese, the cultural environment, the ineffectiveness of high technology in that form of conflict, the support of the American people and Congress, international support, and the capabilities we would need in order to prosecute the war.

But here was his most telling lesson: "We failed," he said, "to analyze and debate our actions in Southeast Asia—our objectives, the risks and costs of alternative ways of dealing with them, and the necessity of changing course when failure was clear—with the intensity and thoroughness that characterized the debates of the Executive Committee during the Cuban Missile Crisis."

I don't know of a better endorsement for robust analysis and assessment from multiple points of view.

The Weinberger and Powell doctrines, as well as the McNamara lessons, can serve as good general rules and guidance, but they are broad and don't reflect the more complex issues of today's conflict environment. We need to draw deeper lessons that help leaders answer today's most profound and challenging questions . . . questions like Secretary Albright's: "How do you commit the military to missions with limited objectives, limited political will, and limited resources?"

FOUR

THE BUCK
STOPS HERE

*Boys, if you ever pray, pray for me now. I don't know if you fellows ever had a
load of hay fall on you, but when they told me yesterday what had happened,
I felt like the moon, the stars and all the planets had fallen on me. I've got the
most terribly responsible job a man ever had.*

President Harry Truman, April 14, 1945

JOB DESCRIPTION: US PRESIDENTS MAKE DECISIONS—
decisions that are often difficult, complex, and produce big consequences.
Their responsibilities are awesome and stressful, thus the moving words
of Harry Truman to reporters two days after the death of President Roosevelt, and thus also the famous sign on his desk: "The Buck Stops Here."
Truman may, arguably, have been the president who was least prepared for
the monumental tasks he faced. Roosevelt had not brought him into his
inner circle, and had not kept him abreast of the significant issues he was
dealing with as World War II was coming to a climax and new challenges
were looming.

In spite of his scanty preparation for the job, Truman more than once
faced the most difficult, complex, and consequential presidential decision:
to use force or not. Some of his tougher and more controversial decisions
were the atomic bombing of Hiroshima and Nagasaki, America's participation in the Korean War, the firing of General Douglas MacArthur, the

reorganizing of the national security structure, and the daring Berlin airlift to counter the Soviet attempt to swallow Berlin. He made these momentous decisions with no hesitation, with only the counsel of his small select staff. He understood what was required of him, whom to go to for advice (his principal advisor on foreign policy was Army Chief of Staff George Marshall, whom Truman nominated as secretary of state in 1947), and what might be the consequences.

Truman may be the consummate American decision maker. He was tough, straight-talking, humble, and experienced in war (he commanded an artillery battery in World War I). All presidents should take a lesson from him. He may not have been well prepared to take on these decisions, but he brought the right character to the office to take them on, and he knew where to go for advice. His down-to-earth, practical approach to decision making reflected the average American's thinking and character.

Every president who commits the nation to a military intervention crosses the decision line at some point. "In January 2003," wrote Colin Powell, of the time when he was secretary of state, "as war with Iraq was approaching, President Bush felt we needed to present our case against Iraq to the public and the international community. By then, the President did not think war could be avoided. He had crossed the line in his own mind, even though the NSC had never met—and never would meet—to discuss the decision."[1] It's hard not to conclude that President Bush, predisposed to attacking Iraq, was not open to contrary advice.

"Let's do it."

We would like to believe a president reaches this point solely on the merits of the situation and after careful and exhaustive analysis, weighing diverse expert opinions, and considering all possible alternatives. But decisions hardly ever work out that way. As they work through the process, presidents handle pressures from every direction.

What else influences presidents? Some come from outside. Others are more personal.

THE PLANTED FLAG

"Let our position be absolutely clear: An attempt by any outside force to gain control of the Persian Gulf region will be regarded as an assault on the vital interests of the United States of America, and such an assault will be repelled by any means necessary, including military force." President Jimmy Carter made this statement in his State of the Union Address on January 23, 1980; it proclaimed the Carter Doctrine that committed the US to defend the Persian Gulf Region, and led to the creation of the Rapid Deployment Joint Task Force (RDJTF) that evolved later into the US Central Command (CENTCOM). The Carter Doctrine was in response to the 1979 Soviet invasion of Afghanistan. The president saw the incursion as a possible beginning of a Soviet advance into the critical oil-rich Persian Gulf region, and this doctrine formed the basis for American military intervention in the region for decades to come, even after the Soviet threat was long gone.

Throughout our history, presidents have established foreign policy positions that directly or indirectly pre-committed military force if specific interests were threatened. These doctrines are named for the presidents who established them—from the Monroe Doctrine to the Bush Doctrine. There are doctrines associated with presidents Theodore Roosevelt, Truman, Eisenhower, Kennedy, Johnson, Nixon, Carter, and Reagan.

The Monroe Doctrine, and the (Theodore) Roosevelt Corollary to it, proclaimed that our hemisphere was off-limits to other nations, particularly Europeans, for colonization or intervention. The Truman Doctrine committed the US to support militarily countries under threat from, or resisting, communist aggression internally or externally. The Eisenhower Doctrine authorized military aid and support to nations facing armed aggression by communist-controlled nations. The Kennedy Doctrine proclaimed support for the containment of communism and the reversal of communist inroads into the Western Hemisphere. The Johnson Doctrine declared that communist-motivated revolution in our hemisphere would not be considered a local matter. The Nixon Doctrine provided for aid to allies facing threats from communism. The Reagan Doctrine called for support of anti-communist resistance movements. The Clinton Doctrine committed the US to act against threats of genocide and ethnic cleansing. The Bush Doctrine stated the right of the US to strike preemptively and intervene where terrorist threats to the US were present.

These and other presidential doctrines allow presidents to measure political and popular support, or to create it, well ahead of a decision to act. In some cases they give a president the justification to act preemptively if a threat line is approached.

On the downside, presidential doctrines, National Security Strategies,[2] policy speeches, redlines, and other forms of defining our interests and articulating the actions we will take to defend them can pre-commit presidents to act. These pre-commitments may tie the hands of a future president who may prefer not to have a planted flag in place. Once a strong position has been staked out, though, it is difficult not to defend it, even if circumstances have changed. Very specific commitments to act can take away presidential flexibility. Israeli and many US political leaders, for example, have constantly pressed President Obama to strictly define a redline on Iran's development, or potential development, of a weaponized nuclear capability. Although Obama has in fact set a broad redline—a nuclear armed Iran is unacceptable; all options, including military action, are on the table to prevent that—his critics want a more narrow articulation of the redline, such as the enrichment of a specific quantity of uranium. The diplomatic art of setting a redline so that there is no mistaking what is unacceptable, yet leaving yourself the greatest degree of flexibility and maneuver room, requires great skill.

Obama's two redlines, on Bashar al-Assad's use of chemical weapons and Iran's development of a nuclear weapon, have been problematic for him. He seemed to waffle on the chemical weapons issue, then he was outmaneuvered diplomatically by the Russians, and when he went to Congress for approval, he looked weak and indecisive. The charm offensive by Iran's new president, Hassan Rouhani, pulled us into negotiations that worried and angered Israel, Saudi Arabia, the United Arab Emirates, and other close allies, who fear Iran is just buying time and angling to get sanctions lifted while they move their nuclear program forward. Other "allies" were eager to profit from the potential economic benefits of lifting sanctions on Iran, while critics feared it would be difficult to reinstate sanctions once trade with Iran began, even if Iran slow rolled compliance with any agreement.

Yet presidents must take a stand.

Other complications loom when, as sometimes happens, we fail to carefully define our interests here or there, leaving adversaries to conclude that such places are fair game. The North Koreans likely interpreted the withdrawal of US troops from South Korea in 1948 and the failure of Secretary of State Dean Acheson in 1950 to include the Korean Peninsula in a defined "defense perimeter" to mean that the US would not defend South Korea. As a result, North Korea's leader, Kim Il Sung, felt South Korea was up for grabs and charged south.

CONGRESS

Article II, Section 2, of our Constitution states that the president is the commander in chief. Article I, Section 8, states that Congress has the authority to declare war. So who's in charge of committing the military?

In the centuries of the United States' existence, our nation's political leaders have found no clear resolution to the Constitution's division of authority. Though Congress has formally declared war only five times in our history, Congress has at times authorized presidents to use force without a declaration of war; and at other times Congress has looked the other way when a president committed the military. Yet Congress has occasionally denied the president that authority. The 1973 War Powers Act attempted to force presidents to gain Congressional approval to continue an action not later than 60 days after its launch. But presidents Ronald Reagan and Bill Clinton have been charged with ignoring the act, Reagan in the early 1980s during the Iran-Contra operations and Clinton in the mid-1990s during the bombing campaign in the Balkans. The battle between the executive and the legislative branches on the authority to use force has raged from George Washington's presidency to Barack Obama's.

Constitutional scholars acknowledge that the president must possess the power to act in the face of a serious, immediate threat, and that Congress must at some point approve the initial commitment, as well as sustaining operations (Congress must fund), and termination (Congress must approve treaties).

Most important, Congress is where the debate should take place. As the invasion of Iraq loomed, many Americans were unhappy about the rush to war without a full airing of the looming conflict's rationale, consequences, and purpose. There wasn't much debate about any of this in Congress—and the little there was came too late.

A month or so before the invasion, Democratic congressman Jack Murtha asked me to address a large group of Democratic House members regarding the invasion and its consequences. As I opened my talk, I could clearly see the congressmen were angry that there had not been a full airing of the issues and that anyone who dared to oppose or question the wisdom of the mission was being unfairly branded as unpatriotic. Their anger grew as I gave my take on the impending operation and answered their questions.

About an hour into the meeting, someone rushed into the room. "It's over," he shouted. "Daschle and Gephardt have gone over to the White House; they're standing beside the president to show support for the war." Senator Tom Daschle was the Democratic leader in the Senate and Congressman Dick Gephardt was the Democratic leader in the House.

There was no reason to continue the meeting; the invasion was a done deal. The room slowly emptied; heads were shaking. The Bush administration had cleverly packaged the invasion of Iraq with the invasion of Afghanistan and shut down debate.

"You know," Congressman Murtha told me before we parted, "I tried to tell Cheney and those guys at the White House that we needed a full hashing out of the issues. There are too many unanswered questions. We can support you if we all understand and agree with what we're getting into, I told them." He caught my eye. "But they won't even respond."

During that same period, Republican senator Dick Lugar, the chairman of the Senate Foreign Relations Committee, asked me and two others to testify before the committee about the coming intervention. Senator Lugar wanted to get a healthy debate going and lay all issues and views on the table—a courageous call, given the Republican administration's headlong drive toward invading. Lugar was a very senior and respected Republican who took foreign affairs seriously. I left the hearing room appreciating his attempt to get an honest debate going (the views of the two others testifying were different from mine). But the ship had sailed.

Congress's failure to face the challenges it was their job to face was forcefully made clear at a dinner talk I gave a few weeks earlier to a prominent group of Richmond, Virginia, civic leaders (including members of Congress from the area). The subject was Iraq. My views stirred strong reactions. During the question period, a man stood up and pointed to the members of Congress. "I'm a Republican," he said. "I support the president. But you members of Congress owed us the debate. I have not heard a full account of the issues." Exactly on target.

Not all members of Congress, however, dodged their responsibilities to watch over Iraq and Afghanistan. Some, like Representative Walter Jones, a Republican from a very conservative district in North Carolina, have been truly courageous. Jones loyally supported the war until the misrepresentations and mistakes became clear to him. The many funerals of service members from his district prompted him to search out the causes of these failures to keep our troops safe. As a result of what he learned, he became a highly vocal critic of the war. "This will probably cost me reelection," he told me, "but it's the right thing to do." He was reelected.

I CAN'T LET THIS GO ON

In April 1991, President George H. W. Bush ordered Provide Comfort, a military operation to protect Kurds fleeing Iraqi forces in the aftermath of their failed uprising against Saddam Hussein's regime following Iraq's defeat in the Gulf War. (Kurds are an ethnic group who also live in neighboring Turkey, Syria, and Iran, and wanted nothing to do with Saddam's Iraq.) I was the deputy commander and chief of staff for this operation. Many of Bush's political opponents charged that he had incited the Kurds to rebel, then left them dangling on their own to suffer the wrath of Saddam's brutal forces. (During the operation, a number of Democratic members of Congress came to Iraq and Turkey looking for evidence of this failure on Bush's part.) Provide Comfort was originally designed as a humanitarian operation to stabilize the traumatized Kurdish refugees trapped under horrific conditions in the hills of southern Turkey. But the operation morphed into a mission to return the Kurds to their homes in northern Iraq and then to shield them from the wrath of the Iraqis with a long-lasting no-fly and no-drive zone. This last mission ended with Saddam's defeat in the Iraq War that was launched in March 2003.

In 1995, President Clinton ordered the US operation called United Shield, which I commanded, to protect the withdrawal of UN forces from Somalia. By then, the president had already been burned by Somalia more than once; he did not relish sending troops back there. But the UN mission to Somalia had failed, and the president felt an obligation to help them out.

Our entanglements in Somalia started in late 1992, when Clinton's predecessor, George H. W. Bush, ordered the US-led Operation Restore Hope to provide security after rising hostilities prevented an anemic UN operation from fulfilling its mandate. During the months that followed, the mission changed, eventually turning into a larger UN operation to fight powerful warlords. Meanwhile, in the aftermath of the infamous Black Hawk Down incident in 1993, the US had withdrawn from the mission. Even so, the president felt an obligation to the nations that had provided forces at our request and were still vulnerable to attack as they withdrew.

In April 1975, President Gerald Ford ordered Operation Frequent Wind—the rescue of Americans and Vietnamese as Saigon fell to the North Vietnamese onslaught. By then, American troops were long gone from Vietnam, and support for South Vietnamese forces had been drastically cut by Congress. Yet Ford felt obliged to rescue not only American diplomats but also South Vietnamese who had worked for the US or were at great risk of retribution by the Communist regime. The images of helicopters lifting frightened people clinging to the skids from the roof of the US embassy have imprinted on that generation . . . and on me.

On October 24, 1984, President Ronald Reagan ordered the invasion of Grenada, a small Caribbean island nation.

It was not a popular decision—especially in the face of the horrific events of October 23, the day before Reagan announced his Grenada decision, when the Marine barracks in Beirut, Lebanon, were bombed by two suicide bombers in trucks packed with explosives. In the attack, 299 US and French troops were killed.

The administration received scathing criticism, reminiscent of the recent Benghazi scandal, for allowing the military force in Beirut to remain after its initial 1982 mission to protect the withdrawal of the Palestine Liberation Organization had been completed. Accusations of mission creep, murky political objectives, and lack of understanding of the threat were hurled against the president and his national security team.

Another military intervention was the last thing his advisors recommended. And there was significant opposition from the international community to the Grenada invasion, including from close allies such as the United Kingdom. A UN Security Council resolution condemning the intervention in Grenada had to be vetoed by the US.

As soon as he learned of the bombing in Beirut, President Reagan went to Camp David in order to be with the Marine security contingent there. He obviously felt a strong emotional reaction to the tragedy and to his responsibility for it.

Under the weight of these pressures, he gave the order to execute Operation Urgent Fury, the invasion of Grenada. Military forces, including the Marines on their way to relieve the decimated force in Beirut, were given the mission.

"Why did he do it under such heavy pressure not to?" I asked an official close to the president who was involved in the decision.

"The President focused on the US medical students trapped in their dorm rooms on the island," he told me. "'Is there a potential threat to their safety?'" Reagan asked. "When he was told there could be, there was only one decision he could make in his mind. Americans were in danger. He had to act."

Decisions often create unexpected responsibilities that presidents must then accept and act on, either because they can't allow a nasty situation to fester or metastasize or because they feel it's necessary to reinforce America's trustworthiness and dependability.

Pointing to the instances in which growing casualties had provoked America's withdrawals from Vietnam, Beirut, Somalia, Yemen, and the eastern provinces of Saudi Arabia, Osama Bin Laden claimed that the United States would never stay the course if the going got tough.

An argument can be made for Bin Laden's claim (he's not the first to make it and he won't be the last), and it can send a powerful message to allies and those we want to enlist with us in a future cause. We have to counter it by making certain our commitment does not flutter away when it's seriously tested. And we have to show that we honor our obligations and responsibilities, no matter how long honoring them takes. As an example, we remain committed in Korea after six decades. And we remained committed to our European allies for seven decades

POLITICAL PRESSURES

"We will stand in Vietnam," President Lyndon Johnson announced on July 23, 1965.

A few months before, he committed US ground combat units to Vietnam with the landing of 3,500 Marines at Chu Lai. It was the most important decision of his presidency. And he would have dodged it if he could have. By all accounts he felt trapped by it.

The trap had many snares. For starters, there was the weight of the legacy of his beloved predecessor John F. Kennedy. Kennedy had accepted the challenge of communist-inspired insurgencies and had pushed for a strong counterinsurgency capability to confront Chinese and Soviet expansion. Publicly embracing the challenge to meet these insurgencies head on, Kennedy had committed significant numbers of advisors and support personnel to the Vietnam conflict, and Congress had authorized significant funding support for the South Vietnamese.

Though Johnson had been elected in his own right in November 1964 and had moved beyond his sensitive position as chief advocate of Kennedy's programs after Kennedy's assassination, Johnson could not easily reverse Kennedy's commitments. Yet his thrust as president was oriented toward domestic issues, as articulated in his Great Society and War on Poverty programs, and not toward foreign military interventions. Vietnam was a distraction.

Worse, if Johnson did not commit major US forces to the conflict, he knew he would be seen as weak. He would be defined as the president who lost Vietnam. (He could not forget the "Who lost China?" accusations from powerful Washington hawks ever since Mao Tse-tung's communists took over in 1949.) Political adversaries and strong anti-communist members of the opposition party such as Richard Nixon and Senator Barry Goldwater, an Air Force Reserve general, a respected hawk, and Johnson's Republican opponent in the 1964 election, would pounce on him for not standing up to the challenge of encroaching communist aggression (the most fearsome "ism" of the time). They'd brand him as soft on communism, the president who let the dominoes fall in Southeast Asia. (Strategists had predicted that if South Vietnam fell, Laos and Cambodia would quickly follow, and then perhaps Thailand, and so on—the so-called domino theory.)

Worse still, the news from the battlefield was not good. The Joint Chiefs and the Secretary of Defense were reporting that South Vietnam was too weak to survive on its own. Unless we took strong action, it could fall.

For Johnson, this was a no-win situation. With all these political pressures weighing on him, he saw no option other than to commit US ground forces to the conflict. By the end of 1965, there were 189,000 troops in Vietnam, and by the end of 1966 that number doubled. By 1969, there were more than 500,000 US troops there. Thirty thousand Americans had been killed by the time Johnson left office in January 1969.

President Nixon was elected on a promise to end the Vietnam War, and he claimed to have a secret plan to end it. In fact, he did not. He actually expanded the war into Laos and Cambodia, in an effort to force the North Vietnamese into peace talks. Even though he had inherited the war, he was under considerable pressure from each end of the political spectrum. From the left, to end it quickly. From the right, to end it honorably, with a sustainable South Vietnam in place as we withdrew. These conflicting pressures were tough to harmonize as he faced an enemy who was aware of his dilemma.

President Obama has faced tremendous political pressure to keep a residual force of trainers and special operations units in Afghanistan; and he is blamed by political opponents for not having remained in Iraq with the same kind commitment. Despite the refusal of political leaders in those countries to approve a remaining commitment, his foes in Congress charge that he didn't do enough to insist on a follow-on capability and that his rush to exit these conflicts has left both countries vulnerable to sliding back into the violence and chaos that previously existed.

PERSONAL PRESSURES

"The pressures and complexities of the presidency," said President Truman, "have grown to a state where they are almost too much for one man to endure."

If that was the case over sixty years ago, imagine what it's like now in our far more complex world. Many influences play on a president's mind after a crisis hits but before he begins to weigh the situation and determine a course of action. These influences may shape the ultimate decision before he commences hard analysis of the facts of the situation, and they may shade the context within which a president makes his decisions—the "outer ring" that shapes his thinking before he can bring his mind into the "inner ring," the analysis of the specific situation.

Presidents are human. They fall prey to the same weaknesses as all the rest of us. They have the same drives and emotions that everyone else has. They make terrible mistakes that they have to live with. They may get caught in a scandal. They worry to a varying degree about how they are perceived by Congress, the rest of government, by the American people, and the rest of the world. They worry about their legacy. These factors, and many others, weigh on their decision making, consciously and unconsciously.

In *Bush at War,* Bob Woodward discusses George W. Bush's emotions in the wake of the horrific 9/11 attacks: "The public tears were perhaps very important. For two days Bush had been responding as president, genuinely but still within the norms of expected presidential behavior. It was perhaps too detached and impersonal. What he had been saying didn't quite seem like him. He had assumed the aura of president, had imposed it on himself. Standing there in the Oval Office and crying made it clear that human emotions trumped even the office of the president."

There's no way any president could avoid a wide range of emotions after the horrific events of 9/11—sorrow, anger, desire for revenge, grief, and the stress of his own responsibility for the nation's response. The weight of what he must do and the struggle to discipline those emotions while trying to make calm and reasoned decisions could only add to the stress. No matter how hard a president tries to avoid taking events personally, emotions sparked by national tragedies and glaring outrages are hard to tame.

Barack Obama has often seemed too detached and cool. Bush often seemed to act out of bravado. How much and what kind of emotion do we want in our presidents? We certainly don't want them to act solely out of emotion, but we do want to see them reflect the passion we feel when events require action.

IN AUGUST 1998, THE MONICA LEWINSKY SCANDAL broke. President Clinton had carried on a sexual relationship with the young White House intern and lied about it. The scandal dominated the news; there were cries for his impeachment.

That same August, during my time as commander of CENTCOM, President Clinton ordered military strikes against terrorist targets in Afghanistan and Sudan in response to terrorist attacks on embassies in Kenya and Tanzania. And at the end of the year, he ordered strikes against Iraqi targets in response to Saddam's obstruction of UN inspectors searching for weapons of mass destruction. Though the president's actions with Ms. Lewinsky were outrageous and indefensible, they created no risk to the security and well-being of the nation; and there was no connection between the decisions to attack and the scandal. Planning for the Iraq strikes was done well before the scandal became public, as a contingency in case Iraqi interference prevented the inspectors from conducting their mission. The Afghanistan and Sudan strikes were an immediate response to an immediate shocking attack.

In the 1997 movie *Wag the Dog*, a US president orders military action to cover up a personal sex scandal. The movie's plot was inadvertently prescient, and when the Monica Lewinsky scandal broke, the two stories inevitably intertwined. "Wag the Dog" charges were flying from Clinton's political opponents.

The tempest of accusations intensified, and from all sides, even though the leadership of the Republican-led Congress supported the president's decisions to strike. Some even charged that the scandal had so weakened Clinton that he was incapable of deciding whether or not to use force! Clinton was caught in a trap of his own making.

Since I was CENTCOM commander at that time and responsible for the execution of the strikes, I attended meetings and briefings with the president and his advisors in Washington and at Camp David on strike planning and execution. On one occasion, as we prepared to conduct air and missile strikes against Iraq, we flew to Camp David to brief the president and members of his cabinet during a time when it was reported that Clinton and his wife had withdrawn to Camp David to attempt a reconciliation. Despite his personal strains and pressures, the president was upbeat and focused during the briefing. Clinton was always brilliant at compartmentalizing the many disparate pieces of his life. And yet the stress he was feeling still slipped through. "I'm damned if I do and damned if I don't," he remarked with a rueful, pained expression after we presented our strike options.

In fact, though he was all too aware of the political and media accusations he faced, Clinton never wavered from his longstanding position: We would use force if the inspectors were prevented from accomplishing their mission.

WARRIORS? . . . OR COMMUNITY ORGANIZERS?

Presidents are not all like Harry Truman. Sometimes they are politically vulnerable to accusations of inexperience and indecisiveness, and so feel they have to establish their decisiveness and strength under stress. These accusations leave them vulnerable; they can be swayed by pressures they might otherwise safely ignore.

During the 2008 Democratic presidential primary campaign, Barack Obama faced a strong challenge from Senator Hillary Clinton. Shortly after Obama came to the Senate, on the recommendation of another senator, he and I met to discuss Iraq. Impressed with his intelligence and personable character, I anticipated that he might rise to higher office, but needed much more time in the saddle. The young Illinois senator had only two years of national experience. Pouncing on that weakness, Senator Clinton charged Obama with inexperience and lack of resolve. The charge was most famously articulated in Clinton's television ads asking who could more effectively handle an unexpected crisis call in the wee hours of the morning, Clinton or Obama. To embellish her "warrior" credentials, Mrs. Clinton falsely claimed to have come under "sniper fire" when, as first lady, she landed at Tuzla Air Base in Bosnia during a visit in 1996. Later video footage of her arrival showed nothing of the kind: on the tarmac a small girl presented Mrs. Clinton with a poem, and then the first lady strolled leisurely toward the terminal. The video quickly led to challenges to her sniper attack claim, and she was forced to admit that she had "misspoke."

Candidates for high office will go to bizarre lengths to demonstrate their warrior and foreign crisis credentials. Even if the Tuzla sniper had been real, the first lady was no better prepared for a 3 a.m. crisis call than the young senator from Illinois.

Obama won the primaries and the presidential election, but the perception that he was inexperienced and indecisive stuck; and these perceptions brought pressures from hawkish politicians like senators John McCain, Lindsey Graham, and Joe Lieberman to take more forceful positions or actions on Libya, Syria, Iraq, and Afghanistan. To date Obama has resisted these pressures and has been determined to withdraw from Iraq and Afghanistan and to avoid commitment to potential long-term, messy involvements in places like Syria. However, this course and his backing down from the redline he drew on Syrian use of chemical weapons and his negotiations with the Iranians over their pursuit of a nuclear weapons capability have only increased the accusations of weakness and inexperience.

THE PERCEPTIONS OF OBAMA'S INEXPERIENCE ARE not totally inaccurate.

On May 1, 2011, in a nearly flawless operation, Neptune's Spear, US Navy Seals killed Osama Bin Laden. Later, photos from the White House Situation Room during the mission revealed faces struggling to comprehend what was happening on the ground in the compound inside Pakistan. For all the intellectual and political savvy of Obama and his advisors, the senior leadership in that room had the look of people who were mystified by what was going on. They had no frame of reference, no visceral experience that gave them a handle on what was happening in that compound.

Some years ago a senior Special Forces officer discussed with me and a few others the brief given to President Carter and senior leaders at the White House prior to launching Operation Desert One (1980), the failed action to rescue our embassy hostages in Iran. The questions they asked, he told us, showed no real comprehension of what was expected to take place on the ground. They were more interested in details, such as the restraints (handcuffs) that our rescue team would be equipped with, than in the broader strategic and operational challenges to the mission.

Contrast this with the experience Eisenhower and his senior advisors brought to the presidency. They had been through two world wars and numerous crises. Truman, who fought in the trenches in World War I, and Kennedy, who commanded a PT boat in World War II combat, could likewise relate to the tactical military environment.

Must a president have been shot at to be able to handle his job? No. Yet if a president's personal experience does not include military service, he won't have that visceral understanding of what he may be ordering troops to do; presidents who lack that firsthand experience must find some other way to grasp the implications of their decisions to use force as these play out on the ground. Achieving that understanding can be a struggle.

General Hugh Shelton, former chairman of the Joint Chiefs of Staff, once told me he wished an experienced four-star general were sitting on the National Security Council (NSC) alongside the president's civilian advisors. "I want somebody in the room, from the start," he explained, "who has credible military experience and can give credible advice." He made it clear that he didn't want a political or "chateau" general in that position.

I knew what he meant. The chairman—the principal uniformed military advisor to the president and secretary of defense—is always brought into the military-related decision making process, but decisions are sometimes reached, or at least formed, before he ever gets to the White House. And it's hard to counter flawed ideas once they begin to set in leaders' minds.

President Obama did choose a retired four-star as his first NSC head, General James Jones, but the appointment did not work out well, reportedly due to friction between members of the council who had more direct access to the president and grumblings from the military over his views on Afghanistan. These tensions became evident in the Stanly McChrystal dust-up in 2010, in which a *Rolling Stone* reporter tagging along with McChrystal's staff wrote a story recounting McChrystal's open criticism of Obama, Vice President Joe Biden, and General Jones. Jones left his position after two years and was replaced by his deputy who was a long-time member of Obama's inner circle.

VOX POPULI

Every president is acutely aware of the expectations and mood of the people. He will hear it in the streets, from the media, from polls, from other elected officials, and from members of other government organizations. These voices can put pressure on a president to act and act very quickly and boldly. It can even force a president's hand before he feels ready to act. Presidents Clinton (Somalia), Johnson (Vietnam), Nixon (Vietnam), and Reagan (Beirut) felt pressure from the American people to end military commitments that in their view had gone wrong. President Obama faced pressures from senators McCain, Graham, and others who urged intervention into Libya and Syria that he did not want to commit to.

The irony is that pressures to act can quickly turn into pressures to withdraw, and the pressures to *not* act can later lead to criticism that you haven't stood up to the challenge. The so-called CNN Effect—horrific scenes of devastation and humanitarian tragedy beamed into America's living rooms—can generate an outcry for intervention. But, as happened in Somalia, when the cost of intervention becomes unexpectedly high and the results are not what was advertised, the outcry can rapidly reverse itself and turn to "get us out."

DECISIONS

Presidents like Eisenhower and Clinton, who listen objectively and seek to fully understand the issues we face, tend to make good decisions. They ensure that all voices are heard and all required data is gathered and credibly analyzed. They guard against private agendas, personal bias, or preconceived notions influencing open and honest debate and discussion. Their primary goal is to gain a clear and unfiltered understanding of the issues and the problems they face. They bring in experienced and trusted advisors to fill gaps in understanding effects, risks, and consequences. They seek a wide-ranging discussion of available options—their merits and limitations. They avoid making hasty decisions, decisions under stress, and decisions by committee.

The secretary of defense must play a major role in this process. A big part of his job is to objectively lay out the options and consequences of each proposed military course of action. He cannot come to the president with a private or narrow agenda, and he must ensure that other influences on the president are weighed against the military reality. This means that he must have made sure that the president is familiar with his military and its capabilities and shortcomings long before any crisis develops. Not every defense secretary fits that model. Hyper-controlling secretaries like McNamara and Rumsfeld limit direct contact between presidents and the generals and admirals who command the services and combatant commands. When that happens, presidential decisions suffer. Others, like Secretary William Cohen, carefully build direct relationships between presidents and military leaders before crises hit.

MILITARY DOCTRINE AND PLANNING ARE BASED ON centuries of experiences that have been continuously examined and debated. The military is obsessed with reviewing past military decisions and studying historic military decision making. Gaming and exercises are another important element in the military's preparation for handling crises. Political leaders have a very different—and, in my view, mistaken—understanding of their responsibilities toward future crises. Few political leaders review their own and past major decisions with anything like the military's intensity and care, much less engage in programs of games and exercises that provide opportunities to prepare for a crisis. It's a rare presidential administration, with its cabinet, the NSC, and other advisory bodies, that does not begin its term from scratch—uninformed and unprepared for the unexpected crises that will inevitably leap up to bite them.

That problem is not intractable. It would not be especially difficult to create a professional—and professionally trained—civilian national security service, just as we have a professional foreign service, to man the national security structure (the Pentagon, the NSC, and other security staffs). Like the foreign service, the CIA, and the FBI, the security service would have a training and development program and a career progression structure.

Neither is the problem on the White House side intractable. Traditionally, presidents do not participate in "war games"—for a powerful reason: potential real decisions might be revealed to enemies. Yet presidents and cabinet members need a mechanism to practice their crisis response skills. It can be structured so that the process stops at decision making with only the options developed and presented.

I recently attended a lecture by a noted military historian, whose specialty is civilian control of the military, on the problems of this relationship. During his lecture, he mentioned my name. That caught my attention; I became even more attentive when he went on to dismiss as naive my recommendations that our political masters who have no military experience must have in place a mechanism that will better prepare them and their staffs to manage crises before crises hit. In his view, our political system doesn't allow for on the job education of our political leaders. They just come and go; they handle challenges as best they can with what they come with. I don't buy that. Our leaders should not have to continue to relearn critical lessons on the job. Must past mistakes forever be forgotten or ignored? Leaders *can* learn from them if they choose to.

FIVE

EUROPE FIRST

Notwithstanding the entry of Japan into the war, our view remains that Germany is still the prime enemy, and her defeat is the key to victory.

George Marshall, Army Chief of Staff,
Memo, Arcadia Conference, December 1941

THE FIRST WASHINGTON CONFERENCE, CODE-NAMED Arcadia, took place immediately after the Pearl Harbor attack on December 7, 1941, in the midst of a two-year war raging around the globe. In the days and years before Pearl Harbor, the United States had no true national security strategy, but nothing focuses leaders' concentration like a devastating attack. American and British leaders and planners quickly came together to lay out a strategy for defeating the Axis Powers. The resulting agreement set the priority: Germany above Japan (aka the Europe First policy). Though this commitment wasn't without US critics (after all, it was Japan that attacked us), the urgency of the task to get a strategy articulated drove that commitment without much debate.

The world was already two years into the war. Japan and Germany were gobbling up territory with effective and sophisticated military machines. Allies were in dire straits; too many had fallen—France, for example, had surrendered to Germany in 1940—and more would fall. A coalition plan had to be put together; priorities, such as which theater should take precedence, had to be agreed upon; our industrial base, long idled by the Great

Depression, had to be revived and given direction; and our military had to be built up at a rate, and to a size, unprecedented in our history.

It may have been too early to know where we would finally be headed (we could not then foresee the war's end state) or what our timelines might be, but we needed to set clear—though necessarily temporary and provisional—guidelines. We needed a clear statement of our direction and goals. We were behind our enemies in strategic direction and purpose. We desperately needed to catch up quickly.

The strategy evolved rapidly through a series of high-level conferences attended by top leaders and talented diplomats and generals. In December 1941, while we were still reeling from the devastating attack, it might have been impossible to even imagine a strategic direction or design for fighting this war, but men like Roosevelt, Marshall, and Churchill knew the process had to begin and would evolve as events progressed. They possessed the strategic character and visionary thinking that understood the urgency of mapping out a future direction. (Roosevelt and Churchill had in fact been communicating and strategizing for several years. Among other actions, in 1939 FDR had prodded Congress to repeal the Neutrality Acts, thus allowing sales of weapons and supplies to Britain; two years later, he urged Congress to approve the Lend-Lease Act of March 1941.) Unlike many in the past, and many more in recent years, these leaders were not transactional in their approach to prosecuting the war in that they were not about fighting a series of disconnected battles and campaigns that had no strategic purpose or ultimate objective. As an example, Marshall and Eisenhower resisted Churchill's pressure to engage in operations that did not lead directly to achieving the strategic goal of bringing the war to the heart of Germany as soon as allied forces were capable of achieving it. Churchill's dreams for sideshow missions in the eastern Mediterranean and elsewhere were rejected. The strategy that Roosevelt, Marshall, and Eisenhower developed not only led to unconditional surrender of our enemies, it changed and redefined America.

The negative and positive experiences of World War II—from our unpreparedness in December 1941, to the strategic design and purpose that carried us to victory, to the brilliantly successful military operations on land, seas, and skies—followed by the increasingly dangerous world that emerged after the war, taught us many lessons, and during the Cold War we maintained a strategic underpinning to our security decisions. Strategic thinkers and actors like Marshall, George F. Kennan, and others provided the security, economic, and diplomatic strategies that helped us navigate the dangerous decades from the end of the war to the collapse of communism. But, regrettably, that level of rich strategic thinking and planning, ceased with the end of the Cold War. In recent decades we have so far failed to think and act strategically. Our leaders mouth grand phrases, such as "new world order," "peace dividends," and "military transformation;" they plough apathetically through the bureaucratic processes that are supposed to lead to effective strategies; and they half-heartedly produce documents such as our national security and military strategies that are rarely read or understood; but they never give serious thought to how we should respond to this new, complex world.

George Marshall would never have accepted what passes for strategy today.

IN 1996, ALMOST EXACTLY FIFTY YEARS AFTER THE end of World War II, I came to CENTCOM as the deputy commander; I took full command the following year. Up until that moment, I had always understood that four-star generals were deeply involved in designing and implementing strategy. I imagined that they frequently engaged in serious strategic dialogue with our political leaders. And so, as I settled into command, an immediate priority was to study both the recent evolution of strategic guidance for the region under my responsibility and the current strategic documents that would provide me, and our command, direction for the days ahead. All this came with my job as commander of a Unified Command. I was charged with developing what was then called a theater engagement plan, a strategy for implementing the national strategic guidance for the region assigned to CENTCOM. The other combatant commanders had a similar responsibility to design a strategy for their regions.

I wanted to ensure that our strategy fit into the larger national strategies and complemented the adjacent regional command strategies. After all, I was educated at our military schools to expect meaningful strategic guidance. I had learned that carefully thought-out strategies underpinned all our national security efforts and that my contributions to our strategic foundation were critical elements in our overall security strategy. I pored over the past two administrations' National Security Strategies (NSS, the grand strategy that is supposed to guide all other strategies) for guidance affecting our region—the National Defense Strategy (which guides the military and nonmilitary requirements for our security), the National Military Strategy (the military-specific guidance), the Quadrennial Defense Review (the four-year set of very specific directions for our forces), the counterpart strategies developed by the agencies of government other than the Defense Department, and the US ambassadors' Country Plans (the country-specific direction for our relationships and interests in a given nation). I even studied the strategies of the other combatant commanders and the service chiefs. Stacks of documents filled tables in my office, and I waded through all of them. I was in for some surprises.

I found shocking inconsistencies from document to document. Terms were different, or had divergent meanings. Priorities varied. Directions and policies were different. There was no centralized direction or coherence, no common or global focus. I could only conclude that each was produced in isolation from all the others, as if our government were a feudal system where each baron followed his own lights to develop his own goals and courses of action.

In theory, strategies from above should provide a clear framework and guidance for strategic development and implementation down and across government departments and agencies. I had expected a smooth flow from the NSC, our grand strategy at the top, down to my level. I didn't get it. Even the geographic divisions of responsibility were different from agency to agency. CENTCOM had part of the Middle East, part of Africa, part of Central Asia, and part of Southwest Asia. These assigned areas of responsibility were covered by four separate State Department regional bureaus with overlapping regional responsibilities in Central Command's,

Pacific Command's, and European Command's areas of responsibility. The State Department bureaus with responsibility for Africa, the Middle East, Southwest Asia, and Central Asia formed policies and strategies that straddled the unified commands. A Middle East policy that was significantly shaped by our relationship with Israel, for example, was difficult to coordinate, since Israel was in the European Command's area of responsibility, and most of the rest of the Middle East was in CENTCOM's. In those days, as the CENTCOM commander, I was a low man on the strategic totem pole, but I could clearly see the strategic dysfunctions. They remain today.

It was obvious to me that no one truly monitored all the strategic documents to shape consistency, coherence, and compliance with guidance from above. I suspected, and later became convinced, that few if any decision- or policy makers even read them with any care. These documents were intended to drive policy, to guide allocation of resources, and to form the underpinning for debate. That was not happening. The feudal barons just did what they thought best.

The Theater Engagement Plan, the strategy we developed for CENT-COM, had several complementary elements. My aim was to build military and other relationships in our region, to deal with and contain the threats to our mutual interests there, to protect those interests, to establish the right balance of military presence, and to develop a coalition approach to handling problems. We sought to build a collective structure for security and the containment or elimination of threats. And I wanted to do this with a minimal presence of US military force, yet with enough punch to retain the ability to respond rapidly and effectively should the need arise. These elements, taken together, seemed to be in keeping with the general course that my seniors desired, even if that was not spelled out in the strategic documents. Sometimes, you have to push the strategy up.

GOALS AND VISIONS

"Strategy"—officially defined—"is the art and science of developing and using political, economic, informational, and military forces as necessary during peace and war, to afford the maximum support to policies, in order to increase the probabilities and favorable consequences of victory and to lessen the chances of defeat."[1] More simply stated, it is the articulation of ends, ways, and means we apply to achieving a political objective. As the old saying goes, "If you don't know where you're going, any path will get you there." Strategy is about knowing where you are going, or where you want to go.

Strategy can take many forms. It can be a very broad principle or set of principles, like deliberate isolationism, which guided us for a century and a half, or containment and deterrence, which guided us through the Cold War. It can also take the form of an elaborate plan or design, as the strategy for fighting World War II became over time. Or it can be a very specific guiding tenet designed to meet a specific threat or crisis. Although our Cold War goal was to not go nuclear unless we were attacked by nuclear weapons, our strategy did not reject the possibility of a nuclear first strike against an overwhelming Soviet conventional force attack (an invasion of West Germany for example).

To be clear, I'm not talking solely about a strategy for the use of military force. National strategy goes way beyond that. The Marshall Plan, formally the European Recovery Program (1947), was an economic and governance strategy that contributed as much to stabilizing and protecting Europe during the Cold War period as the NATO military alliance did. The establishing of the World Bank, the reorganizing of our government structure under the 1947 National Security Act, and the articulation of the Truman Doctrine all combined with the military components to form a total grand strategy for managing the postwar environment.

BUILDING STRATEGIES

The United States does have in place a highly structured process for developing strategies. The requirement for security strategies is derived from the National Security Act of 1947 and further amended by the Goldwater-Nichols Department of Defense Reorganization Act of 1986. The president is required to present an NSS to Congress within his first 150 days in office, to update it each year, and to submit that update with his budget. In theory and in law, our overarching strategy, the NSS, must be constantly in place. It's our Grand Strategy. It's the way we direct the planning, developing, managing, and implementation of the programs and capabilities necessary to protect our interests, our people, and way of life. It should also set priorities. Economic and security considerations, for example, have caused President Obama's administration to set a Pacific First or Pacific Pivot strategy which places that region as the top regional priority.

Once the NSS has been developed, Congress should then, in theory, review it and provide the resources and funding to support it . . . or else deny them. The NSS is supposed to give Congress a point of reference as it decides funding issues. If they support the strategy, presumably they will okay funding. If they don't support the strategy, they will presumably deny funding or request clarification. Balance of powers. From the NSS stem supporting strategic plans through all agencies of government designed to express how they intend to achieve their part in the larger grand strategy.

Three problems come with this process.

First, little actual attention is paid to the NSS, normally prepared by the National Security Council within the executive branch (White House). It is rarely completed on time. Instead of forming the conceptual basis for discussing and debating national security issues, it is ignored. I seriously doubt that many members of Congress even read the NSS.

Second, politics and narrow political needs are too often substituted for strategy. Political agendas, congressional pork, current and uninformed popular opinion, and other factors replace strategic analysis. For example, how many redundant military bases continue to operate in districts of powerful congressmen? How many plants produce possibly unneeded ships, planes, vehicles, or weapons? How many times have we seen our service chiefs complain that programs and equipment that were forced on them by specific, congressionally directed funding were not what they needed, or came at the expense of other, more critical programs?

Third, we all know that you rarely get the crisis you have prepared for, or fight the war you plan for. At such times you hope you are balanced enough in your basic strategy to shift strategic gears to meet the challenges you face. A conventional military, for example, thoughtfully developed and designed in the 1950s to fight a hot war in Central Europe against the Soviet Union, found itself in the 1960s mired in fighting insurgencies in steaming jungles in the tropics of Southeast Asia and in Central and South America. Our Cold War strategy did not prepare us for this.

President Kennedy took on this challenge of proxy warfare, and his successors inherited that challenge. To the contain-and-deter strategy that included a nuclear capability and a highly ready and technologically advanced conventional military force, had to be added a secondary strategic path that included a highly skilled unconventional force that could operate in the difficult environment of a third-world insurgency. Yet, our fundamental strategy required us to stay prepared and organized for the greater threat from a direct conflict with the Soviet Union. Because we had a strategy, we knew the risks we faced in altering our military structure. We accepted the challenge of fighting insurgencies, but only as a secondary mission that would not detract from our primary focus.

THE VISION THING

During the 1988 presidential campaign, an interviewer urged George H. W. Bush to pay more attention to longer-term objectives and to setting forth inspiring national goals. "Oh, the vision thing," he replied dismissively, as though setting national goals was a pointless exercise.

Interestingly, though, his administration handled the Middle East challenges they faced with strategic deftness. On the other hand, they let the collapsed Soviet Union dismantle itself without serous strategic thinking or design aimed at influencing the outcomes to make them more favorable to US interests. There was other fallout. Immediately after the Soviet breakup (1991), problems broke out in the Balkans and eastern Europe. And issues like "whither NATO?," future relationships with Russia, and engagement with the former republics of the Soviet Union did not get the strategic attention they merited. We are paying a price for this today as the crises in eastern Europe continue to dominate the news.

Handling these issues required a Marshall-like strategy. Although there were tentative steps in the right direction, nothing like that was forthcoming.

Secretary of State James Baker launched an effort, headed by Ambassador Richard Armitage, to engage our allies in what was termed a new Marshall Plan. The idea was to solicit support from our free-world allies to establish a positive political relationship with the republics of the former Soviet Union and the former Warsaw Pact nations; to help them to adopt, and adapt to, true democracy and free market economies; and to build a friendly military-to-military relationship. This required resources and commitment that our allies weren't ready to provide.

Armitage worked tirelessly with the various ministries of the former communist countries and shuttled around the capitals of our allies to pull this strategy together. (I was on his team, primarily coordinating military support for his mission.)

Despite Armitage's hard work and vision, the full commitment that Truman and congress gave to our strategy and its implementation in the Marshall era was not there—no doubt caused by the absence of a clear looming threat like the one we faced in the aftermath of World War II, when the US and western Europe feared Soviet expansion. However we account for it, we are still dealing with the effects of our failure to build a strategic design after the Soviet collapse. The fruits of that failure include troubling events in the former Soviet republics of Georgia and Ukraine that threaten stability in eastern Europe, Secretary of State Hillary Clinton's ridiculous offer of a reset button to her Russian counterpart after the relationship between the two nations had deteriorated (the button itself was mistakenly labelled with the Russian word for "overload" rather than "reset"[2]), and the willy-nilly rush to sweep new members into the NATO alliance when no member—new or old—understood what that membership meant and required. Did anyone consider that this expansion would be an "in your face" to Russia? (Again, whither NATO?) We should ask ourselves whether Putin's Russia was inevitable; or might a greater investment in building the right relationship by us and our European partners have led to a different evolution in Russia's political leadership and direction.

Formulating strategy is hard. You have to imagine the future you might face, decide how to shape that future to your advantage, and design and implement a course of action to take you there. The alternative to building a meaningful strategy is the transactional, day-to-day, make-it-up-as-you-go-along approach—a proven recipe for disaster. The unfolding of the Obama administration's handling of Syria is an example. So far, the administration has not controlled the track they are on. They have been reactive, not proactive.

Forcing yourself to build a strategy, as with developing any plan, produces a much deeper understanding of what you face and what needs to be done about it. It forces leaders to define their goals and vision for the future. It allows them to foresee risks, potential courses of action, and alternative futures

The first step in designing any strategy is to identify the vision. What kind of security, prosperity, and set of values do we want to achieve and maintain in the future? Next, the strategy lays out the goals—broad statements about how we plan to reach our vision. As the strategy moves down the ladder, supporting strategies developed by the various agencies of government form their own specific objectives, that is, how they plan to contribute to achieving their portion of the broader goals. They then develop the action plans and resource requirements needed to reach their objectives. Since we can't afford everything, it's critically important to set priorities and articulate risks in those areas where we can't support an objective. For example, we have in the past set security and economic priorities for regions of the world and even for specific allies. During the Cold War, Western Europe was our highest-priority region. We continue to have special relationships with countries such as the United Kingdom, Canada, and Australia. But we do have limits. We can't do everything and be everywhere. Cultural affinity, common governance systems, mutual security interests, resource and energy dependencies, and critical economic ties are among the factors that can help us choose our highest priorities. One caution, however: regional priority or single nation selection is old-think in this globalized world; new ways of prioritizing, such as newly emerging economic powers, global alliance members, or democracies may provide better choices in defining priorities.

STRATEGIES MUST BE DYNAMIC. CONDITIONS CHANGE and the unexpected happens. Today's global environment is highly fluid, crisis-prone, and often disordered. We no longer live in the relatively ordered, albeit more dangerous, world of the Cold War. We must constantly monitor day-to-day operational decisions in order to understand how they affect the overall strategy. Sometimes these can create an opportunity, and at other times a challenge. I learned this lesson from an officer at CENTCOM.

"CENTCOM is a crisis management command," my staff was fond of saying. We went from one crisis to another. My successors have had crises in spades. The current CENTCOM commander has on his plate Afghanistan, Iraq, Iran, Syria, Egypt, the Arab Spring, terrorist groups, shaky allies, and many other challenges.

I tracked our strategic plan separately from our day-to-day crises and contingency activities and plans. A different staff directorate and different planners worked on each. Consequently our strategic and contingency briefings and discussions were separated.

One day a planner on my staff, a lieutenant colonel, suggested that both had to be looked at together, as a single continuum. "A decision or action you take today, sir, in reaction to an unforeseen event, can significantly impact the strategy. It can delay or speed up our timelines. It can create a strategic opportunity or a strategic challenge that must be dealt with immediately. It can change the course of the strategy." In other words, he was saying, you have to adapt your thinking and long-range planning to today's real events and make decisions on dealing with those events based on your long-range objectives. At the time we were tightening the noose around Saddam. The sanctions, no-fly and no-drive zones, punishing attacks for crossing redlines, and other actions were slowly making Iraq far less of a threat to anyone. That was all good. These day-to-day actions, however, could eventually lead to the regime's collapse. Should that have occurred, what would be our strategic plan for managing the collapse? What kind of Iraq was desirable in the aftermath, what effect would it have on the region, and how could we influence all this?

This caught my attention. I put the colonel in charge of a small group of officers assigned to track the bridge between our strategy and day-to-day ops. Our strategy was the responsibility of our Plans Directorate (J-5), and our contingency and crisis response activities were the responsibility of our Operations Directorate (J-3). We clearly needed a connecting organization—a small group in the staff who would monitor all the strategic planning efforts and updates, whose members would sit in on all our contingency and crisis response activities and look for disconnects, challenges, or opportunities that could alter the strategy or impact the contingency and crisis planning. We set up the (awkwardly named) Campaign Objectives Analysis Group (COAG), and it worked. The holistic view of strategy, crisis response, and day-to-day engagement in the region gave us greater insights and clearer direction in our decision making.

Now we had better answers to questions like these: If a crisis required the use of force, were the bases we used or the coalition forces available to meet this challenge in line with the strategic relationships we wanted to build? If we responded to a humanitarian disaster, was that an opportunity to lead with forces in the region whose image, training, and experience we wanted to promote? If a military action we took could change the balance of power in the region, how would that affect our larger strategic goals?

STRATEGY EVOLVES EVEN IF YOU ARE ABLE TO START out with a clear set of goals. Time and events will alter those goals. As you deal with unexpected events that have long-term consequences, you have to continually rework your strategy. In an ideal world, you can set your strategy then act. In the real world, a crisis requires immediate action. That action can have long-term consequences, affect your overarching strategy, and cause a specific, or satellite, strategy to be built to manage the crisis.

In August 1990 Saddam Hussein's military attacked and occupied neighboring Kuwait. The invasion caused us major problems. We did not foresee it, it gave Saddam control over immensely increased oil resources, and it threatened our allies and interests in the region. Meanwhile, Iraq had been a Soviet client state, the Cold War had just ended, we were seeking a peace dividend (the long-awaited allocation of funding to nonmilitary priorities) and a new—and calmer—world order, and we did not want to launch a unilateral intervention that might draw international criticism or upset the former Soviet Union's fragile transition to democracy. George H. W. Bush's administration faced further dilemmas. They did not want to end up with a large military presence in the Middle East. Nor did they want to end up with an occupation of Iraq, with all its potentially warring factions and other vexing complexities. Yet the crisis demanded a response. There wasn't much time to develop a detailed strategy, and the end state was difficult, if not impossible, to foresee or define.

The administration decided on several initial policy approaches. It sought and received a United Nations resolution that authorized the use of force. This provided international support, legitimacy, and approval for military action. It also gave political cover to allies inclined to join the cause; however, it limited the authority to use force only to the expulsion of Saddam's forces from Kuwait. Some hawks saw this limitation as unacceptable, but the administration viewed it as prudent.

Several Islamic nations offered to join the anti-Saddam coalition. This had many advantages. Ejecting the Iraqis from Kuwait would not be seen as an anti-Islamic crusade; the Islamic nations would help share the costs of the war; we would retain positive relations with our allies in this sensitive region; and they would aid us in the postwar containment of Iraq. But there were conditions. The Islamic nations joining the coalition desired a separate but coordinated military co-command (a difficult problem for the cohesion and unity of command normally necessary to military operations). To address this condition, US military leaders, from Secretary of Defense Dick

Cheney to Chairman of the Joint Chiefs of Staff Colin Powell to CENT-COM Commander General Norman Schwarzkopf, constructed the complex bifurcated command structure required and made it work.

We successfully expelled Saddam's forces from Kuwait, but we now faced myriad strategic issues left behind. When the Kurds rebelled in northern Iraq, the Iraqis tried to crush the rebellion, and we came to the Kurds' aid. Another UN resolution and another quickly assembled coalition saved the Kurds and established a security zone that protected them from Saddam's forces.

Meanwhile, the Shia in southern Iraq also rebelled, and we established a partial security zone (no-fly restriction) in that part of Iraq to protect the insurgent Shia population. Sadly, the Shia rebellion failed and led to a drawn-out insurgency with nasty consequences. Saddam drained the maze of swamps in that region that provided a livelihood and a (relatively) safe haven for those living there, and they were forced to fight their insurgency from sanctuaries in Iran, creating a relationship that proved problematic once the Shia majority in Iraq came into power after our overthrow of the Sunni-dominated regime of Saddam Hussein.

So here we were in the early 1990s with a commitment to contain Iraq (and also Iran) for an unknowable period of time and with no clear end state.

The Clinton administration continued that commitment—officially called the Dual Containment Policy (Iraq and Iran). It now required additional components over a number of years: a stronger set of relationships to support our expanded military presence, cost-sharing for the continuing operations (no-fly and no-drive zones, maritime intercept operations, support for the UN WMD inspectors, etc.), and direct allied participation in these operations. General Joseph P. Hoar, the new CENTCOM commander (1991–94), successfully built the necessary closer relationships in the region. His successor, General J. H. Binford "Binnie" Peay (1994–97), put in place pre-positioned military equipment, shared basing with host nation forces, combined exercise programs with our regional allies, and scheduled rotational forces from outside CENTCOM—providing forces and capabilities that could meet an immediate crisis without an overwhelming and burdensome presence in the region. CENTCOM accomplished the containment of Iraq and Iran with the help of resources and funding from allies in the region and without permanently assigned forces and US bases. As a result, we could defend against mischief from Iraq or Iran and quickly bring in larger forces to deal with a threat requiring offensive action, but, with this structure, we could just as easily reduce our presence if tensions and threats subsided.

Beginning in 1997, as the successor commander of CENTCOM after generals Hoar and Peay, I continued these policies and added a robust command and control structure in the region. We also bolstered our commitment to the defense of our allies in the Persian Gulf and supported their efforts to build a military capability that complemented our forces in the region. When Saddam got out of line, we systematically reduced his capabilities to threaten his neighbors or to defend himself. Most notably, we incrementally reduced his air defense system and command and control capabilities through air and missile attacks when he failed to comply with UN WMD inspectors' demands or crossed other redlines. By the time I left CENTCOM in 2000, we had effectively neutralized his air defense system and greatly weakened his ability to communicate with and control his forces.

This was a case of strategy evolving over time. Our goals became clearer as elements fell into place. We contained and degraded the threat that Saddam posed, but avoided assuming the burden of rebuilding Iraq with all the inherent problems and costs that went with that task. Although the way ahead to an acceptable total end state—such as removal of the regime with minimal cost and burden to us—was not clear, the most efficient and effective ways to contain and degrade the threat had become clearer. We had effectively put Saddam in a box and stripped him of his ability to threaten his neighbors, while avoiding taking ownership of a messy Iraq.

This strategy was abandoned when the second President Bush invaded Iraq in a kneejerk manner, ignoring the objectives, planning, and insights developed over two previous administrations—including his father's. The invasion of Iraq in 2003 came with costs that previous administrations had wisely avoided.

WHEN STRATEGIES FAIL

The George W. Bush administration went to war in Afghanistan without a fully articulated and workable strategy; and they later opened up an unnecessary two-front war by invading Iraq without a carefully thought out strategy for either theater of operations. This was brought home to me powerfully in conversations with two of my successors at CENTCOM. "We never knew what was expected of us," they told me. "We did not have the strategic guidance we needed to fight these very strange wars intelligently; and we were not invited to contribute to developing it."

It was never clear what the administration's strategy was. Were they trying to implant democracy in a quick shake-and-bake action—as though democracy can "take" in a large, disparate population like a vaccine? Did they see something that few other experienced hands saw when they backed exiled insurgent wannabes like Ahmed Chalabi, who claimed they could transform Iraq and the region? Did they really believe our invasion of Iraq was about weapons of mass destruction, and did they see that as a greater priority than searching out and destroying Al Qaeda? Even if one of these possibilities turned out to be the Bush administration's actual strategic purpose, none of them demonstrates the slightest understanding of the environment they threw themselves and our military forces into. No true strategy can be developed without an honest, unbiased, and credible process of gaining that understanding. But the Bush administration's leaders were unwilling to listen to voices other than their own; a small group of like-minded people with private agendas drove the process, and they formed in their minds a rationale for action that was built on biased views and the most doubtful of assumptions.

When I commanded CENTCOM, I'd had close relationships with the decision makers in Washington. Rarely did a day go by that I didn't talk to the secretary of defense, the chairman of the Joint Chiefs of Staff, or other senior government officials. These were not one-way conversations. They wanted input, assessments, and recommendations. Sometimes my views differed from my bosses'. Sometimes that rankled them and they let me know. Yet never did they fail to welcome my views or give them a full hearing.

In the administration of George W. Bush, such relationships no longer existed.

The political leadership, the policy developers, and the operational commanders must be in sync. We should never fail to align policy, politics, strategy, operational design (the way we implement the strategy on the ground), and the tactics in the field. These elements naturally tend to pull apart. The policy makers at the top must stay connected and involved in the actions on the ground, and those at the operational and tactical levels must ensure that their actions are conducted within the intent and framework of the levels above. The communications most go up and down the chain. Americans have always been critical of single direction, top-down direction with no input welcome from the lower end. We thought this a weakness in the Soviet system. Something to be exploited. Yet, we reverted to that system in the recent conflicts we have been engaged in.

History can inform us of what happens when we get out of sync. General George B. McClellan in Virginia in the Civil War, Douglas MacArthur in Korea, William Westmoreland in Vietnam, and numerous other examples demonstrate the consequences of misaligned and disconnected levels. More recently, the disconnects between Washington policy makers and the commanders in the Balkans, Iraq, and Afghanistan created friction that resulted in turnovers in commanders reminiscent of what Lincoln experienced with his generals.

As a combatant commander, I operated most often at the seam where strategy and operations meet. They should influence and inform each other. Without a clear strategic direction, operations are dangerously adrift. Without awareness at the strategic level of the operational environment, useless actions result. How Did MacArthur get so far off the reservation that Truman had to fire him? Why have so many commanders paraded in and out of Baghdad and Kabul? Throughout the more than ten years of war in Iraq and Afghanistan, we were either searching for a strategy or an operational design—or both.

WHOLE OF GOVERNMENT

Experience has taught us that the military can't go it alone if we are to ultimately succeed. Our recent conflicts give this truth more meaning. The "whole of government" must be committed, as the current fashionable Washington phrase has it. We need to integrate the "hard" power of the military with the "soft" power of diplomacy and development. Today's term of art is "smart" power. Joseph Nye, an exceptional strategic thinker and experienced national security policy hand, defines it this way: "Smart power means developing an integrated strategy, resource base, and tool kit to achieve American objectives, drawing on both hard and soft power."

In 2006, I was a member of a Commission on Smart Power sponsored by the Washington-based Center for Strategic and International Studies. Our commission was chaired by Joseph Nye and Ambassador Richard Armitage, another highly regarded policy thinker and a former deputy secretary of state. We recommended that the US should complement its military might by focusing on five critical areas: building stronger international alliances, partnerships, and institutions; elevation of the role of development efforts in our foreign policy; increased emphasis on public diplomacy to build stronger relationships; expansion of economic integration; and greater investment in technology and innovation to resolve issues such as energy security and the effects of climate change. These broad goals were fine, but the difficult question is how to implement them.

I am currently co-chairman of the National Security Advisory Council, which is part of the US Global Leadership Coalition, an organization that is committed to promoting the development of a balanced set of capabilities across our government—in other words, smart power. The council's members include 150 retired three- and four-star generals and admirals—an indication of how significantly we in the military feel about improving partner capabilities in the other agencies of government. We have long seen the need to get our military out of the nonmilitary functions required to stabilize a conflict environment and to bring into those environments people with real expertise in these areas and provide them with the capacity necessary to ensure success.

A MILITARIZED FOREIGN POLICY

Our foreign policy and national security strategies have often been criticized—justly—as overmilitarized, a truth both Secretary of State Hillary Clinton and Secretary of Defense Robert Gates strongly acknowledged while in office. We've allowed the military to become too easy to use and the other agencies of government too hard to use. In Iraq, the Department of Defense took over such roles as overseeing governance, economic, and political development, when the State Department and other agencies are better equipped to handle such tasks. I could never understand why my CENTCOM war plans did not include political, economic, and social development planning and execution responsibilities. I tried to change this after the Desert Crossing war game demonstrated the weakness in a military-only plan for an environment such as Iraq where many nonmilitary problems would have to be addressed. But the other agencies of government I approached were unable or unwilling to commit to the planning. It's not only critical to integrate all our elements of power into our thinking and planning at the strategic and operational levels, but those who are responsible for implementing the actions must also be integrated into our training, exercises, and teams that deploy to our foreign interventions.

In the days before our 2003 invasion of Iraq, I asked two generals in charge of units spearheading the attacks who would be responsible, during our entry into Iraq, for connecting our occupying forces to the population, providing humanitarian aid, settling local disputes, and reconstructing the local governance and economic systems.

"We've been told that's not our job," they told me. "There's a vague reference to some kind of follow-up force that will do all that." That follow-up force was the Office of Reconstruction and Humanitarian Assistance (ORHA). Though it was headed by a superb retired Army general, Jay Garner (I served with Garner in Kurdistan during Operation Provide Comfort), ORHA did not have the capacity, structure, or clear lines of authority for the nation-building tasks they faced. Needless to say, during the early days of the invasion when it was critically needed, the ORHA force never arrived in any significant way, and the military initially took on those jobs . . . or tried to. Later, a hastily thrown together organization was rushed into place, the Coalition Provisional Authority (CPA), which made a series of inept decisions like disbanding the regular Iraqi military (after years of promising the Iraqi military that they would be left essentially intact if they did not resist), closing state-owned factories and putting people out of work, and poorly managing ill-conceived contracts with civilian contractors. The CPA reported to the Pentagon, hardly the department best suited for national reconstruction, learned little from their mistakes, and got no better over time. This was the cost of failure to create a plan that went beyond the military dimension.

Although the official definition of strategy includes the nonmilitary dimensions of intervention, these aspects rarely find their way into actual strategic plans and war plans. As a result, the bulk of the nonmilitary tasks are shouldered by the military, as I learned for myself during my recent assessments in Iraq and Afghanistan. Uniformed military personnel were engaged in numerous functions that were totally out of their range of skills and expertise. The military were running zoos, recreational swimming pools, mediation groups, anticorruption task forces, governance development teams, and many, many other nonmilitary activities.

In 2009, at a smart power conference in Washington, DC, I proposed that if the other agencies of our government could not take on their responsibilities in post-conflict situations, we should make the military's de facto assumption of them legitimate. I recommended that the military's Civil Affairs organization become a unified command responsible for integrating all the agencies' efforts and providing the planning, administrative, and logistical support for the interagency teams on the ground. Just as our Transportation Command brings together all the air, sea, and land transportation capabilities, Civil Affairs would bring together the agencies involved in managing post-conflict conditions.

Not everyone appreciated my suggestions. And the Clinton State Department reacted strongly to them. Within days, Dr. Jeffrey Stacey, a political science and international relations professor working in the Office of the Coordinator for Reconstruction and Stabilization, gave an official response. His office, he claimed, has a "substantial standalone budget" and "sizable staff," and had created a "Civilian Response Corps . . . an expeditionary force primarily for deploying to conflict zones" who were engaged in activities all across the globe. Sorry, Dr. Stacey, but during my visits to Iraq and Afghanistan I must have missed all those funds being spent and people making a difference in conflict zones. Uniforms far outnumbered the suits and skirts involved in nonmilitary reconstruction programs. The Office of the Coordinator for Reconstruction and Stabilization had zero effect in Iraq. "It was dead on arrival," a senior diplomat at the State Department told me. The State Department was brushed aside by Rumsfeld as the Defense Department assumed control of the reconstruction.

Shortly after I retired, the Senate Foreign Relations Committee organized a high-level Policy Advisory Group, co-chaired by Senators Dick Lugar and Joe Biden, to examine this problem. Many other committee members actively participated. I was asked by Senator Biden to serve on the group.

During the meetings, it became clear to me that the recommendations were headed toward minor fixes, such as adding people and money to the other agencies and organizing small offices at their headquarters to deal with these issues. But John Kerry (then a senator) wisely cautioned us to think bigger. He rightly felt that we needed to address issues beyond providing resources. My experience backed that caution. We needed to address deficiencies in the other agencies, such as the absence of an extensive planning capability and their inability to take on large, complex projects. If we don't want the military to continue to be left with the hard, essentially nonmilitary work of nation-building, then we need to develop a serious interagency commitment to develop these capabilities, and we need a serious whole of government strategy to go with it. It is not there now. Some in Washington have called for a second Goldwater-Nichols Act that would integrate the agencies (the original act integrated the military services) and provide for the structure, resources, and other requirements necessary to put agencies such as the State Department and the Agency for International Development on an equal footing with the military. Those who argue that this would be too expensive fail to understand the cost when the military gets stuck with these tasks.

When I made my assessments in Iraq and Afghanistan, I saw that virtually every department and agency of government was represented in these countries, and the vast majority of agency people I witnessed toiling away in these difficult environments were dedicated and skilled, but there were far too few of them to accomplish the mission they had been sent to accomplish.

WHERE ARE THE MARSHALLS?

Thoughtful people in and out of government have frequently asked why we no longer seem to produce George Marshalls . . . or George Kennans . . . or Henry Kissingers. The question goes beyond security goals and visions. A great nation must produce strategic thinkers and actors—those who can implement a strategy as well as design it—of all kinds if it expects to stay on course and meet future challenges. Few with the right intelligence, skills, and experience make it into the key positions that require these abilities. Appointees to leadership positions where strategies are developed are more often chosen for political loyalty than for strategic talent.

The military tends by tradition to put more emphasis on developing strategic thinkers and actors than other organizations. But bitter experiences from lack of strategic direction on the battlefield have given the military added incentive. Somebody has to do it.

The US Army developed a promising program, the Army Strategic Leadership Development Program, conceived by General Peter J. Schoomaker, who was army chief of staff from 2003 to 2007, to broaden his generals' perspectives, expose them to strategic issues, and build up their strategic skills. He wanted them not only to get a better grasp of strategic design, strategic thinking, and strategic communications, but also to become participants in deciding the strategic direction of the army and our national security. The program pulls groups of general officers away from their assignments and has them experience strategic planning from other fields, such as major corporations. It also provides them with concentrated, group-guided discussions on all aspects of strategic issues, such as strategic communications, character, and design. It is offered in basic, intermediate, advanced, and senior level increments for each of the four general officer grades.

I asked Pete, a friend, why he started the program.

"Think about it," he said. "We get educated about strategy from early in our officer careers, but we never, or rarely, get directly involved in the development of strategy and the strategic decision making that goes with it until we are generals. I want all my generals exposed and involved at that level from the time they pin on their first star."

As young officers we use to talk tactics with relish. That was our business. Pete's program showed me how generals could talk strategy with the same relish, excitement, and engagement.

We not only need ways to develop military strategists, but also economic, diplomatic, communications, cyber, and other strategists. War college and equivalent level education courses are not enough. They teach the theory and basics splendidly, but direct involvement in strategic planning and implementation is necessary to truly grasp strategy development. Regional military commands and State Department regional bureaus should be co-located and integrated for collective planning. Interagency task forces need to be structured and trained to be able to quickly and effectively team up to meet contingency missions.

In 1986, as a newly promoted colonel, I was assigned to the Chief of Naval Operations' (CNO) Strategic Studies Group. I thought this would build on my strategic education the way a National War College course had previously done. I was wrong. I learned much more.

At that time (still during the Cold War), our naval forces operated under what was called the Maritime Strategy, which addressed how naval forces would engage Soviet forces in a global conflict. It emphasized how we would counter any attacks by threatening their flanks in Europe and by cutting their sea access to needed resources. In our initial meeting, the CNO, Admiral Carlisle Trost, told us he wanted us to examine how the Soviets were responding and reacting to this strategy. After we had determined that, he wanted us to develop updates to this strategy and counterstrategies. We were given the highest security clearances. To ensure we had a full understanding of both sides, we had access to our own deeply classified programs and to any intelligence we needed. A career diplomat, a former US ambassador to Russia, Marshall Brement, headed our group. He gave us insights into elements beyond the military dimension.

The nine of us in the group spent a year working on the project. It was not theory, an education exercise, or a game (although we did game out some of our recommendations). We had all been through that. It was the real thing. It was a rare opportunity to work and contribute at a strategic level. As we went through the process, we saw clearly the importance of the other elements of our power and how they had to be integrated into any strategic planning. Afterward, the Maritime Strategy was updated to include our findings and recommendations.

Careful selection and involvement of our brightest minds in strategic development early in their careers is one way to build a cadre of true strategic thinkers. Interagency programs that bring together members from all agencies of government should be formed to work on real-world strategic projects as we did in the navy program. These can be set up through think tanks that focus on strategic issues.

In order to ensure the strategic development of rising leaders, we need to guide their education and career assignments, and let them be exposed to the highest levels of leadership. There is not a natural progression from the tactical level to the operational and strategic. It's not just a matter of scale. Each level brings in more diverse components and requires thinking and acting in far more expansive time horizons.

I have been a senior advisor and mentor to classes at our Joint Forces Staff College, where an impressive year-long course in planning is given. The course includes interagency students, most of whom go on to planning assignments in various commands and agencies. Courses like this and later performance in follow-on planning assignments are excellent ways to tag future strategists.

According to Churchill, George Marshall was "the true organizer of victory." Successful strategies come out of powerful strategic thinkers like Marshall, who are put into positions that effect sound strategic foundations in plans and execution.

LOOKING AHEAD

At this moment our strategic and policy direction is confused. The Obama administration has announced a shift or "pivot" to the Pacific. We've been repositioning military forces to the region and opening up new bases in places like Australia. To what end? Is there a changed or heightened threat there? What interests require a military prioritization of the Pacific region? The US government intends to invest a lot of funds to develop military facilities in Guam and the Northern Marianas. At a time of constrained military budgets, this seems ill-considered. The forces stationed there would have limited training opportunities, add to the stresses of additional deployments, and be far removed from the strategic lift assets that need to move them.

In my view, the demands on our military are greater in the Indian Ocean, the Middle East, Africa, and our own hemisphere. Extremists, drug cartels, pirates, uprisings, political turmoil, and other threats are centered in those other regions. China is not the only rising power. Mexico, Brazil, Nigeria, Turkey, Indonesia, and India, are all among nations with resources and potential to become significant powers. And Russia has risen to again play a significant role on the world stage and is creating turmoil in eastern Europe. The distributed global powers we increasingly face means we must pursue and protect new interests and establish new security cooperation structures that have to be viewed in a global vice regional context.

It's not about "pivoting" or "rebalancing" toward one region. It's about the agility to respond anywhere on the globe.

SIX

MY FELLOW AMERICANS

Good evening, my fellow Americans. Tonight I want to speak to you of peace in Vietnam and Southeast Asia. No other question so preoccupies our people. No other dream so absorbs the 250 million human beings who live in that part of the world. No other goal motivates American policy in Southeast Asia.

President Lyndon Johnson,
Address to the Nation, March 31, 1968

THESE WORDS OPENED THE ADDRESS OF A WEARY-looking Lyndon Johnson to the American people on a memorable night in 1968. His speech—in the aftermath of North Vietnam's unsuccessful but game-changing Tet Offensive—announced steps to limit the war: an offer to cease the bombing of the North and a proposal for initiating peace negotiations. Two realities were staring LBJ in the face: Costly military actions in Vietnam, although winning on the tactical battlefield, were failing to achieve ultimate victory, and the American public was becoming increasingly disillusioned with the war. These two realities were mutually reinforcing. And LBJ couldn't do anything about either. Waves of negative news reports from Vietnam had caused the American people to lose trust in the president's and his administration's war message and frustrated his attempts to bring the North Vietnamese to the peace table. Then came the climax, the president's shocking announcement that he would not seek reelection. The war in Vietnam had destroyed his presidency.

Johnson inherited that war. He didn't want it, he wasn't prepared for it, and, as the war wore on, he found himself ill-advised by those he relied on for guidance. He tried mightily to explain the war to the American people, but the disconnects between the explanations and the reality were increasingly affecting support for the war.

I watched that speech on TV. A few months earlier I had been in Vietnam. I was now training young lieutenants to go there. In another two years I would go back again to a very different war—a war, I realized, that no longer had the support of the American people.

Wars don't always fail on faraway battlefields. They can also fail at home. The Tet Offensive was an operational failure for General Vo Nguyen Giap, the North Vietnamese commander and architect of the Vietcong strategy during the war. It achieved none of his tactical objectives, and it created a bitter rift between the North Vietnamese leadership and the Vietcong guerrillas in the South, who felt they had been sacrificed by the North's leadership. Yet, while Tet may have been a defeat for Giap on the ground in Vietnam, it was a victory for Giap on Main Street USA.

In 2013, as President Obama readied the military to strike the Assad regime in Syria after they had crossed his redline on the use of chemical weapons, he found himself with an unsupportive American public that was tired of war and mistrustful of Washington decision makers. He seemed surprised to learn that domestic and international support wasn't there. Even though Syria had egregiously violated the Chemical Weapons Convention, signed by 191 nations, and the administration had produced heart-tearing images of gassed children dying in the streets of Damascus, he could not sell his case for military action. Greatly embarrassed and with immense loss of face, he backed off and sought approval from a reluctant Congress.

Does a war make its own case, or does a president have to make that case? It depends on the war.

Since 1943, the year of my birth, our nation has had thirteen presidents. Every one of them has delivered at least one "my fellow Americans" address to authorize military action, justify it, update its progress, or announce its end. The president is "the communicator-in-chief."

These addresses have had varying impacts on the public. Some, because of the occasion—after Pearl Harbor or 9/11, for instance—powerfully moved the people. They fanned emotional fires already lit by direct attacks. Some failed to light emotional fires and persuade the people because the rationale for war was not compelling, an ongoing conflict had failed to produce the results that had been promised, or a president lacked charisma and communication skills.

Franklin Roosevelt had an ability to connect directly with his audience. His fireside radio chats gave comfort, reassurance, and solid information during the dark night of the Great Depression and through the struggles of a world war. His chats resonated with Americans and kept them supporting his efforts to move the nation forward.

John Kennedy, young, brimming with energy, and charismatic, approached Americans with an exciting and inspirational message. He convinced the people to support his challenge to oppose communist expansion. They came to love him . . . a love cemented by his tragic death. Others, like Jimmy Carter, turned the people off. Carter attempted to move the people with a warm, comforting "fireside chat" approach while wearing a V-neck sweater with an open collar at the Oval Office desk. But his message of economic austerity, energy conservation, and diminished expectations depressed the people, and his support withered. His perceived weakness in the face of Iran's taking of US hostages from our embassy in 1979 and the failed attempt to rescue them contributed to his failure to be re-elected.

President Reagan was the Great Communicator. His naturally warm, sunny, fatherly personality, together with decades of movie acting and years of public speaking on the political, broadcasting, and corporate stump shaped and fine-tuned his communicating skills. "It was like my father was in the White House, and that reassured me," a friend remarked to me after a Reagan speech.

President George W. Bush often came across as a "cowboy," too fast on the trigger, overly-willing to commit the military too quickly. His doctrine of preemptive military action and his swaggering style worked for him in the immediate aftermath of 9/11, but these wore thin as two wars ground on without successful endings.

President Obama has been the reluctant warrior. Although detractors have argued that his reluctance is a weakness, his caution has fit with the American peoples' mood; Iraq and Afghanistan have left the nation exhausted by war, and he proved his tough-guy credibility by the committing of Special Operations Forces to the daring Osama bin Laden mission and increasing the drone strikes in places like Afghanistan, Pakistan, and Yemen. That Obama tough-guy image didn't last long. His actions during the Libyan and Syrian crises, his confusion and waffling during the recent military takeover in Egypt (was it a coup or not?), made him appear befuddled and indecisive. Awkward terms like "leading from behind" and confusing decisions to conduct military strikes—now on, now off—opened questions about his resolve and willingness to use force.

Some presidents have gone to extremes to control the narrative. Woodrow Wilson saw the need to influence American public opinion and support for our involvement in World War I as so critical to the war effort that he created a controversial separate government agency to deal with it. The Committee on Public Information was established in 1917 and disestablished a year later. Wilson found himself spending more time defending the organization from charges of propagandizing than realizing the benefits of the agency in developing his message, coordinating its distribution, and monitoring the media.

The bully pulpit has always been a critical tool for presidents. They have staggering powers, but their power is not absolute. They don't rule by decree, and support from Congress is at best uncertain. They need to persuade the people to back their programs. The bully pulpit is even more essential to a president as he contemplates using force. Though they may wish it otherwise, few presidents will risk committing our military to action without the support of the people. As LBJ and George W. Bush learned, the loss of support can destroy or seriously damage the legacy of a presidency.

Once military actions have been launched, presidents need continuing support to sustain them; and because radio, TV, and the Internet now provide instantaneous coverage of virtually the entire world, presidents need to obtain the nation's support now, not tomorrow, next week, or next month. In the days of old a king would order his subjects into battle, and they could do little to affect his decision; but in democracies it's not the king's subjects who march into battle, it's men and women who vote for presidents and Congress . . . men and women who are the sons and daughters of parents who vote for presidents and for members of Congress. And because they are citizens, the millions of other Americans who vote for presidents and Congress have a stake in a president's decision to take military action. Their voices, both direct and through the ballot box, can block a president's intention to use military power. Or even end it after military actions have been launched. Initial support may be withdrawn if the people perceive that the cost or chances of success are not what they expected or were led to believe. In today's high-intensity, instantaneous media environment, the events on the battlefield that drive their support, or cause it to be withdrawn, can be followed in real time. And they can be interpreted by many disparate sources.

Journalists, politicians, and other observers crawl around battlefields and beam reports of their findings directly into living rooms all over the world. Government officials seek personal advantage in leaking information, intelligence, internal discussions, and decisions (with few questions about whether their leaks will harm or benefit the nation). Everyone in the chain of command holds press conferences and interviews, on and off the record. Soldiers' cell phones and laptops allow them to send their take on what is happening back to their families' living rooms, or via Facebook, to their friends' mobile devices. TV talking heads and editorial writers provide opinion and "expert analysis" even before the smoke of battle clears. News networks like Fox and MSNBC look at events from vastly different and opposing—even hostile—perspectives. The result: people are bombarded by an overwhelming variety of interpretations of events. Some are accurate and some are not.

Everybody plays in this game. The enemy, however unsophisticated, distributes his views and counter-justifications. Political opponents in our own country instantly challenge any aspect of a military action that may damage the other party.

Leaders have to be ahead of every news cycle. To wait for the perfect response is to lose the battle of the narrative.

A new dimension of war has developed.

THE BATTLE OF THE NARRATIVE

Words and ideas are now as important to victory in today's conflicts as rifles and bullets. It's not enough to know the truth and to be truthful. You have to successfully communicate the truth and your intentions to a dazzling variety of audiences. Successful communication starts at the top, with the president and leadership in Washington, but it must work its way down through the leaders on the battlefield to the lowest ranks. Everyone in the chain of command has become a messenger.

To support all this communicating, an elaborate structure of information providers has emerged—public relations, public affairs, and communications consultants—who send volleys of data and analysis to a dedicated press corps that prowls the halls of Congress, the White House, the Pentagon, *and* the battlefield. The deliverers of the communications have become essential to planning and executing military operations.

My visit to Afghanistan in 2011 included a briefing by a navy rear admiral who was in charge of "the communications strategy and the command mission narrative" for that mission. This was designed to provide "the story": why we are here, what are we doing, how are we doing, what do we intend to do, what is the enemy doing, and many other aspects of the operation that were designed to counter misperceptions and adverse propaganda as well as to generate continued support for our forces and their mission.

In today's battles, dedicated staff personnel—primarily at the operational but sometimes even at the tactical level—work on messaging and communicating with the same diligence that their colleagues apply to operational planning and execution. I was no stranger to the Battle of the

Narrative but the work they now produce has become a far more sophisticated, vital, and important part of the fight than it was just over a decade earlier when I retired. Information technology has opened up a world of instant communication, information sharing, and opinion shaping. Military commanders must now add another component—information—to the shaping of the field of battle. They have to shape the narrative.

The work they produce is not intended to be propaganda; it is developed to counter the propaganda, misinformation, and misperceptions.

In this battle it's essential not to be reactive. You have to lead with your version of events and intentions before someone else defines them and you. Target audiences are many: the folks back home, our allies, the local people, the enemy, and the international community.

Operations such as these fall under a broad category called Information Operations (IO), which encompasses all our communications and messaging. Its scope ranges from media relations to delivering and shaping the message to cyberattack to protecting cyber systems; a significant number of people and organizations are dedicated to it. Today's battlefield is loaded with public affairs units, visitors bureaus, psychological operations units, communications strategy planners, and a host of others trying to stay in front of the information fight. A recently created four-star Cyber Command handles the cyber end of the business.

I was director of operations during my first tour in Somalia—several packed months that included far more time than I expected in planning and managing the information campaign. We ran a Somali language radio station and published a newspaper to keep the locals in the country informed and to counter the propaganda generated by hostile warlords who owned media outlets. I gave frequent briefings to US and international media and distinguished visitors. I met daily with the fourteen warlords, the numerous clan leaders, and other local leaders throughout the southern half of Somalia to share information, issue warnings, and prevent misunderstandings. I dealt with hostile propaganda and false rumors. And I reviewed and approved the content of leaflets dropped to support our tactical operations. These functions consumed as much of our time as providing humanitarian aid and engaging hostile forces, our principal reasons for being there. As time went on, it grew clear to me that these activities were becoming increasingly essential to military operations.

The battle of the narrative is a real battle. And the UN operation that succeeded us lost it. That loss contributed to the disastrous events that led to the eventual withdrawal of their force. They adopted a more confrontational approach to dealing with the warlords that they were unable to back up, and that led to increased violence.

All our military operations are closely watched by people all over the world; and all our military operations are subject to powerful political pressures from all over the political spectrum. These realities require clarity at every level in communicating our purpose and progress. Everyone from the president to the sergeant whose squad is manning a checkpoint has to understand and clearly communicate what we are trying to do in a consistent and credible way.

Today a relatively junior tactical leader's decisions or actions can have high-level impact, good or bad. Senior military leaders have a term for it—the "strategic corporal." There are too many examples of high-level harm stemming from the behavior of junior-level people—for example, the actions of the guards at the Abu Ghraib prison in Iraq, the urination on dead enemy bodies in Afghanistan, the murderous rampage by a US noncommissioned officer in Afghanistan, and other scandalous events we all know about. Events like these are aberrations; they don't darken the heroic, honorable, and humanitarian actions of the vast majority of our troops. But they do create negative reactions in America and throughout the world that risk support for the mission, and sometimes spark protests and further hostilities. Our leaders must act quickly to limit damage from outbreaks like these. They can't be allowed to fester unaddressed.

And, naturally, senior leaders themselves have high-level impact. They have to watch their words. Too often, unfortunately, they don't. Generals—or even presidents—now and again get carried away with excitement, enthusiasm, anxiety, frustration, or bravado and blurt out statements or send out memos, emails, or cables that prove to be at best embarrassing and at worst damaging to the mission. President Bush's "bring 'em on" taunt in July 2003 in response to mounting deaths of American troops in Iraq after hostilities had been declared over was not helpful to a soldier who has to face the enemy the president was challenging, and the loose comments of General Stanley McChrystal's staff to a *Rolling Stone* reporter expressing personal opinions about the president, vice president, national security advisor, and other political leaders cost the career of an excellent general. Communications like these call into question the competence, judgment, and moral compass of our leaders. Americans want to know that their sons and daughters are in good hands and that the mission is just. That means that leaders must show in their communications to the American people that they are competent, strong, and compassionate.

THE MILITARY AND THE MEDIA

During World War II the military and the media were on friendly terms. In the decades that followed they became far more confrontational.

In World War II reporters were admired and respected; many were seen as heroes. President Roosevelt personally greeted with his warmest praise our greatest and most famous war correspondent, Edward R. Murrow, on his return from Europe. Murrow's gripping accounts of the London Blitz and reports from the battlefields of Europe had riveted Americans to their radios. Down in the mud and the blood telling the soldier's story were reporters like Ernie Pyle (who was killed by a Japanese machine gun blast on a small island during the invasion of Okinawa). Reporters like Murrow and Pyle were revered. The people loved them and the soldiers loved them. They told the story of the war and those who fought it. They built a bond with the military and with the people.

The rules of reporting were clear then. Military censors controlled what could and couldn't be reported. Yet few reporters were driven to challenge the war's purpose, strategy, or operations. Few prowled around the battlefield looking for atrocities, scandals, and other negative stories. Just the opposite. As a result, no one saw the relationship between media and military as anything other than positive.

Certainly a case can be made that the job of journalists is to give an accurate account of what they have witnessed, and not to just be supportive of the troops or the mission. And certainly the kind of censorship that was okay in World War II would never be accepted today. Today the media's access to the field is much more open and unrestricted. We hope that open access frees journalists to tell it like it is—fairly, balancing good and bad, successes as well as failures. Most of the time, that's what happens. But not always. Some journalists file negative reports that those in the field, rightly or wrongly, feel are unfair or violate a confidence. When that happens, trust is lost.

Trust between the media and the military took a terrible hit during the Vietnam War. It has never completely recovered.

In a 1995 report on the relationship between the media and the military, Frank Aukofer, a journalist at the *Milwaukee Journal Sentinel,* and retired navy Vice Admiral William P. Lawrence surveyed military officers and members of the media on a variety of relationship issues, with troubling findings.[1] 64 percent of the officers questioned believed that "the news media coverage of the events in Vietnam harmed the war effort." Only 17 percent of the journalists questioned agreed. It has become a military tradition to be suspicious of the media. For many years the bond of trust has been, at best, tenuous. Sadly, many in the military see the media as an enemy.

Did the media harm the Vietnam war effort? Possibly. But that's not the best question to ask in this context. Better questions would be: Did journalists report accurately? Were their reports balanced? Were reporters deliberately blind to successes? Did they cast out their nets exclusively for failures and atrocities? If the answers to these questions are "no," "no," "yes," and "yes," then a strong case can be made for harm. In my view, reporting toward the end of the war was not only antiwar but increasingly antimilitary.

To be fair, Vietnam was not World War II. The nature of our involvement, the new form of conflict, the lack of measurable progress, and the disconnects between realities in the field and explanations from leaders made this war different. For these and many other reasons, as the war wore on, journalists drifted away from telling the soldier's story toward challenging the war. That change inevitably left the military suspicious and angry. In the eyes of those on the ground, journalists were hostile witnesses who promoted the negative and ignored the positive. The troops in the field saw too many journalists whose eyes were on fame and personal success, even if at the cost of bending the truth. Today we remember the My Lai massacre and not the countless stories of the grunts sweating and bleeding and trying to do the right things in a confusing environment.

The hostility between media and military that existed as Vietnam was winding down and in the years that followed did not exist in the war's earliest days. For his heroic actions in caring for the wounded during the intense fighting in one of the earliest major battles, the Battle of the Ia Drang Valley, reporter Joe Galloway was awarded a Bronze Star. His account of that battle, *We Were Soldiers Once . . . And Young*, written with Harold G. "Hal" Moore, the commander during the battle, was a bestseller and became a popular movie starring Mel Gibson.[2] But Joe, a good friend and a soldier's reporter, may have been a throwback. When he and I talk about the war, I can't help but think of him as a battle-hardened version of Ernie Pyle. As the war wore on, too many of Joe's journalist colleagues proved to be a different breed.

Although he was often critical of the conduct of the war, another reporter, Bernard Fall, earned the respect of the Marines with whom he patrolled in the tough areas of I Corps in Vietnam. His books, *Street Without Joy* and *Last Reflections on a War*, became required reading for young officers like me. He lost his life while covering operations with the Marines.

In the aftermath of Vietnam, the military leadership knew they couldn't just climb into a hole and avoid reporters. In order to get our story out in the best way possible, they instituted a new component to officers' development—media training for mid-level to senior officers. The training assumed we would be facing an adversary; it did not prepare us for a friendly relationship, but for the media "ambush," the hostile interview, or the tricky question designed to catch us off guard—"gotcha journalism."

Today, especially with the rise of cable news networks, the distinction between reporters and opinion shapers, editorial writers, and advocates has become cloudy and confused. Too often reporting is neither objective, neutral, nor balanced. Celebrity journalists on cable networks have too often become the centerpiece of the story. They don't just report the news; they have opinions about it. They put the spotlight on themselves, not the news. A longtime CNN hand once told me that when Ted Turner first established CNN, he made the news the star. No longer.

What happens when reporters take a position? Does the reporting become shaded by the position? Does the reporting lose objectivity? If you come into my command post on the battlefield with strong pre-formed views, are you there to report objectively or to find evidence to support your views? Should we clearly identify and separate those who report from those who editorialize or advocate? Sure, it's hard to keep total neutrality as we narrate our experience, and I have no problem with reporters editorializing or advocating if they clearly announce what they are doing. But when they are reporting, reporters should take their best shot at neutrality and objectivity.

I HAVE BEEN PAINTING A GLOOMY PICTURE. BUT IN fact the military and the media are not at war, and they never were. There are even signs of tentatively renewed friendship. Highly qualified, high-integrity journalists now cover the military with skill and perception, and military officers are becoming less suspicious when they engage with journalists. Young officers whom I've talked to in today's military don't have the same cautious and suspicious approach in dealing with the media that my generation had.

When I retired in 2000 after thirty-nine years of service, I left with the view that the media was like terrain or weather—just another factor you have to take into account as you conduct operations. If there was a story—maybe favorable, maybe unfavorable—you had to realize that you could not control it or influence it, nor should you try to. Like other professionals, journalists and reporters come in many varieties, from highly competent and honorable to incompetent and deceitful. In my experience, the former greatly outnumbers the latter. I ran into maybe 10 percent who were incompetent or who betrayed a trust. You will find that 10 percent in any walk of life.

At the other end of the spectrum, you will find the 10 percent of truly outstanding journalists—the high-integrity reporters who give up great stories in the interest of security, or who come back to you to ask for clarification before reporting a "juicy" story, or who delay publication because the event they are reporting has not yet unfolded to their satisfaction, or because they don't feel they see into it with sufficient depth.

In today's world a prudent person about to be interviewed by any reporter will lay down the rules. Is the interview on or off the record? Are your comments quotable or on background? It is now standard practice for both sides of an interview to establish the ground rules from the outset.

I have come to trust many in the media, and some have become friends. I have learned from my journalist friends that the relationship works both ways.

This lesson hit me with particular force back in December of 1998 during my time as commander of CENTCOM. We were in the middle of Operation Desert Fox—attacks against Iraqi targets in response to Iraqi efforts to frustrate the activities of UN WMD inspectors—when the Pentagon made a strange decision to brief the press on the battle damage assessment (BDA, the way commanders assess the progress or effectiveness of military strikes). It's unusual to brief BDA, and especially unusual for Pentagon people to do it. Statistics may be briefed to the press, but not as battle damage assessment. The BDA is a commander's assessment tool, not a tool for briefing reporters.

The Pentagon briefing did not go well; reporters hit the briefers with a barrage of questions they couldn't answer. This is not surprising. You can't understand a battle damage assessment unless you know the commander's plan and intentions. And it's extremely hard to judge their effectiveness until operations have gone on long enough to make a significant impact. For example, the BDA may show that after several days of strikes, only 17 percent of the air defense targets were destroyed. That may raise questions about the effectiveness of your campaign; 17 percent doesn't sound like very much. But if all you needed to do was inflict minimal destruction and suppression to get to the key targets, and if the 17 percent destruction had reduced air defenses enough to be no longer a threat, then you were on course.

Reporting BDA early in the course of the operation and without knowing the commander's intent naturally led to confusion and questions. I received a panicked call to come to Washington to handle the next briefing and put Humpty Dumpty back together again. Doing that in the middle of conducting strikes on Iraq was a distraction I didn't need.

I knew that I couldn't just hit reporters with our latest BDA in the form of raw, unexplained numbers. They could never understand that. They needed context, such as how battle damage assessment fits into the larger picture of what we were trying to achieve. So I began the brief with a "BDA 101" to give the reporters necessary context. Once they had context, our BDA made sense to them, and they followed up by asking good, sharp, intelligent questions.

After the briefing ended, a seasoned Pentagon reporter came up to me and told me how pleased she was to get the information I'd given them. "We need that kind of information badly, and we don't get enough of it," she said. "We don't get enough of the kind of access we need, or the kind of background information we need. The result too often is unnecessary misunderstandings."

Her words remained with me, and the experience reinforced my belief in the value of educating journalists in all things military. You can't assume that those who cover the military beat come with a full understanding of all the complex things we do. Old seasoned hands may have gotten it from long experience, but we in the military need to do a better job of educating all the reporters we encounter, not just the old guys. And commanders need to invest time and effort in that job. We shouldn't just leave it to uniformed public affairs folks.

THE PENTAGON USED TO PREPARE A DAILY COMPILA-tion, called "The Early Bird," of media items that contained reports on defense issues or the military. The first thing I did each morning was to read it before the intelligence reports and before the situation reports. I knew that, without fail, the first calls I would receive from the five-sided building in Washington would be about anything in there that had to do with my command.

Every profession lives in its own bubble—some never venture or see outside of it. The military lives in a different culture from journalists. We have professional training, experience, and a language that few of them share with us. In order to understand what they are seeing and hear-ing, reporters need context. They need to know how specific actions and events fit into a larger picture. If we don't provide that, they will fill in the blanks with all manner of misinformed accounts. These stories don't come from hostility or malice. They come from our failure to give them what they need.

There are many reasons why we can't always do that. But we should do our best to try.

In 1995 I was directed to lead the operation to protect the withdrawal of UN forces from Somalia. We were given the mission months ahead of the execution date. This kind of time to plan is a godsend for command-ers, especially since we had many extremely difficult and complex military tasks to perform: a nighttime amphibious withdrawal, a passage of lines, and a relief in place; we had to accomplish these actions under fire with a mix of international forces.

In the midst of planning, I was informed that we would take with us a press pool—a team of ten to twenty reporters from print and TV who channel their reports to all the media. Reporters do not like pools: they have to operate under military supervision, live in military quarters, and get moved by military transport. They want independence and freedom of movement. As they see it, a press pool is under too much military control.

Our pool reporters originally planned to hire a separate ship that would join our task force but give them freedom to come and go ashore as they liked. That idea was nixed by the Pentagon.

As we headed for Mogadishu, a dozen or so unhappy journalists boarded our ship, many of them seasoned veterans of missions like this one. I knew I couldn't just let them stew; I didn't need an angry press pool festering inside our task force. I had to meet with them, listen to their concerns, and then do my best to take care of them. Soon after they arrived on board, I invited them to sit around a conference room table in my stateroom. This is what they told me: "As long as the military carries us to wherever they want to take us, we'll never be sure we're seeing and reporting the really significant actions. And since we depend on access to the ship's probably overstressed communications facilities to file our reports, we can never be sure that we will be able to file our reports on time." Bottom line: they feared missing the story or getting it out late. A number of other journalists, mostly foreign, were roaming around Mogadishu who might scoop them (several of them were killed or kidnapped by Somali criminals as a result of the risk they took).

These were genuine and reasonable concerns. Reporters need access to the big events, and they need to be able to get their stories out as soon as possible. (My deputy commander, an Italian admiral, had been hit with similar concerns from the foreign press accompanying our coalition partners in the force.) I gave lots of thought to the best way to satisfy their needs without compromising those of the mission.

I called my staff and commanders together to see what we could come up with to smooth the journalists' feathers. They laid out several ideas. Here is what we proposed to the pool: I would assign to them officers and noncommissioned officers (NCOs) whose job it was to take care of their needs, make sure they had a link with us, and handle separate transportation that we would provide to take them where they wanted to go if security conditions permitted. I would brief them ahead of time on what was about to happen, so they had context, and I would recommend the best place to be when an important event went down. I assured them they would have direct access to commanders, including me, if circumstances permitted. And I assured them that they'd have timely access to communications facilities; they'd be able to file on time. I only had two requests. I asked them not to reveal future operations. And I asked them to comply with requests to embargo information they'd been given until after it no longer risked compromising security.

They were not happy, but they reluctantly agreed.

Fortunately, as the operation played out, we were able to provide them with most of what they needed, and they sent their editors and producers the kinds of stories they wanted.

After the operation was completed, and UN forces had been safely removed from Somalia, I met the pool members again. This time the meeting went smoothly and without suspicions. They had come to understand that we'd done our best to listen to them and take care of their needs, and they were grateful. So was I. They had done a terrific job of reporting. To show my appreciation, I gave each of them one of my commander's coins (presented to troops and others who do something exceptional); to show theirs, they gave me a framed photo, taken on the last night ashore as we fought our way off the beach, signed by each of them. I was silhouetted against a backdrop of blazing flares.

Many in that pool have crossed paths with me often after that, and many remain friends of mine. I learned a lot from them. I realized that they sincerely wanted to do their jobs in the most professional way. We both came to appreciate each other's efforts to work together.

But let's be honest. In the real world, the military and the press will not always work smoothly together. We give it our best and move on. Or, to paraphrase the Rolling Stones: You don't always get what you want, but sometimes, if you work real hard, you just might get what you need.

My son, a Marine infantry officer, has had several tours of duty in Iraq and Afghanistan. After he returned from a tour in command of an infantry company in Afghanistan during the Marja operation, I asked him how he and his officers and troops viewed the media.

"We really like embedded reporters," he told me—reporters who spend months with the units and share the hardships (shades of Ernie Pyle). "But we don't like celebrity journalists who do touch-and-goes. They already know what they're going to say or write. They're just there to validate that." That problem has been with us since Vietnam.

The concept of "embedded media" was developed near the start of the Iraq and Afghanistan invasions. Reporters and other journalists are placed in a unit for long stretches of time, sharing their experiences and hardships; with rare exceptions they become members of the unit.

When embedding was first adopted, I wasn't sure it was a good idea. Would embedded journalists' real-time reports mean that commanders and political leaders would have to constantly react to events before the context and full facts could be determined? And would the presence of embedded reporters distract small unit commanders from the focus they needed to keep on their operational duties?

The reality has turned out better than I feared. Embedding has been a good move overall—another sign of progress in the mutual efforts to repair the break between the military and the media.

The power of the press is great, and we do all we can to ensure its freedom. It can shape and influence decisions and actions to a far greater degree than most people realize. It informs the American people and provides scrutiny over all our government, helping to hold officials accountable. It cannot and should not be ignored.

CYBERWAR

Critical terrain in the twenty-first-century battleground is not only located on a map, but also in the airwaves and cyberspace. Information and communications are the lifeblood of military commands. Dominate these and/or control as much as possible your adversaries' information and communications capabilities, and you are assured victory in today's military environment. It's a wild and lawless territory. General Mike Hayden, former head of the CIA and NSA, aptly described the cyber domain as "a manmade, ungoverned, digital Somalia."

Cyberspace opens a window into everything you own. You see out, bring information in, and communicate through it. To ensure your window works the way you want it to, you have to accomplish three essential tasks: You have to use the most advanced technology to develop state-of-the-art systems; you have to protect your window so it can't be broken or opened; and you have to be able to break or open the other guy's window. The cyberwar is ongoing. Our systems are under attack daily. The race to out-tech and outsmart each other is rapid and heated. Either you must build better tech than the other guy, or you must steal it.

Some of the earliest cyberattacks hit CENTCOM while I was commander in the 1990s. During a growing crisis in 1997, our information systems were attacked. Attempts were made to enter our systems and either gather information or disrupt them.

Saddam had long been interfering with UN inspectors and taking potshots at our planes enforcing no-fly zones. Everyone in the world was aware that if Saddam did not stop these activities, we were poised to attack Iraq. We'd been building up forces in bases around Iraq; it was clear the president intended to strike. As tensions mounted, the number of attacks on our classified and unclassified cyber and communications systems increased daily, which caused us even more worries than we might otherwise have had because of the imminence of military action. We were fully engaged in a raging battle in cyberspace, and no kinetic (conventional) shots had yet been fired

Though we were able to protect our systems, the number and sophistication of the attacks, growing steadily each day, were a serious concern. We had moved into the age of the cyber battlefield. Today's CENTCOM commander knows that cyberattacks will be a routine part of his day-to-day environment. Some may originate from a curious teenage hacker or a potential enemy's rudimentary probes. But the most dangerous will represent a continuous, sophisticated attempt to penetrate our most critical information and command and control systems by large nation-state organizations dedicated to conducting cyberwarfare.

In cyberwar, there is no immediately visible destruction, no immediately obvious casualties, and no immediate panic. Yet, the effects can be devastating to our security. We responded forcefully to the Pearl Harbor and 9/11 attacks. We may need to respond just as forcefully to a cyberattack, whose catastrophic effects could be just as bad as Pearl Harbor's or 9/11's, or worse. Think of cyberattacks aimed at disrupting air traffic control, nuclear or conventional power plants, oil refineries, chemical factories, or the electrical transmission network. Our security, technology, industrial, economic, and other vital information is stolen daily. The sophistication of the threat adjusts to each countermeasure we throw up and penetrates our defenses. Attacks don't just penetrate our security and intelligence organizations, but every facet of our society where an enemy can gain from stealing our intellectual property, innovation, and technology.

We must treat the cyber world as a potential battleground and be prepared to engage potential enemies in it. How do we respond? Should we stay in the cyber world and respond with only cyber counterattacks? Or should we respond to cyberattacks with kinetic counterattacks? If a future cyberattack cripples, or threatens to cripple, a vital component of our national security, a president will have to be prepared not only to respond in kind but to use military force. By law we cannot use a cyberattack in and of itself to justify a military counterattack. We are required to base such a response on the consequences of the cyberattack.

These aren't the only issues. Defense against cyberattacks requires intelligence to be gathered and reconnaissance in the non-physical, electronic dimension; data has to be collected; transmissions have to be monitored. That means somebody may be collecting personal data and personal transmissions of yours and mine. And that raises serious civil liberties questions.

Cyberwar presents us with a labyrinth of dilemmas. Do we need new rules and new international treaties and conventions to govern cyberspace? Just as we have addressed the use of chemical, biological, and nuclear weapons in an international set of forums, we will, no doubt, find ourselves doing the same with cyberwarfare. We are beginning to realize how critical cyberspace is to every aspect of our lives and how vulnerable this can make us, especially through our infrastructure and financial networks. I do not believe we can afford to leave this domain unprotected. There must be balance between our security requirements and our access to and use of this powerful informational environment.

JUST WAR

The United States and other civilized nations apply certain moral and ethical standards as they decide to go to war and after combat has begun. The message that leaders send the people to explain and justify a war must speak to these standards. The people need to feel that their nation's cause is just.

For over two thousand years, men have been codifying rules for the conduct of war and laying out criteria for entering and conducting a just war. Over time, the criteria for just war have been generally agreed upon and accepted by most civilized societies; and the rules have been set down in specific conventions and agreements, such as the Hague Conventions (1890, 1907), the Geneva Conventions (1864–1977), and the Chemical Weapons Convention (1993).

These conventions and agreements boil down to two sets of criteria. The first focuses on the decision for war, and addresses issues like the right to go to war, just cause, competent authority, right intention, and probability of success. The second focuses on conduct within war and addresses issues like military necessity, fair treatment of prisoners of war, and "evil" methods or weapons. These rules and criteria give us an accepted moral and legal basis for using military force.

Any narrative making the case for war has to be based and presented on strong legal, ethical, and moral grounds. The just war theory and the applicable international conventions the United States signed have to guide our decision to use force. Popular support fades when the justification for war turns out to be false. We are a nation of values. We want our values to justify our leaders' decisions about war and peace.

THE MORAL JUSTIFICATION FOR A PARTICULAR MILItary action is not the only moral question raised by a war. During wartime, leaders sometime suspend or limit basic rights. How must we judge these actions?

Values we hold dear—such as our right to privacy or our right to free speech—sometimes present a challenge to decision makers. There can be a conflict between their responsibility to protect these values and their responsibility to provide for our security and well-being.

Presidents from John Adams to Abraham Lincoln to Woodrow Wilson to FDR to George W. Bush have felt it necessary to take measures that diminished our rights in order to ensure our protection and security. Examples include the Alien and Sedition Acts, waiver of habeas corpus in time of war, internment of US citizens because of their ethnic heritage, and monitoring of private communications . . . all controversial actions. Do they do far greater harm in the long run than they gain in short-term security? In my view, we have to face the fact that presidents may have to impinge on civil liberties to protect us. This, however, should only be done with the approval of Congress, on a temporary basis and only for as long as the threat requires, and under some sort of judicial oversight.

After a war is over, it's easy to look back and criticize decisions that curtailed civil liberties or violated our sense of justice or ethical and moral behavior. But in the heat of the moment, when the lives of our loved ones and the well-being and future of our society are at stake, what do we expect? If our leaders are faced with a catastrophic or existential threat, can the end justify the means? During these events, is the greater good more important than individual rights?

We elect or appoint leaders to make these calls and we rightly examine their decisions critically when the crisis has passed. But can this be fairly done without understanding the context and environment within which these decisions were made? These issues have again grabbed our attention with the Edward Snowden case that has revealed the extent of NSA monitoring of phones and the Internet, at home and abroad.

It is healthy to examine and weigh the effects of tough decisions that seem to work against common good or individual rights. But no one ethical approach can guide each and every situation. We are stronger for the examination, questioning, and seeking of the ideal answer. Yet we are human and must take into account the environment, times, and consequences.

In this democracy, our troops swear an oath to the Constitution of the United States, not to a leader, and the people do not automatically support a leader's decision to go to war. Through their elected representatives, the people must grant support for the commitment of our military. Even if their approval for the mission is initially given, this isn't blanket approval; the case for war must not only be made, it must be sustained. How the war is conducted will be under constant scrutiny and leaders will be held accountable for decisions that raise questions about legality and moral justification. All this requires confident leadership, superb communications skills, and continuous attention to all activities surrounding and involving a commitment of our forces.

SEVEN

TWO AND A
HALF WARS

A vital element in keeping the peace is our military establishment. Our arms must be mighty, ready for instant action, so that no potential aggressor may be tempted to risk his own destruction.

President Dwight D. Eisenhower
Farewell Address, January 1961

ANY AMERICAN MILITARY DEPLOYMENT ANYWHERE IN the world comes with a particular mix of forces—troops with special skills and training, equipment, transport, weapons, and a variety of other capabilities. American forces fighting in our War for Independence came with a mix of forces of great simplicity—trained, partially trained, or untrained troops, regulars and militias, armed with muskets and maybe bayonets and sabers, maybe a few canons, and supported by horse-drawn wagons. As years passed, complexity grew. The Civil War mix of forces was far more complex than that of the Revolutionary war. And the mix of forces required for the D-Day invasion of Europe was incredibly complex, requiring months of planning and preparation by an enormous staff of planners, both American and British. The mix of forces on today's battlefields may be nowhere near as enormous as D-Day's in sheer numbers, but it's even more complex as technology and innovation have added a tremendous variety of capabilities to be brought to the battlefield and integrated into the fight.

Just to get to the scene requires an elaborate network of planes, trains, and ships whose movements are synchronized by a unified command (Transportation Command). A huge database, the Time Phased Force and Deployment Data (TPFDD), manages, schedules, and aligns movement of massive amounts of equipment and personnel to flow in accordance with the operational plan's scheduled order of arrival.

At the receiving end an equally elaborate process, known as Reception, Staging, Onward Movement, and Integration (RSOI), is put into effect to receive units and logistics at the ports of debarkation and move them into position to conduct operations. Imagine all this occurring when the ports and airfields are not the best in the world, or when engagement with the enemy has already begun, or when these ports and airports are under threat.

Elaborate global command and control systems are activated, or created, to provide the means to pull together the complex coordination and direction requirements.

I witnessed just one part of this massive "system of systems" in action while I was the deputy operations director in the European Command during Operation Desert Storm. The network designed to move everything that CENTCOM (US Central Command) on the Arabian Peninsula needed came through our area. The requirements for over-flight rights, diplomatic clearances, security, en route basing, and refueling were tremendous. The largest unit ever deployed, the US Army's 7th Corps, had to be moved to Saudi Arabia from its bases in Europe. This move required extensive planning and coordination as German rail systems, road systems, and North Sea ports had to be contracted, coordinated, and organized to move the Corps in the sequence dictated by General Norman Schwarzkopf's operational plan. All this was only one part of the effort going on to bring forces to the fight; it was all an enormous and complicated process.

The old saying that "colonels talk tactics while generals talk logistics" came to mind as I observed this complex undertaking. But, to be fair to the colonels, in today's US military everybody talks logistics, because getting there is half the challenge. And once we get them there, unloading and sustaining the force is a stupendous additional challenge.

HOW DO WE CREATE THE FORCES WE WILL NEED FOR today's and tomorrow's battlefields?

According to Title X of the US Code (the Code of laws of the United States), the job of the service branches—the Army, Marine Corps, Navy, and Air Force (in peacetime, the Coast Guard is run by the Department of Homeland Security; in time of war it may be transferred to the Department of Defense)—is to train, organize, and equip their service forces. The service secretaries (Army, Navy, and Air Force) and service chiefs put together the capabilities and structure they think will best meet the needs of projected threats or missions that they expect their services to handle. They attempt to ensure they have those right capabilities by exhaustive analyses, program planning and development, and testing. They then produce their wish lists. These, and the associated costs, are consolidated and prioritized by the Department of Defense and submitted to the president and eventually to Congress as a defense budget. Congress debates costs and priorities, and eventually decides what will or won't be funded. This process may sound simple and straightforward, but it is often fraught with politics, service rivalries, lobbying, and strategic debates. As a result, far from everything a service may want gets funded.

Eventually the sausage is made, and the services have a structure . . . until the next go-round.

In the early days of our republic, the services fought battles simply and directly, without the many intermediate levels of forces and commands we have today. Archibald Henderson, the commandant of the Marine Corps from 1820 to 1859, tacked a note on the door of his home at the Marine Barracks on 8th and I streets in Washington, DC: "Gone to fight the Indians." Today a Marine Corps commandant would not command actions on a battlefield. Combatant commanders now have that responsibility. They command one of six regional commands (Central, Pacific, European, Northern, Southern, and Africa) or three functional commands (Special Operations, Transportation, and Strategic). Their primary job is to integrate and employ the forces provided by the services, and then to provide feedback to the services on capabilities they feel are missing, in short supply, or need to be made more interoperable for better integration on the battlefield.

The Office of the Secretary of Defense (OSD) and the Joint Chiefs of Staff (JCS) oversee and direct the planning, allocation of forces to the combatant commands, and other functions that tie together the service provided forces and their integration and employment by the combatant commands.

Of course, this is a simplified explanation of a far more elaborate, complex, and extremely powerful system. Huge staffs labor long and hard to make this process work.

WHEN THE JAPANESE ATTACKED PEARL HARBOR, HAwaii, on December 7, 1941, Dwight D. "Ike" Eisenhower was a newly promoted brigadier general with little command experience, serving in the world's seventeenth-largest army (the Romanian army ranked above it). The US military was in every respect inferior to the mighty military machines of Germany and Japan that we would face. Four years later, our country had the most powerful military in the world, tailored to fight in both the European and Pacific theaters, dominant in every measurable way . . . and the sole possessor of atomic weapons. Eisenhower was a five-star general in command of formations whose size and number he could never have imagined in 1941. From that time until the inconceivable future, we have had, and will continue to have, a powerful standing military force, the most powerful in the world.

The US Constitution gives Congress the power to "raise and support armies" and to "provide and maintain a Navy." But for a century and a half, the young nation, blessed by geographic and political isolation, did not require large forces, particularly ground forces. If necessary, we could mobilize in time to meet any emerging threat. Government arsenals supplied the weapons and equipment needed, or acquisition of needed gear from a small number of companies could provide for our requirements. Pearl Harbor, the worldwide war, and the existential threat from the newly powerful Soviet Union and Red China, changed all that. Ike witnessed the large, complex bureaucracy rapidly grow over the two decades from World War II to the end of his presidency (1953–1961).

Eisenhower's Farewell Address famously warned of the growing power of a military-industrial complex (in his original draft it was a "military-industrial-congressional complex"). He recognized and warned that the ever-tightening web linking Congress, industry, the military, and money should be carefully monitored and controlled. Yet he understood that we could not solve that problem by weakening the military.

Pundits and editorial writers often cite his warning about the growing military-industrial complex. Far fewer cite other warnings in his address, such as the one stating that "our arms must be mighty." Everyone knows the zero-sum guns-and-butter dilemma. If you spend on defense, you have less to spend on our nation's other needs. This former general, who had led America and its European Allies in a war that threatened our very existence, had become the leader of the free world facing a menacing Red threat and the president of a fast-growing nation that would only expand to its potential by satisfying numerous critical and costly domestic needs. He was acutely aware of this difficult choice. He knew that costs, risks, and security had to be weighed and carefully balanced against our country's other needs.

So did his successors.

But how mighty a military? How much can we afford? How should we structure it? These questions have plagued every presidential administration and congress since the end of World War II. If you know whom you are going to fight, where you are going to fight, and who might fight by your side, then it's relatively easy to determine the kind of military you need, where to put it, and where you can afford to take risks. But only rarely, if ever, have we had that luxury.

Prior to World War II, private industry did not build all our weapons. We either built our armaments in government arsenals as we needed them or we acquired them through limited contracts with private companies. But after the United States plunged into World War II, that approach no longer ensured the top-quality edge we needed. Factories long idled by the

Great Depression were retooled to forge what FDR called "the arsenal of democracy." World War II and the Cold War generated a half-century-long arms race. We dared not become complacent. We abandoned the arsenal concept; private industry and competition now gave us the innovation and technological advancements we needed to stay ahead of our potential foes. Further, the Soviet Union's launching of the *Sputnik I* satellite in 1957 inaugurated a "space race" and prompted the United States to invest heavily in science education and technical training. The good news has been that the American defense industry delivered the edge we needed. The bad news has been that the goalposts keep moving as our potential adversaries' technology advances, or they steal ours, and as the cost of further advances in sophisticated technology rises.

As the threats we faced changed in the decades following World War II, we adapted the structure of our military forces to the new realities. When the Soviet Union emerged as a nuclear power in the 1950s, we oriented our military primarily toward fighting the Soviets and their Warsaw Pact allies on a nuclear battlefield. The emphasis was on nuclear deterrence. We built the TRIAD—the three-pronged system for delivering massive retaliation: long-range bombers, inter-continental ballistic missiles (ICBM), and sea- and air-launched cruise missiles—and added to that high-end conventional forces, including massive tank, heavy artillery, and air support units, that were prepared to fight on a nuclear battlefield. American strategists expected World War III to ignite with a Soviet–Warsaw Pact invasion of Western Europe that we would meet in the Fulda Gap (a broad plain in central Germany). But we could not ignore Asia; we had to be prepared for a war with Red China or North Korea, a two-front war once again. Since fighting on the ground in Asia was thought to be as futile as fighting the tide, our goal was to avoid a ground war in that theater. We positioned strong defensive forces in Korea and Japan (where US bases remain). But this also meant we needed a strong naval and air power capability in that region to prevent Chinese expansion and to threaten the vital sea links that China required to meet its trade and energy demands. Since the crises with China in the early 1950s in the Taiwan Strait, the navy's Seventh Fleet and the threat from strategic airpower based on Guam, Japan, and elsewhere have served as key deterrents to potential Asian enemies.

The alarming prospect of a mutually suicidal nuclear war caused the communist powers to change their strategy toward us, and, by the early 1960s, communist-inspired insurgencies were threatening US interests in the third-world periphery (though the threat of a clash of massive armies on the plains of central Europe remained). Newly elected President John F. Kennedy took on that challenge, and his administration developed a counterstrategy of "flexible response." We now needed to be capable of fighting "two and a half wars"—the label given to our new strategy. It required a force to meet the challenges of two major theaters of war (e.g., Soviets and China) and a small one (e.g., a third-world insurgency) at the same time. To the high-end forces needed to fight on a nuclear battlefield had to be added forces designed to fight at the lower end of the combat spectrum, where insurgent, guerrilla, and other irregular forces operate (e.g., light infantry, special operations forces, civil affairs, etc.). This new strategic vision required not only a larger military but new kinds of military forces, such as highly mobile helicopter-borne forces and US Army Special Forces, with their specialized skills in missions like foreign internal development and counterinsurgency. Structuring and providing resources for these changes required elaborate planning and new doctrine. We added extensive new war plans and command structures, and greatly increased our presence overseas, through foreign alliances, military assistance programs, bases, and pre-positioned stocks and forces in critical parts of the world. Since the US was operating under the strategic concept of containment and deterrence, these moves were designed to check communist attempts to spread their ideology without direct confrontation with us and our NATO allies on a conventional or nuclear level. We would contend and compete through a kind of proxy warfare.

In 1973 the Department of Defense's Office of Net Assessment (ONA) was created. Its mission is to provide assessments on future threats and emerging technologies applicable to the military. It was designed to be an in-house, high-level think tank for DOD. In the 1970s and 80s, the Soviet

Union launched an effort to significantly modernize its military concepts and structure. This effort became known as the Revolution in Military Affairs (RMA). The Chinese and the US (through ONA) followed suit. The RMA was about transforming the military through innovation, conceptual change, technology, and restructuring.

The Defense Department's quest for transformation has never truly been realized. There had been only slight changes by the time the Cold War faded away (1989–91). Since then, we have struggled to find a strategic vision that made sense of the post-Soviet world. Without such a vision, we have had little to guide us toward the kind of military forces we need.

With no looming existential threat, strategists in the 1990s tossed up all kinds of ideas aimed at retooling the military. Everyone recognized that our military must continue to evolve and modernize, but towards what end, and for what purpose?

Some called for a "strategic pause" to allow us to rethink our military. Meaning: "We can risk a pause in modernizing until we have time to think through a new strategic assessment." Some called for a serious commitment to achieving that elusive military "transformation." Since we no longer faced an existential threat, we no longer needed a threat-based military structure and should move toward a structure based on selected capabilities, such as maintaining air and naval dominance, while seeking revolutionary changes to our structure, doctrine, and equipment. That meant keeping a safe qualitative or technological edge in some established capabilities, while investing in radically new force structures based on high-tech capabilities, such as unmanned aircraft and cruise missiles. Some called for a more measured— that is, less radical—balance of forces between the services that would be able to respond to any level of emerging threat. And some believed that the promise of a peace dividend allowed us to take a big risk and shift a substantial portion of resources allocated to supporting the military on a large scale to other pressing national needs such as education, energy independence, health care, and infrastructure. The surprise 9/11 attacks and the Global War on Terrorism put retooling our military structure on hold.

Secretary of Defense Donald Rumsfeld came into the job in 2001 hell-bent on transforming the military. He had a vision to strengthen—and pay for—our technology advantage by streamlining—that is, cutting—manpower, the biggest single expense in our military. His aim: "Shock and Awe." Our high-tech military would so overwhelm enemies with speed and precision strikes that only a small force of boots on the ground would be needed to pick up the pieces. That was the theory, anyway.

Early in 2001, soon after I had retired as a four-star general, I was asked to participate with a think-tank group contracted to work for the Joint Staff at the Pentagon to study what the new military should look like. The group had a strange makeup. Of the several retired four stars in the group, I was the only ground officer. As soon as the study director read our Pentagon-provided parameters and guidance for the study, it became clear why. Ground forces were to be cut drastically. The Army would lose four to five divisions. Marine ground forces would also be reduced. The emphasis was on high-tech systems—airpower, precision munitions, space-based intelligence systems, and the like. Shades of McNamara, I thought, and his high-tech line along the Vietnam DMZ (demilitarized zone) that was supposed to detect infiltration by using electronic sensors in place of patrols walking the ground. It failed.

When I told the others that, in my view, this approach was blind to current realities, a retired air force four star I know well put his arm on my shoulder. "Tony," he said, "the era of large ground formations is over. All we need now is a few, lightly armed, 500-man gendarmerie units to walk the ground after we're through." The 9/11 attacks and the Iraq and Afghanistan wars suspended the work of the study group.

After the unimpressive debut of Shock and Awe in Iraq—the troops called it "Aw Shucks"—we increased the size of the Army and Marine ground units and surged additional ground forces into Iraq and Afghanistan. Missions like fighting insurgencies require control of the populace and terrain; they require manpower and lots of it. So much for the little gendarmerie.

"THE ARMY YOU HAVE"

"You go to war with the army you have—not the army you might want to have at a later time," Secretary of Defense Donald Rumsfeld replied to a soldier, during the Iraq War, at a staging base in Kuwait. The young soldier had complained to Rumsfeld that their vehicles' lack of armor had left them dangerously exposed to the growing improvised explosive device (IED) threat. He and his unit mates, he told the secretary, had to scrounge from scrap heaps to jury-rig armor for vulnerable vehicles. To the folks back home, this did not seem right; and Rumsfeld, always direct and blunt, was criticized—not for the first time—for his lack of sympathy. How could we, the wealthy United States of America, send our troops into combat with less than they needed? But the reality was not so simple. The forces we had in place on 9/11 had vulnerabilities that the enemy quickly exploited. The far more powerful IEDs we encountered in Iraq and Afghanistan presented a threat we didn't expect (but certainly should have given the terrorists' heavy reliance on explosive devices). If you can't foresee or plan for every possible threat, the best you can do is adapt quickly to the ones you didn't expect.

And, in fact, soon after Secretary Rumsfeld's encounter with the soldier in Kuwait, the Pentagon and the defense industry came up with a solution to this problem—a rapidly produced family of armored vehicles called MRAPs (mine-resistant ambush protected). Good news for our troops for the lifesaving protection they provided . . . but they added cost to a stretched defense budget that had to be offset by canceling or reducing other planned future equipment programs.

OUTSOURCING WAR

The end of the Cold War meant big cuts to defense spending. But how? How could we become more efficient?

One idea that caught fire was to significantly increase civilian contracting. Military personnel, it was thought, were performing functions that others could perform more easily, efficiently, and cheaply. Recruiting, training, providing benefits, and housing troops costs lots of money. Should we be paying these costs for services like food preparation or maintenance of equipment or routine military base functions? You don't need fully trained soldiers for these services. Contracting them to others who could perform them more cheaply, and just as well, seemed logical.

As the years passed, contractors occupied ever increasing niches all through the military establishment. At some stages of the Iraq conflict, contractors in that country outnumbered military personnel.

Although contracting probably saved money, it caused serious, unforeseen problems. For starters, the enormous number of contracts. The State Department, for example, handled large contracts for construction, police training, and security services. The number of contracts grew . . . and grew . . . until the State Department's slender capacity to manage them was overwhelmed. The result: contracts were poorly written, contractors' pay was delayed, and contracts and contractors were not effectively monitored. Other agencies handling contracts had similar failures.

Another big problem broke out when contractors broke local laws, most notoriously when contractors providing security were accused of killing innocent locals. When our troops run afoul of local laws, they are legally protected from local enforcement and local justice. That doesn't mean our troops can get away with committing crimes in other countries, but crimes they commit fall under US laws—such as the Uniformed Code of Military Justice (UCMJ) and Status of Forces Agreements (SOFA) between nations—and not local ones (unless covered by SOFA). That's not true of contractors. Since offenses they committed were not covered by the UCMJ or SOFAs, contractors were subject to local laws that might not be acceptable to our notion of justice. Disputes over jurisdiction raged. And as they did, host nation governments, Iraq and Afghanistan, banned some contractors from operating in the war zones.

When the call went out for contractors to take over jobs our troops had been doing, everybody assumed there'd be plenty of contractors ready and able to take on the jobs. It turns out that wasn't the case. But it wasn't long before companies popped up out of nowhere and rushed to the battlefields to offer their services. It was a new kind of fast-growing market with little barrier to entry. Performance suffered. Too many contracting companies failed to deliver the work they promised. Others underbid the job and failed to satisfactorily complete it. Too often local sub-contractors were hired who could not deliver. Some of the jobs contracted sparked serious backlash back home. Many Americans and congressional leaders were uneasy when security services were contracted to companies like Blackwater, which became infamous after Iraqi government officials and US government employees charged Blackwater employees with recklessly causing unnecessary civilian deaths, a few Blackwater employees were accused of committing criminal acts, while others engaged in firefights alongside US troops, bringing charges that they were "hired mercenaries."

I have seen the contracting business from both sides, in the military and as a member of boards of directors of companies whose businesses included government contracting. Rightly implemented, contracting is useful; it frees up our troops to focus on the military job of fighting the war and is a less expensive way of handling many support tasks. But in recent times contracting has been poorly implemented, badly thought out, and has grown too big too fast. Mistakes were made by both the government and the contractors. There were administrative errors, monitoring flaws, and legal limbos.

We need to fix all those problems. We also need to decide what should be contracted and what shouldn't. It's clear that Americans and our Congress feel security missions, such as those performed by Blackwater and other private contractors, should be in the hands of US troops or government agencies, not contractors. It's wonderful to save taxpayer money, but it cannot be the only factor to consider when making contracting decisions in wartime. We also have to settle the legal status of contractors both for their own protection and so they will be properly held accountable for their actions. The writing of quality contracts is another issue that must be addressed. That is in the best interests of the government and the contractors. Poorly crafted contracts lead to misunderstandings and mistrust. The vetting of contractors and monitoring must also be more robust and timely. Timely payment to contractors should follow timely inspections and formal acceptance of work completed.

To get these fixes done, we need a robust government contracting agency that handles all government contracting outside of the Department of Defense.

In his final report as special inspector general for Iraq Reconstruction, Stuart Bowen recommended that we establish uniform contracting, personnel, and information management systems that would be used by all personnel involved in stabilization and reconstruction activities, both the military and contractors. Bowen's detailed recommendations would go a long way to fix the contracting problems we faced in Iraq and Afghanistan. His reports superbly analyze what worked, what didn't work, and why. We need to follow up on his recommendations with actions so that we can gain the benefits contracting can bring and avoid the contracting mistakes of the past. Consolidating the contracting work under one agency for the non-DOD requirements would provide a single point of administration with collective expertise. The Government Accountability Office (GAO) is an excellent candidate to directly oversee such an organization.

THE TOTAL FORCE

As the war in Vietnam escalated, President Johnson's secretary of defense and other senior officials urged the president to formally call up the National Guard and Reserve units to join the conflict, as had been done in previous wars. The Guard and the Reserve are the components of our military that are closest to the people; they are our local sons and daughters and our close neighbors. Involving them in a war directly involves the American people . . . meaning that the war can't help but touch closer to home. Conducting a major war using only draftees and regular forces (in those Vietnam days already strained to meet the worldwide Soviet threat) risked putting a barrier between the war and the public. It's not *their* war. Or anyhow, it may not have seemed so.

The president decided to fight the war in Vietnam using only active forces. He did not call up the Guard and Reserve. His explanation for this decision was thin. He wanted to make the conflict appear to be relatively small, manageable, and under control, he claimed, so as not to risk appearing so large that China and the Soviets would feel compelled to enter it. We eventually had half a million troops in Vietnam. By then the Soviets and the Chinese knew how big the war was—*very* big. But they stayed out of it, at least directly.

Johnson was far more likely motivated by domestic political reasons. Popular support for the war was decreasing daily. Calling up the reserves, he knew, would bring the war home and inflame the passions of those opposing the war even more.

Johnson was in a lose-lose situation. No matter how he chose to make war—with reserves or with volunteers and draftees—opposition passions were certain to be inflamed. As time went on, a significant number of Americans didn't want the nation to be involved in that war, and large numbers of young American men didn't want to fight in it.

After Vietnam, we came to see the decision not to call up National Guard and Reserve units as a serious mistake. The military realized that these units should be more than simply available duplication and reinforcement; they must connect with active forces in a way that ensures we would require both in any significant future conflict. They could and should offer to our active forces skills and capabilities that the active forces did not normally have or maintain. This concept, once implemented, evolved into what became known as the Total Force concept. You could no longer go to war without the Guard and Reserve. They came to have capabilities, such as transportation, military police, civil affairs, and logistics (these functions fall under categories called combat support and combat service support), that either did not exist in the active force or didn't exist in the numbers needed to conduct serious missions. Lines between active and reserve forces were largely erased, and they are now seen as interchangeable.

MY FIRST ORDER OF BUSINESS WHEN I TOOK COM-mand of CENTCOM was to visit all our military units deployed in the Middle East, a major part of our area of responsibility, including a number of National Guard and Reserve units. As I traveled from base to base, in such places as Bahrain, Saudi Arabia, Kuwait, Qatar, and Oman, I was impressed with the skills, competence, and training that I observed in these units. They were providing security, flying missions, and working in virtually every other area required of our forces in that part of the world at that time. They deserved recognition and thanks, and I made a note to acknowledge their contribution to our command when I returned to CENTCOM headquarters in Tampa.

Back home, as I dutifully worked through the list of taskings to the staff that came out of my visits, I asked my chief of staff to prepare letters for the Reserve component commanders who had units deployed in our CENTCOM area and for governors and adjutants general of the different states who had Guard units there. Two days later a huge stack of letters was plopped on my desk for signature. I was astonished. "I had no idea that so many Guard and Reserve units were making these kinds of deployments in peacetime, and on a routine basis," I said to my deputy, who also was surprised at the number.

The Guard and Reserve deployments—so many of them, and so often—raised questions. How do these deployments affect our citizen-soldiers? I wondered. It's great that we have them, but these have to be serious hardships. Their civilian jobs, community, family responsibilities, and quality of life have to be disrupted.

Looking for answers, I visited several units recently returned to their home bases.

Some units, I learned, had been deployed many times, for months at a time. Though the morale and desire to serve of both officers and enlisted were impressive, the multiple deployments had taken a toll. When units left home, local police or fire departments had been stripped of person-nel, small businesses had had to struggle to keep jobs open for deployed employees, and families suffered a financial crunch as breadwinners' salaries were reduced.

After I returned to headquarters, I remained convinced that the Total Force concept was good and necessary, but I wondered if we overdid its peacetime commitments. "We've run them hard in peacetime," I said to my deputy. "How much do they have left to give? What happens if we find ourselves in a major conflict that requires a significant call-up?"

Unfortunately, 9/11 made that necessary, and our incredibly dedicated citizen-soldiers have paid a big price. All kinds of bad outcomes have overwhelmed them—rising unemployment rates, family conflicts, business and community disruptions . . . and, worse, long-lasting injuries to both body and soul. There is a definite role for these forces and they bring the talent and motivation to serve that is extremely valuable in dealing with today's kinds of conflicts. We just need to be wise and prudent in how we employ them.

AS THE TOTAL FORCE PROGRAM SETTLED IN, AND AC-tive and reserve units grew increasingly comfortable with it, we discovered that the Guard had expertise and experience from their civilian lives that we had never imagined—not only combat skills, but also priceless skills in saving lives, rebuilding institutions, and reconstruction after the worst combat is over.

In 1997 the five Central Asian republics, states formerly in the Soviet Union—the "Stans"—were added to Central Command's area of responsibility. These nations were often prone to natural disasters—earthquakes, mudslides, wildfires, floods—that they were poorly equipped to handle. When disaster struck, loss of life and property were typically heavy. As it happened, some of our guard units came from states like Arizona and California, where earthquakes, mudslides, and wildfires are frequent; they are often first responders when disaster strikes. When these calamities occur, they have skills, training, experience, and organization that no one else has. We quickly discovered we could use all these.

As we opened up relationships with the Central Asian nations, we tasked National Guard units with relevant experience and training to work with local disaster relief organizations in response to natural disasters. Our units brought their expertise to the local organizations, shared their skills and equipment, and worked with them to save the injured and help the people recover and rebuild. The results were gratifying. Our disaster relief services helped build strong relationships in the region.

In Afghanistan and Iraq, the unique contributions—and the workload—of the Reserve and Guard grew ever more essential.

My son, a regular active duty Marine officer, served a tour in Iraq in a Reserve Marine infantry battalion. I asked him afterward how that experience compared to serving in a regular unit.

"In 2007 when we replaced an active duty battalion in Haditha," he told me, "our sector was rebounding. It had been a hotbed of insurgency; now it was becoming more secure. As time went on things were more under control, the insurgency became less violent, and we turned to helping the people recover. The mission evolved from less and less combat to more and more engagement, reconstruction, and stabilization; and the Reserve unit brought with them a wealth of civilian skills greatly applicable to these tasks. The Marines and Sailors in the unit were older than in an active duty battalion. They tended to have more life and civilian career experiences and more college degrees (one corporal in my unit was a surgeon in civilian life). Their civilian skills were now more applicable to the tasks required in the phase of the operation we were now in."

He went on to describe some of the things the unit was able to accomplish, "One task we took on was to repair, rehabilitate, and restart a long-offline oil refinery. As it happened, one of our officers came out of his civilian life with those skills. He was a mechanical engineer with Shell Oil, and his stateside contacts helped to get the refinery back online."

My son's story reminded me of my earlier days as a young captain running a combat skills course at Camp Lejeune, North Carolina. Reserve Marine units and Reserve Navy Construction Battalions (CBs) often came there in the summers to train. We gave them the required training in combat skills, and they in turn virtually rebuilt our austere training facilities. Reflecting on my past Vietnam tours, it struck me that these skills would have been invaluable as we tried to build relations and improve the environment in villages and hamlets. To have those skills embedded in actual combat units would have made us much better received and trusted.

Because the Guard and Reserve have become ever more valuable to our military structure, we have to become ever smarter in how we use them. During peacetime we shouldn't overuse them in roles that our active forces can and should handle. We should tap into their inherent civilian skills as well as their military capabilities. And we should make sure we do not waste their unique contributions to our ability to make war and peace.

JOINTNESS

The most significant and long-lasting change in the structure of our military forces since the creation of the Air Force in the late 1940s took place in 1986, following the passing of the Goldwater-Nichols Act. Before the act, the military services were rivals—sometimes friendly, sometimes bitter, but always in competition for scarce, zero-sum resources. When one service wins, others may lose. Much of that changed in 1986.

Since the passing of the act, our military has worked hard toward greater "jointness" (the integration of the forces from all our services to gain a more effective and efficient force from the resulting synergy). The services initially fought integration, fearing it would create a "separate service," a group of "purple mandarins" as one service chief quipped. (Purple is the color, and term, given to anything joint. It is what comes from blending Army green, Marine Corps red, Navy blue, and Air Force light blue.) The service chiefs knew that Congress normally resolved problems caused by lack of integration by imposing an overarching organization on top of the agencies they felt needed to be better integrated. This is what happened when the Department of Homeland Security and the Director of Central Intelligence were created in the aftermath of 9/11. The imposition of another layer of authority doesn't solve the problems of integration and coordination if outsiders are plopped on top of agencies that are suspicious, protective, and resentful of each other.

Goldwater-Nichols allayed the service fears by stipulating that the personnel who filled the joint structure would come from, and return to, the services. It also added a service component to all joint structures. This meant the services were totally integrated in joint organizations and manned the billets within them. Jointness was not above and distinct from the services.

I was there during all the stages of this process and saw firsthand how we all built together truly joint forces. It took time and goodwill.

We started out with wary deconfliction, where the battlefield was nominally joint but lines and measures were constructed to keep the turf clearly separate and the linking of effort only came at the topmost level. It eventually moved to coordination as trust was built and the value of the synergy created became apparent. Cooperation at lower levels and mutual support grew. It finally reached true integration, and the mix of troops at the lowest levels was decided by best capabilities needed and not by uniforms.

Today our senior officers are carefully educated in joint concepts, doctrine, and organization and are provided with extensive experience in joint operations. By the time you become an admiral or a general officer, you are familiar with how the other services work, and how to work comfortably and efficiently with them. You cannot reach star rank without that joint experience and certification. That doesn't mean you've lost your identity as a Navy, Marine, Army, or Air Force officer. There is still strong service pride, and that's healthy, but there is very little corrosive service prejudice. Sure, issues, personalities, and competition for resources can still cause friction, but these conflicts rarely wash down to the battlefield. As we face several years of constrained defense budgets ahead, we must be careful, however, that this environment of stiff competition for dollars does not recreate the bitter rivalries we experienced in the past.

BROTHERS IN ARMS

"The only thing worse than fighting with allies," Churchill said, "is fighting without them."

Allies want consistency in policies and commitments from the United States. If they commit to us, they want a solid commitment to them. I listened to angry and exasperated leaders in the Middle East on a visit shortly after President Obama announced talks with Iran. They stuck their heads above the parapet and wanted assurances that they aren't going to be left in range of Iran's wrath if a poorly negotiated deal is made and American protection and commitment to them wanes. Many allies in the region joined us in Desert Storm, Somalia, the Balkans, and Afghanistan and let us use bases on their turf to support our operations in Iraq, Afghanistan, and elsewhere. They expect that we will be there if they are challenged by a hegemonic power with a long memory like Iran.

Having international partners on the battlefield can bring many advantages. They can share the burden, bring international legitimacy to the mission, and provide cultural awareness, sensitivity, and interaction on the ground that we may lack. And allies also often come with specialized and valuable expertise that our forces don't have—such as extensive experience in peacekeeping and humanitarian assistance. But there are downsides.

I have taken part in numerous coalition operations and have commanded several. They are always a serious challenge, requiring considerable diplomatic skill, patience, and understanding to ensure operations go smoothly, especially when staff meetings look like the bar scene in *Star Wars*, with a bizarre assemblage of disparate uniforms with differing political motivations, worldviews, capabilities, and operational approaches. I have encountered coalition requests for "fresh" foods (meaning live goats and chickens), medical malpractice insurance for their troops we treated at our military medical units, and even assurances that their forces would not engage in actual combat!

Coalition forces can arrive with very different goals, political direction, and perspectives toward the mission than we come with. Although they may bring such advantages as cultural affinity with the people of the country where we are operating, cultural and historical incompatibility with the United States or with each other may create problems on the ground or within the force. There can be command and control issues, military interoperability issues (if equipment, doctrine, and capabilities differ), and intelligence issues (e.g., we may not want to share sensitive intelligence). Some well-meaning allies contribute forces that come with a heavy support requirement that we have to fill. We have to weigh the value of the allied flag against the burdens it may bring.

Operation Restore Hope (1992–93), the initial response to the Somalia humanitarian disaster, ended up with forces from twenty-six nations that spanned the spectrum of capability, political motivation, and experience. Some were self-sufficient and highly committed. Others were heavily dependent on US support and reluctant to risk serious engagement. Before we ended our mission and passed it back to the UN, we were looking at adding to the initial twenty-six allies more than fifteen other potential contributors to our task force. The State Department loved the multiple flags, but the law of diminishing returns was clearly setting in.

More and more we find ourselves teamed up with disparate collections of military forces from nations we never dreamed of sharing a battlefield with. The differences between our forces and theirs create significant challenges, and the search for a common organizational structure goes on.

The question of who leads in coalition operations is always controversial. It's hard to imagine the US not leading large-scale or combat operations for reasons of capacity and the political difficulty of placing US troops under any authority other than US operational control. We have accepted that arrangement in operations with close allies in smaller operations, such as in East Timor, where the Australians led and our role was to support them; we have of course also accepted it in a NATO context (but the top leadership of NATO has always been a US commander); and we have accepted it from time to time under the UN as we did in Somalia (although the deputy UN commander was a US Army general who retained command of US forces in the UN operation).

The United Nations has proven highly effective in peacekeeping and humanitarian operations. They bring together international forces that somehow do the job. But the UN does not do war fighting or peace enforcement missions well. For the more muscular missions, something else is needed.

Can NATO fill that slot?

The North Atlantic Treaty Organization, established in 1949, is the greatest and most powerful alliance ever constructed, and its member nations have invested significant amounts of their treasure in the military force they contribute to NATO and to achieving alliance standards. For decades NATO stood tall against the Soviet and Warsaw Pact threat. But the collapse of the Soviet Union and the Warsaw Pact (both in 1991) has raised many questions about NATO's future.

When the Cold War ended, I was serving in Europe. One of the first questions that was asked was "whither NATO?" Should it be disbanded? Could it be restructured to meet other challenges? What is its purpose now that the threat it was created to meet is gone? The Russians certainly saw no purpose in its further existence. They wanted it to go away—understandably. But most members wanted it to remain . . . in some form or other. And Eastern Europeans eagerly rushed to join.

Today, nearly twenty-five years after the Cold War ended, the question "whither NATO?" remains. During those years it has become more a political than a military alliance, and it has grown from sixteen members to today's twenty-eight.

Have these additions, and fading commitment from original members, diluted military capability? Yes.

Article V of NATO's charter reads, "an attack against one is an attack against all." For the first time in NATO's history, Article V was invoked, on September 12, 2001, the day after the 9/11 attacks, and NATO forces were sent to fight in the Afghanistan War. Once there, they got mixed reviews. That's not good enough. They need to do much better.

NATO has a choice. It can come out of Afghanistan with a renewed sense of commitment and a determination to become a more cohesive and capable global force. Or it can continue to devolve into a paper alliance—a handful of marginally capable militaries and a near-impotent flock of others going through the motions.

If NATO chooses renewal, it must reestablish and enforce throughout the member militaries a strong set of military standards, like those they maintained during the Cold War. Commitments to levels of funding, training, and equipping have been allowed to slip. Nations that cannot or will not commit to the standards should be rejected for membership, or given a lesser membership status and a prescribed program that will, over time and upon fulfillment, lift them to full membership.

Now that the UN has demonstrated that it cannot handle the more muscular and difficult missions like Somalia, a revitalized and reoriented NATO, with a more global mission and membership, could fill a much-needed role in the world. In 2014 the NATO nations will hold their biannual heads of government summit. This will present an opportunity to revisit its charter, expand it into a more international force, assess its performance in Afghanistan, and seriously discuss the need for greater burden-sharing by all its members, and its future role.

If NATO fails to step up to the plate, however, we need to take on the task of creating another organization, one more global in its outlook, to fill the role of handling military commitments beyond the scope of the UN's capacity and political willingness to take on. This is a much more difficult task than reforming NATO, but the alternative—trying to gather "coalitions of the willing"—will not work, and we can't continue to carry the burden alone or with minimal allied support.

THE AMERICAN BATTLEFIELD

There is an American style of war—our way of making war. We're the best in the world at fighting our kind of wars; and when we fight wars our way (for example, the First Gulf War), we win.

How do you characterize the American style of war?

We love technology. We blanket the battlefield with high-tech, chip-driven devices and precision munitions. If our electronic eyes can see it, we can hit it with great precision. We like a big battlefield that we can control, that allows us to stretch out and overwhelm the enemy. We want short-duration conflicts in which we dominate the tempo of operations and casualties are minimal; we compel the enemy to fight on our terms. We are obsessed with intelligence and invest greatly in all sorts of systems that dissect the battlefield and the enemy every which way from Sunday. We don't like "boots on the ground" for any prolonged period. We are enamored with special operations forces that can strike with great skill and disappear into the darkness. And we need to have absolute moral certainty in our cause.

When a conflict doesn't lend itself to this approach (and more and more conflicts do not), we have difficulty adapting. But adapt we must.

"It's not the strongest of the species that survives, nor the most intelligent that survives," Charles Darwin observed. "It is the one that is the most adaptable to change." Darwin's words are as true for our military as they are for the evolution of species. In my four decades of military experience, through numerous military operations, this is the most important lesson I have learned. Our military thinkers have dreamed up all kinds of new schemes aimed at winning on the battlefield. We've tried to overpower potential enemies. We've tried to out Shock and Awe them. We've tried to surpass them in training and education of our leadership. But in the end, the most important attribute on the ground is adaptability. Whoever adapts first, best, and consistently, prevails . . . most of the time. To paraphrase Sun Tzu, this requires knowing yourself, your adversary, and your environment extremely well.

One of the most impressive military leaders and mentors I have known, General Alfred M. "Al" Gray, once told me that a standing military structure should be seen as a large "reservoir of capabilities." He felt that in today's unpredictable world we cannot have a rigid structure organized for specific missions as in the Cold War days. Then we knew the potential enemy, battlefield, and allies. Today we do not have that kind of knowledge. That means we need a highly ready collection of capabilities that can rapidly be task-organized for a host of possible missions that do not have a defined place, time, foe, or set of partners. When the call to arms is sounded, we have to draw from that reservoir the forces and capabilities necessary to achieve the mission effectively and efficiently. Think of it in sports terms. You don't know what game you may be called on to play. It could be baseball, football, or basketball. To meet that challenge, it makes sense to have a stable of triathlon-style athletes who have the required collection of basic skills—speed, strength, smarts, and endurance. When the whistle blows, you draw out the skills needed and organize them into the team you need.

We must also be agile in an uncertain world. Since we don't have a crystal ball to guide us through an unsure future when unexpected challenges materialize, we need to be able to quickly shift the priorities in our structure, acquisition, and training. The same kind of adaptability is required on the battlefield.

Today it's very difficult to determine the kind of military we need. Do we have a potential high-end threat? China? Russia? Which capabilities should we invest in to keep a qualitative edge? Since we can't keep all our capabilities at their highest possible levels, which ones can we risk weakening? Can we accept a more narrow advantage than we have thought necessary in the past? Or none at all? How much of the force do we keep on active duty and how much should go into the reserves? What is the best force structure to meet the challenges of transnational threats such as terrorism, instability, insurgencies, and international criminal activities? And, perhaps the biggest question: What can we afford?

We can't keep guessing at these questions. Admittedly, we live in a very unpredictable world, but we know that the threats to us will be split between "low-end" and "high-end." We will need to deal with extremists, criminal organizations, environmental and natural disasters, humanitarian crises, and other "low-end" missions. Forces and technology that best fit these missions need to be developed and at the ready. We also need forces and capability at the ready to face "high-end," potentially existential threats—weapons of mass destruction, missile delivery systems, cyberattacks, and threats from space-based systems.

MIX OR MESS?

After leaders make the decision to commit our military to action and choose a set of strategic goals for it, they shape the mix of forces they will send to accomplish the mission.

In recent times, that has not come easy. Different leaders have differing views of how to do it. The forces assembled to take on Saddam Hussein's army in the First Gulf War (Operation Desert Storm) were shaped by the Powell Doctrine, which advocated "overwhelming force" in order to achieve a decisive outcome. A massive force was assembled in the Persian Gulf and built up to leave no doubt as to the outcome. The quick and decisive defeat of Saddam's forces and the limited casualties clearly paid off. Soon after Desert Storm I traveled around Eastern Europe and the former Soviet Union as an envoy from the European Command; we were beginning the process of military-to-military engagement with our former enemies. The reaction to our overwhelming victory in the desert and the total superiority of our forces and equipment amazed the Eastern Bloc officers I met. After all, Iraq was using their equipment and doctrine. Soviet tanks, planes, air defense systems, and command and control facilities were no match for our capabilities.

There are missions that are best handled by overwhelming our adversaries and ending things quickly, and there are times when our advantages in technology might allow us to use minimal force to resolve things. The trick is to know when to apply which kind of force. If we need to control people and terrain, we need boots on the ground. That wasn't understood in selecting the reduced force sent into Iraq by the Rumsfeld Pentagon. It worked fine to remove Saddam's regime, but not to handle the aftermath, and a surge of forces was necessary later to try to recover from the loss of momentum.

At times, differing views of the forces required for a mission have created tensions between the political and military leaderships. Such frictions are not just recent. In the Civil War, President Lincoln and General George B. McClellan clashed repeatedly over the forces required to defeat the

Confederate Army of Northern Virginia. Civilian leaders are concerned about costs and public reaction to committing large numbers of troops. Military leaders match forces to missions and tasks and calibrate the minimizing of risks to success. Both have a valid basis for their positions, but each side must understand the requirements, costs, and risks in order to reach a mutually acceptable decision on the force structure.

I left CENTCOM with a war plan in place that mapped in detail our plans for another conflict with Iraq. We had looked at a number of triggers, from a response to another attack by Saddam's forces to an invasion of Iraq after some other Iraqi outrage, such as a proven WMD program. We had developed this plan over a decade; four previous CENTCOM commanders had worked on it. Our troop numbers and forces were determined by exhaustive assessments of threats from the Iraqi military and hostile forces outside Iraq, the chaos that could erupt from long-suppressed ethnic and religious rivalries, and the demands of a military occupation to administer and provide security during reconstruction. Our plan went through several iterations. The Pentagon leadership during the two Clinton administrations reviewed, war-gamed, changed where necessary, and approved each iteration. Forces were allocated and structures and procedures put in place to rapidly execute the plan.

That plan was based on a deep understanding of the region and of conditions inside Iraq. It not only called for a force that could race up to Baghdad and quickly remove the Saddam Hussein regime, but for the additional force necessary to create security and stability in the aftermath of the invasion. This was not just a matter of numbers but of specialized skills and training. Iraq was not France in 1944. It was a serpents' nest of hostile tribes and factions in a land with porous and dangerous borders.

When they decided to invade Iraq, the Bush administration ignored the CENTCOM plan. Defense Secretary Rumsfeld declared it "old and stale" and "on the shelf." Hardly. Like all serious plans, it was dynamic—constantly updated (based on reassessments of the threat, the changing environment, and our own capabilities) and tested in real and simulated exercises.

In early 2003 in the run-up to the war, Army Chief of Staff General Eric Shinseki's testimony before the US Senate Armed Services Committee laid out the forces and numbers the mission required. It was his view that "something on the order of several hundred thousand soldiers" would be needed in taking down the regime and handling the post-Saddam environment. Shinseki was an experienced planner; his assessment reflected precisely what the plan called for.

The civilian leadership in the Pentagon had other ideas, and Shinseki was left to hang out in the cold, his judgment crudely dismissed. Worse yet, the military leadership who had approved the CENTCOM plan, and in some cases had been involved in developing it, passively submitted to burying it as did the Joint Chiefs of Staff who had approved it.

As a result, we paid a tragic price on the battlefield, and tens of thousands of Iraqis paid an even more tragic price during the civil war that followed our "liberation" of their country. We have left behind a $1 billion embassy . . . and a violent, poorly run country tottering on the brink of civil war.

As my predecessor at CENTCOM, General "Binnie" Peay, was preparing to leave and turn over command to me (I had been his deputy for the previous year), we took some private time together to share thoughts about the future of our area of responsibility. General Peay told me that it was important to make my own decisions and not feel bound by those he had made. Because our command encompassed a highly dynamic and volatile region that required constant rethinking of how we dealt with it, he assured me, any changes I made to what he put in place would not be seen by him as disloyal or in a negative light. "The only thing I will caution you on," he emphasized, "is not to reduce the number of troops in the Iraq war plan. There will be pressures on you to do it, but it would be a big mistake. Hold the line." Prescient advice my successor should have heeded.

We need a better method to determine how best to shape the right forces to fit a mission in a way that blends political considerations with military judgments. This would lead to a more streamlined relationship and coordinated process that brings closer together the many military and civilian staffs of the services, unified commands, Joint Chiefs of Staff, the Office of the Secretary of Defense, and the National Security Council. The planning should be done in a more collaborative manner, with planning staffs working together rather than developing plans at lower levels then passing them up the chain for approval.

Much of the disharmony we see today stems from distrust between civilian and military leaders. Political leaders and advisors question the military's motive in asking for forces. They believe that generals and admirals are thinking of their own needs and not the needs of the nation, and are trying to justify their enormous panoply of capabilities and fulfill their lifelong dream of commanding grand forces in the field. The military complains that dilettantes capture the ears of political leaders and claim to know better than generals what our country needs to ensure our security.

The answer goes back to the Washingtons, Grants, Marshalls, Eisenhowers, and Powells. Presidents, secretaries of defense, and national security advisors need trusted uniformed military leaders at their sides advising them, military leaders who appreciate the political aspects and pressures of using force but also understand the needs on the battlefield. By the same token, we need political leaders who understand the military's requirements.

And it's not just the political-military relationship that needs work. If we are going to continue to find on battlefields an increasing mix of diplomats, aid workers, institution builders, contractors, and warriors, then we need a more informed understanding of each other's needs and functions.

EIGHT

THE NEW BATTLEFIELD

I do not propose to send our young citizen-soldiers into action, if they must go into action, under commanders whose minds are no longer adaptable to the making of split-second decisions in the fast moving war of today.

General George Marshall

MY FATHER FOUGHT IN WORLD WAR I, MY COUSINS IN World War II, and my brother in Korea. My wars were Vietnam, many interventions like Somalia and Iraq, and actions against terrorist targets. My son's wars have been Iraq and Afghanistan. During my years on active duty a new kind of battlefield emerged. My father, cousins, and brother would have easily recognized the military I entered in 1961. All of us prepared for the same kinds of wars. But the military from which I retired would have been absolutely alien to them, not in its structure but in its missions. We prepared for and engaged in missions they could never have imagined.

Over the years, the spectrum of conflict has greatly broadened, and the battlefield environment has become far more complex. Civil War general William Tecumseh Sherman's application of "hard war," as he termed it, is no longer imaginable. Sherman felt that in order to end a war, its horrors and realities had to be brought home to those who supported it. In his view, civilians weren't observers; they were involved. If they suffered, it was unfortunate but necessary. It was their war as much as it was the soldier's war.

That hard policy changed in later wars. We came to care about civilian populations, but not as a priority during the fighting. We would do what we could not to harm them, but otherwise, we would take care of them after the fighting had ended. The Marshall Plan of the late 1940s asked Americans to pay to rehabilitate and transform the societies that had been our enemies, and the American public was also asked to unite with those former enemies under treaties, such as the NATO treaty, for mutual protection. That was the first time in history that the victor bore the total costs of war. The crippling reparations exacted less than three decades before, at the end of World War I, were not repeated. We shaped changes in those societies that turned out to be far superior to any gains victory in combat would, or could, have given them. Some years ago I attended a ceremony in Stuttgart, Germany, honoring Dwight Eisenhower. The mayor, Manfred Rommel, son of Field Marshal Erwin Rommel, was a lead speaker. "I loved my father," he said, "but I'm glad that Eisenhower was the winner in that war."

The bombing of cities in Germany and Japan was a difficult decision, but afterward we repaired those societies. No victor had ever done that. And, more than physical reconstruction, we offered to help build new economic, social, and governance structures that led to the prosperity and freedoms these nations now enjoy . . . and probably would not have otherwise achieved.

And now we face a new battlefield in which civilians are not relegated to the aftermath of the conflict. It's unthinkable today to fight wars that disregard the effects on the civilian population *as* you are fighting. We worry about "collateral damage" and the welfare of the people caught up in the conflict, and we often take extraordinary measures and risks to protect them even though we face enemies such as terrorists, warlords, pirates, and drug cartels that do not share our concern about civilian casualties. In Sherman's day the enemy's military force was the chief focus of military efforts. That's no longer true. The uncommitted civilian population has increasingly become the center of gravity. Today's enemies fight to gain control of peoples' hearts and minds; we must do the same.

Today, our enemies tend not to be nation-states but movements or international and local gangs. Combat power counts less, the narrative counts more. The battlefield is not defined simply as geography or terrain but as people's minds, and that "contested ground" is cluttered with media, diplomats, aid workers, and politicians. We have rules. The enemy doesn't. Victory is elusive, ill-defined, and non-traditional; measuring success or failure is difficult. Technology is only marginally helpful. No longer can actions be taken sequentially. Simultaneity is the rule. You can't make fighting the battle your first priority, then pick up the pieces and tend to the population later. You take care of everything at the same time. Humanitarian assistance, building a governance system, repairing infrastructure, improving the economy, and installing social programs are just some of the activities that may take precedence over combat operations. Because of media attention, small, tactical events can have strategic impact whose effects can be good or bad. A humanitarian action that gets attention can change a people's attitude toward our forces and aid acceptance. An act of bad judgment by an immature service member can have a devastating opposite effect.

These are just a few of the differences.

Wars like World War II or Korea—in which destructive battles are fought in cities and through civilian populations, and where millions of innocents become casualties—are growing increasingly rare. We're not likely to see battles like World War II's Stalingrad or Battle of the Bulge. High-end conventional warfare is tremendously destructive (over fifty million Europeans died in the two world wars), and it sits on the threshold of nuclear war. It has therefore become increasingly unthinkable. Yet, because the possibility, however remote, still exists, and because an existential threat can challenge us at that level, we need a military fully ready to handle—or deter—it.

Vietnam and later military actions brought a new dimension to the battlefield. They became "hybrid wars"—combining conventional military operations with a heavy dose of other objectives like "winning hearts and minds" and reconstructing societies *while* fighting. Organizations such as civil affairs, psychological operations, provincial reconstruction teams, female engagement teams, human terrain mapping teams, and other population-oriented units, some first seen in Vietnam, are more present on battlefields and integrated into combat organizations than ever before.

Military theorists differ about what all this means. Some argue that because this latest generation of warfare has so radically changed the character of war, radical changes are required in the way conflicts are handled. Others argue that the nature of war has not changed, it is immutable; but modern warfare (since the Peace of Westphalia in 1648) has evolved, and is now in its "fourth generation." The first generation was war waged by states, the second was attrition or firepower warfare, the third was maneuver warfare, and now, the fourth, is warfare conducted by non-state entities (perhaps cyberwar and robots will be the fifth generation). However we finally decide to characterize twenty-first-century warfare, nonmilitary considerations are now fully blended with military dimensions, and this change has certainly altered how we fight wars. Whether or not today's warriors face greater challenges than those faced by warriors in previous generations of warfare, the young Zinni now under arms experiences a far different battlefield than his grandfather did.

The modern general must not only be expert in his military profession of arms, he must also be part anthropologist, part economist, part sociologist, part political scientist, part everything else that brings expertise to the structuring of a stable and viable society capable of thriving in the twenty-first century. When he exits the battlefield, he is now expected not only to leave behind a vanquished enemy, but a functioning, stable society.

A president can no longer just look for a good fighter to plot the operational scheme that leads to victory in arms. He must also find a person who can reconstruct a society.

THE OPERATIONAL ART

"The art of war is simple," wrote Ulysses S. Grant. "Find out where your enemy is. Get him as soon as you can and keep moving on." Grant was fortunate. His president knew what he wanted. Lincoln's strategic direction required a total defeat of the armies of the Confederacy, and he wanted that defeat as soon as Grant could make it happen. The president needed victory before a problematic election in 1864 that might result in a negotiated settlement that could compromise his strong positions on slavery and the union. Support for the war was weakening after the years of drawn-out fighting and humiliating defeats. Lincoln's big problem was to find a general who could give him his victory. He needed a fighter—a warrior leader. He had wasted too many frustrating years when his only choice had been to tolerate incompetent, overly-cautious generals.

President Lincoln found his man in General Grant—a leader who could translate the president's strategic goals into military action.

Understanding the politics and policies behind the mission and translating strategy and strategic goals into battlefield action—the true definition of generalship—have always been difficult. They involve planning the campaign, structuring of the forces, assigning missions and tasks, establishing command and control structures, and many other necessary battlefield functions. All this begins with an operational design that lays out the overall approach to the operations from beginning to end.

An operational design is the conceptual approach that aims to achieve the political and strategic objectives on the ground. You define the problem and centers of gravity, and then analyze the objectives and other elements that frame the best way to understand and tackle the mission. It should not be confused with the operational plan. After you structure the design and get agreement from everyone who needs to agree to it, the planning begins. The result is an action program that will implement the elements of the design. It's like putting up a large building. You need an architect, a structural engineer, and a construction site manager. Each has a critical role. If their ideas and plans are not in sync, you have a disaster. The operational level is the structural engineer. He must take the architect's (political and strategic leaders') concept and translate it into a design that will work effectively and efficiently; and he will have to ensure that the construction site manager (tactical level commander) has the guidance and wherewithal to make it work. Anyone who has built a house knows these relationships have to be in complete sync. There needs to be a constant up and down communications flow, or else you end up with serious problems. The vision of the architect has to be matched by the practical considerations of the engineer, and these have to harmonize with on the ground realities faced by the site manager.

Grant's operational design, the way he would fight the war and achieve Lincoln's goals on the battlefield, began with his role as general-in-chief. He redefined that role. To him, this meant practically that he took operational command of all the forces in the field. Up until then the operations in the west and those in the east had not been coordinated. He did not want the job as it had been defined up to then and as the sitting general-in-chief, Henry Halleck, had understood it. Halleck sat in Washington as an administrator and provider. Grant wanted Halleck to stay on in that role, but step down to the position of chief of staff, where he would continue to take care of those administrative duties while Grant directly controlled operations at the front. To that end, he established an overall command and control structure to coordinate all the regional efforts under one scheme, with Sherman commanding in the west and General George G. Meade commanding in the east.

This came as a surprise to General Meade, who commanded the Army of the Potomac, the eastern force facing off against General Robert E. Lee's Army of Northern Virginia. He expected that Grant would take direct command of his army. In fact, Meade welcomed that; he didn't feel up to the task. He had been reluctant to take the army command in the first place, and he was still under a cloud of criticism after his failure to follow up after the victory at Gettysburg when he might have delivered a fatal blow to Lee's retreating army.

Ironically, General Lee had argued for the same type of operational command structure as Grant's, to coordinate the efforts in the west and east, but President Jefferson Davis refused. As a result, Grant had Sherman in the west and Meade in the east now fighting a coordinated campaign, while Lee had no ability to coordinate the western operations with his own.

Grant knew he had to bring the war to a close as soon as possible. He knew Sherman would drive relentlessly across the heart of the South through Georgia and South Carolina to the sea, severing the Confederacy's communications and support network. In the east, however, Grant felt compelled to attach himself to Meade's army to ensure that the old tactics—fighting a battle, withdrawing to camps to recover (often over a winter), then restarting the fighting—were ended. Like a tenacious bulldog, Grant would engage Lee, bring to bear the full weight of his forces' superiority in men and matériel, and not let up. He could lose battles, but this operational approach was bound to wear down Lee's Army of Northern Virginia, especially with Sherman cutting him off in his rear from the support he desperately needed to fight on. In the end, Grant gave Lincoln his victory.

GETTING WARS RIGHT

Just as Lincoln was fortunate to have Grant, Franklin Roosevelt was fortunate to have George Marshall at his side throughout World War II—a master at fusing strategy with military operations on the ground. As with Grant, Marshall's task was to deliver unconditional surrender. A monumental task was laid on his plate—building a modern military force, training it, getting the competent leaders it needed, pulling together a massive coalition, and, together with Admiral Ernest King, the chief of naval operations, designing a two-theater war strategy. He delivered. And FDR did not need to search while the war raged for another general capable of managing all those complicated functions.

War had changed. Marshall could not take to the field as Grant had done. He was fighting a complex global war. He had to be drawn into politics and policy as well as the grand strategy being crafted by a complex set of allied relationships.

Not all presidents have been so lucky. Presidents George W. Bush and Barack Obama, faced with Lincoln's dilemma, have gone through numerous generals, looking for one who could convert strategic goals into an operational design that produced victory at an affordable cost and in the time expected. More than a few generals since 9/11 have been asked to retire early or have been flat out relieved of command. The case against these generals is strong, but it's also ambiguous.

The Bush and Obama strategies and directions have been vague and inconsistent. None approached the clear directions Lincoln gave to Grant or Roosevelt gave to Marshall and King. Was the job supposed to be about destroying Al Qaeda? Or rebuilding nations?

Why did we invade Iraq? What exactly were we doing there? Did we invade simply to take out an unfriendly regime and then leave? Did we go in knowing we would soon find ourselves involved in an insurgency that threatened to metastasize into a civil war? Were we there to rebuild that society?

Why did we invade Afghanistan? Were we there simply to defeat the Taliban and make sure they no longer gave Al Qaeda sanctuary? Or was our job to rebuild that nation? How did we miss the perpetrators of 9/11 after unleashing all the force we threw at them?

In the years following the 2001 Al Qaeda attacks on America, we drifted into two costly nation-building commitments in Iraq and Afghanistan, a drift that resulted in years of stagnation on the ground. No one at the higher political or military levels planned for this; but they should have foreseen it. Their failure to understand what we would get ourselves mired into *before* we went in created the stagnation. It was not inevitable. As a result we were constantly trying to play catch-up.

During those years, we searched for a saving operational design . . . and for a savior to lead it. Should we limit ourselves to just combat operations? Should we adopt a counterterrorism (CT) approach and use special operations forces, drone attacks, and the like to go after Al Qaeda surgically? The Bush administration shuffled through the deck of available generals looking for their guy . . . and pulled out a man with a plan—General David Petraeus, a brilliant officer with a reputation for innovation and out-of-the-box thinking. He and other deep thinkers had resurrected and refined a counterinsurgency (COIN) doctrine originally fashioned forty years earlier. It was now offered as the solution to all the president's problems.

It was well-thought-out and meticulously detailed—theory *and* execution carefully spelled out. It called for an operational strategy to "clear-hold-build." With the more than 20,000 troops added by the 2007 surge, we would clear neighborhoods, hold the security posture we then established, and rebuild the society. It requires fighting the insurgents while building up the local military and police forces, governance systems, economic institutions, social programs, and other components of a society.

Big questions: What kind of society do you want to get to? And how do you get there?

We like to think that our own society and system of governance are the best models available, and we like to think we can transform other societies to be just like us. But how do we move cultures rooted in centuries-old mores, religious beliefs, and tribal and clan structures, whose legal and governance systems are closer to feudalism than to democracy? How do we pull a democracy out of a culture where practices of corruption are deeply ingrained, boundary and sovereignty delineations have no relevance, the mistreatment of women and minorities is based on archaic beliefs and traditions, economic practices are primitive and traditional, and education is rare? How do we lift societies like this anywhere near the twenty-first century?

It's tough enough to change a war-torn Germany or Japan, but a Somalia or an Afghanistan? We can't want the change more than they do. General Petraeus's COIN manual warns up front that "COIN campaigns are often long and difficult. Progress can be hard to measure, and the enemy may appear to have many advantages." It should have added that they can be expensive in treasure and casualties, require large numbers of troops, fall on an unreceptive populace, and fail to implant permanent change. Buyer beware!

Since no one else had a better idea, Petraeus's revisions of older doctrines became our operational design. Once again, we would work to win hearts and minds. Since political memories are short, we forgot the costs and lessons of going full-throttle with this approach. A ragtag gang of terrorists effectively dragged us in and mired us down in exceedingly difficult and costly long-term operations in nations that did not significantly threaten us. All our own doing.

General Petraeus not only gave us the operational design, he became the man to lead the effort on the ground, first in Iraq and then in Afghanistan. He was actually asked to step down from his position as overall theater (CENTCOM) commander to take command on the battlefields, a la Grant. Back to the future.

Petraeus certainly had noble intentions, as reflected in his ten-point guidance to his command in Afghanistan in 2010:

- Secure the people where they sleep.
- Give the people justice and honor.
- Integrate civilian and military efforts—this is an interagency, combined-arms fight.
- Get out and walk—move mounted, work dismounted.
- We are in a fight for intelligence—all the time.
- Every unit must advise their ISF partners [international security force—the Coalition forces].
- Include ISF in your operations at the lowest possible level.
- Look beyond the IED (improvised explosive device)—get the network that placed it.
- Be first with the truth.
- Make the people choose.

Hardly fire-breathing, Shermanesque directives. The Petraeus operational design took us down a path that was not in the minds of our political leaders when we started the campaigns in Iraq and Afghanistan. But by then, they thought they had run out of other options.

When the Bush administration launched their wars in Iraq and Afghanistan, I'm sure they believed the people in those countries would see us as shining liberators and hail our arrival—or so they promised on the Sunday morning talk shows. Kill a few bad guys, set up some military and police training and give them some equipment, arrange a quick election, build some social programs, and you can walk away proud of the good you've done. Profound naiveté.

When the Obama administration took over in 2009, they were seriously divided about how to proceed in Iraq and Afghanistan. "Should we continue the counterinsurgency approach?" they wondered. "Or should we favor a straight counterterrorism approach or some other less costly design?"

Obama made up his mind. He wanted out. He hurriedly extracted us from Iraq, leaving a fragile and tentative situation plagued with governance issues, malign outside influences, violent attacks, and brooding religious and ethnic rivalries that could erupt into violence at any time (and has).

In Afghanistan he has ordered cuts in troop numbers and set a deadline for extracting our forces, ignoring pleas from the military and others that the cuts are coming too soon and that a residual force should be left behind to stop Al Qaeda from regaining a sanctuary there.

In Vietnam, forty years earlier, William Westmoreland tried to achieve the opposite of the Petraeus design. He worked to achieve the decisive set-piece battle that would finish off General Vo Nguyen Giap. He wanted another Dien Bien Phu (1954), but a reversed Dien Bien Phu in which he would control the outcome and the Vietcong this time would be defeated. Giap was wise enough to know that he was no longer fighting the French, whom he could beat in that kind of battle. Ironically, looking only at what the political leadership sought, Petraeus may have been the better general for Vietnam and Westmoreland for Iraq and Afghanistan.

The question keeps returning: What is the center of gravity? Should the emphasis be the fight or the people? Modern conflicts tend to be about the people. But we should be cautious. Nation-building is costly in many ways. We could have, and should have, first focused all our efforts on the destruction of Al Qaeda.

Vice President Joe Biden and other political leaders in the Obama administration who favored greater focus on destroying terrorist groups and less on building societies might have welcomed the Westmoreland approach. For them the answer was the enemy first.

Today President Obama seems to be moving in the Biden direction. His administration appears to be shying away from the Petraeus approach that aims to change the culture that breeds or gives sanctuary to extremists. Special operations raids and drone and missile attacks are now replacing the "boots on the ground" conducting hearts-and-minds operations. The president's reluctance to get involved in Libya and Syria further leads to the same conclusion.

There is no single right answer to the people-or-fight dilemma. The answer has to be situational; it depends on where we are, whom we're fighting, and why. In no small measure it also depends on what we can afford and what the American people have the stomach for. We have to realize that we can't always (or ever?) shape societies in our own image . . . or, in some cases, change them at all. Our best course, sometimes, is to let time and less costly influences play out and hope these societies will slowly adjust to modernity. Of course, if elements in a society threaten us, and if the society is unable or unwilling to deal with these threats themselves, we reserve the right to eliminate them. But reshaping societies cannot be an automatic byproduct of every decision to take care of a threat.

We learned that lesson the hard way in Somalia, where we allowed ourselves to be drawn into a long-term nation-building mission after becoming initially engaged in a well-intentioned, supposedly short-term, humanitarian mission. We were stung by the price of that mission creep. And today, twenty years later, Somalia still poses threats. Somali pirates roam the seas off the Horn of Africa; and Al Shabaab, the Somali brand of Al Qaeda, conducts terrorist acts, such as the recent shopping mall attack in Nairobi in 2013, from Somali bases. We deal with these threats by patrolling the seas off the Somali coast to interdict pirates, by launching special operations raids into Somalia to hit extremist targets, and by supporting African nations that provide peacekeeping forces to help the weak Somali government. No one would think of suggesting a COIN strategy for Somalia.

The doctrines of containment and deterrence were designed to deal with the communist threat. A strategy and operational design were crafted to implement those doctrines. They worked. We had a standoff, but we didn't have a major war. Imagine what would have happened if we had not had that clear overarching political and strategic guidance and our military leaders had been expected to blindly fish around for an operational design to deal with the threat absent a strategic direction. Chances are that we'd have ended up with a more provocative military posture that got us into a shooting war with the communist nations. I can imagine Air Force General Curtis "Bombs Away" LeMay's operational approach. Shades of Doctor Strangelove!

GENERALS

Successful operations require successful leadership.

In World War II the US Army produced an abundance of outstanding leaders at the field army, army, and corps levels, units whose troops numbered in the hundreds of thousands and whose armaments exceeded those of the total army prior to the war. How did that happen? No organizations as large as these existed in our very small pre-war army. Did a common thread tie these successful commanders together?

Yes. And the thread was a single man, General George Marshall. Marshall was not only a brilliant strategist, he was an equally brilliant judge of men and the qualities needed for leadership. Virtually every high-level World War II military leader had been listed in Marshall's now famous (but maybe legendary) Black Book. Although historians debate whether or not he actually had a Black Book, nobody debates his uncanny ability to identify successful battlefield leaders.

As he traveled around the army in the years before the war, Marshall, then army chief of staff (1939–45), noted his impressions, good and bad, of officers he met. By 1941, he had begun to settle on the people he felt we would need in the fighting he foresaw. His judgments were tough. In his view, the vast majority of senior army officers were too old to command troops in the war he saw coming. Only one of these older officers, General Walter Krueger, received command (of the Sixth Army in the southwest

Pacific). The others were put out to pasture or were given nonoperational command positions. Junior officers he brought forward for promotion included Eisenhower, Omar Bradley, George Patton, Maxwell Taylor, and Matthew Ridgeway—a who's who of great World War II combat leaders.

In the decades that followed, we have chosen our military leaders in a more bureaucratic fashion.

CHOOSING SENIOR LEADERS

For much of our history, generals have gained command through political appointment or influence, a situation that plagued presidents Washington, Lincoln, Jefferson Davis of the Confederacy, and even Army Chief of Staff Marshall, who complained about officers who tried to use political influence to get promotion. Fortunately, that is no longer a worry. Our system has done away with direct political appointment. (The Senate must still individually approve top generals and admirals—three and four stars are individually nominated by the president. One and two stars are selected by service boards and the lists are sent by the president to the Senate for confirmation.)

All of us can remember from our civics classes that our founding fathers wisely divided our government structure into three parts to gain a balance of powers—the judiciary, the legislature, and the executive. In an interesting way, our generals and admirals are made to answer to all three. We swear an oath to the Constitution, we must be confirmed by Congress after swearing we will answer to them if called upon, and we are nominated and report to the commander-in-chief. It is not unusual for these obligations to cause conflicts.

Today we have an exhaustive process for developing senior leaders capable of handling the management and executive challenges of peacetime leadership. By the time an officer becomes eligible for the top grades, he or she has been through numerous education programs and a variety of command, staff, and other assignments. Even so, we have had problems finding wartime leaders . . . or at least so it seems.

Presidents from Truman to Obama have been frustrated with their senior combat leaders.

During Harry Truman's presidency (1945–53), The National Security Act of 1947 formally created the Joint Chiefs of Staff (JCS)—a chairman, vice chairman, and the service chiefs sitting as members—whose primary duty has been to advise the president, secretary of defense, and other leaders on military matters. Note: they *advise.* They have no real command authority (though in their service chief roles they have authority to train, organize, and equip their own services). For that reason, their power to affect events is limited. Truman, who had witnessed serious service rivalries and disagreements during the war, was pleased with the new JCS. It looked like an excellent remedy for the various top-level dysfunctions in our military.

Have the Joint Chiefs lived up to Truman's hopes? Sadly, no.

Where were they when Truman had to relieve Douglas MacArthur in Korea? Passive . . . unable to break through the confusion their limited authority imposed. Where were they during Vietnam? In his powerful and groundbreaking book, *Dereliction of Duty,* Major (now Major General) H. R. McMaster describes a hapless, ineffective Vietnam-era JCS. "The Joint Chiefs of Staff," he wrote, "became accomplices in the President's deception and focused on a tactical task, killing the enemy."[1]

More recently, there have been calls for a new *Dereliction of Duty* that tells the story of JCS failures in the Iraq and Afghanistan conflicts. Even though the Persian Gulf War was by every measure a success, the JCS was criticized for interference with the combatant commander (General H. Norman Schwarzkopf Jr.) and other aspects of the operation, and the air force chief was relieved of duty for indiscreet comments. The new *Dereliction of Duty* has yet to appear, but military writers, such as Thomas E. Ricks in *Fiasco*[2] and *The Generals*[3] and others, have found serious fault with the performance of senior leaders. Our top commanders in Iraq and Afghanistan shuffled in and out of those countries at a rate that George Marshall would not have stood for. It seemed for a while that General David Petraeus was the only general the political leadership trusted to run a war!

Though a few recent generals have been effective and respected, the criticisms are nevertheless troubling. It's hard not to conclude that the leadership structure is wrong—overcomplicated. Like all huge, long-lasting bureaucracies, it has become bloated and confusing—a Rube Goldberg contraption.

Before the creation of the Joint Chiefs Staff, the Army and Navy service chiefs controlled operations. Then the JCS was created to provide a joint perspective. Though they were still the service chiefs (now with the Air Force and Marine Corps added), they did not control operations. After the creation of the JCS, the operational line of command went from the secretary of defense to a few commanders-in-chief—the commanders of the European Command, Pacific Command, and so on; the JCS were only advisors. The service chain of command went from the service chiefs to the service secretaries to the secretary of defense, and only involved train, organize, and equip responsibilities. The Goldwater-Nichols Act (1986) created the combatant commands (their commanders were called commanders-in-chief) and formalized their operational lines to lead directly to the secretary of defense. The act further required the combatant commanders to communicate to the secretary of defense through the chairman of the JCS. Secretary Rumsfeld later stripped the combatant commanders of their commander-in-chief titles, signaling that he intended to return centralized control to the Pentagon. Meanwhile, confusion between combatant commanders and the JCS over who controls forces, budgets, and "joint" representation, and who approves operational plans, has frequently resulted in friction, as was the case in the lead-up to the Iraq and Afghanistan wars when harsh words were reportedly exchanged between the CENTCOM commander, General Tommy Franks, and members of the JCS over how operations would be conducted and how the forces would be organized.

A few years ago, I was asked by a professor in the government department at a college where I was teaching to explain to his class the Pentagon structure. After I'd done my best to explain and diagram the Pentagon maze on the blackboard, a desperate-looking student raised her hand.

"Professor Zinni," she asked, "will we be tested on this?" I assured her that neither I nor her professor would be so cruel.

While commander of CENTCOM, I was visited by a congressman, a member of the House Armed Services Committee (HASC) who had served in the military. His committee experience and prior military service had given him solid knowledge of military affairs. During his visit he turned to me. "You'd be proud of us [at the HASC]," he announced. "We cut the joint exercise budget by a third."

"Congressman, why would I be proud?" I replied. "That's my exercise budget." I didn't command forces from each service in isolation. I commanded joint forces. They all had to fight together as a single united force. That meant they had to exercise together as a single force.

"Well!" he snapped. "The Joint Chiefs told us joint exercises draw away time and resources from their requirements to train and exercise their forces."

"Are they speaking as the Joint Chiefs or the service chiefs?" I asked. He looked confused. "The service chiefs certainly need to train their forces," I explained. "But so do I if I'm going to meet our requirements."

"What's the value of joint exercises?" he asked. "They didn't see much value in them."

I smiled. "Well, sir, if there is no value in exercising the war plan you may have to execute, in the climate, conditions and terrain where you may have to fight, and with the allies that may have to fight with you, then we should scrap the joint exercise program totally."

He still looked confused. He never got what I was trying to tell him, that the Joint Chiefs were first and foremost service chiefs; Joint came second. Creating the JCS was an attempt to cure the service rivalries that were evident in World War II. Having a "joint" body sitting in the Pentagon did not create true service integration. Hence the Goldwater-Nichols Act. The JCS members were each in a difficult position and faced with a kind of Catch-22. How do they balance their Title X responsibilities to train, organize, and equip their own services with the requirement to integrate and employ their forces with those of the other chiefs when someone else, the combatant commanders, has that responsibility? The time and budget demands of those functions compete with each other. The interests can clearly conflict.

In my view, we should change the makeup of the JCS. It should be a standing body made up of *former* service chiefs and *former* combatant commanders on a final tour of duty. This would bring to that body much broader experiences and a much richer joint experience, and it would encourage uninhibited opinions and advice. It would still retain its purpose as an advisory body.

ALL OF US IN THE MILITARY START OUT ON THE SAME paths. We learn our service responsibilities, we learn our military occupational specialties (MOSs), and we experience diversity in assignments outside our MOSs. It's a solid career development track. But as we get more senior, our skills, strengths, and limitations are more clearly discernible. We also face greater responsibilities that require levels of experience and specialization that can't be met by plugging in just any senior officer. Acquisition, recruiting, manpower management, and other functions now require specialized schooling and extensive past experience before senior positions in those fields can be filled. Regional assignments in combatant commands at senior levels are tough to handle if there is no past experience or education in these areas of responsibility. Operational planning has become much more sophisticated and is difficult to master at senior levels without an extensive background. We need to make sure our senior leaders have been educated and trained in these skills and put on tracks in their career assignments that lead them to the top in areas that require more than just good general leadership ability.

Meanwhile, our defense leadership structure has become too bloated. Given today's budget crunch, we ought to look at cutting headquarters and staffs, as well as consolidating functions. This needs to begin in the Pentagon. Do we really need nine separate staffs there? The secretary of defense, the service secretaries, the JCS, and the services, along with other DOD agencies cram into the largest office building in the world. Too many layers and too much duplication. To begin with, I would eliminate, as some have suggested, the service secretaries (the secretaries of the Army, of the Navy, and of the Air Force) and their staffs. The combatant commands report to the secretary of defense and communicate through the chairman of the JCS. The services could do the same. Many staff functions such as planning, intelligence, and manpower management could be handled on a collaborative basis. The staffs can pool their resources for these functions and save on structure, resources, and personnel and avoid duplication. We have seen this kind of consolidation in support areas. Medical support, for example, has one support system for all services. It's time to bring this concept to staff organizations. In the corporate world, organizations have been streamlining staffs and eliminating duplicative staff levels for over two decades, but in government (military included), bureaucracies continue to grow.

JUNIOR LEADERS

Our junior officers and noncommissioned officers are exceptional. The shift after Vietnam to the all-volunteer and professionalized military has produced highly skilled junior leaders who have mastered sophisticated technology and complex battlefield environments. Any successes we can point to in Iraq and Afghanistan were achieved—and achieved quickly— by the companies, battalions, and brigades on the ground. We learned from the bottom up.

I am amazed at the skills our junior leaders must master—the technical proficiency requirements they must possess, the joint and combined capabilities they must understand, the nonmilitary tasks they must perform and know how to support, the vague or nontraditional missions they must accomplish, and the media and political scrutiny they must face. My generation had its own unique challenges, but we didn't experience anything like this.

Junior leaders have clearly seen and understood what needs to be done from where they have operated, on the ground and in the villages. Senior leaders who bring rosy predictions, ineffective strategies, constantly shifting operational direction, changing rules of engagement, and lack of understanding of the ground fight make the job of the junior leaders at best difficult . . . or at worst impossible. The best senior leaders do their utmost to see what the battlefield is like from the bottom up.

All the great planning in the world can't translate into success unless the lowest-level leadership on the ground is competent enough to implement it, understand it, and, most important, buy into it.

ARMCHAIR GENERALS

We are fortunate in our governing system, which subordinates the military to civilian control. In this way, our founding fathers made virtually impossible historic abuses such as a military takeover of the government or military autonomy, such as often occur elsewhere in the world. Lincoln, Truman, Carter, Obama, and other presidents have successfully stood up to and removed powerful, insubordinate, or incompetent generals. That is as it should be. As a senior officer you may express your views in the chain of command. If you do not feel your voice has been heard or if you disagree with a decision, you have a choice: you can salute smartly and execute the orders to the best of your abilities, or you can resign or retire and express your views as a private citizen. You can, as we say, throw your stars on the table and leave.

To be sure, it's not always the general who is at fault when the relationship between a general and a political leader goes bad. Too often—as during the Vietnam and the Iraq wars—presidents and defense secretaries ignored sound advice from generals who attempted to give their advice. In such cases, blame for the disastrous outcomes that followed cannot be hung exclusively on the military. Politicians who advocate disastrous courses of action or do not provide the sound, well thought-out, and complete direction necessary should also be held accountable—though that rarely happens. Today we see members of Congress and cabinet members who never met an intervention they didn't like . . . but you can't find their fingerprints when accountability time rolls around.

No president should put the prosecution of a war entirely in the hands of a general. By the same token, no president should become an operational commander (aka micromanager) running tactical events from the basement of the White House, as LBJ did during the Vietnam War.

During the Clinton presidency, Secretary of Defense Bill Cohen made sure the president knew his generals and admirals. Several times during the year, each of us had time with the president and were encouraged to give our views. When decisions were being made to commit our military, Cohen ensured the commander was in the room during the decision-making process, and that his input was listened to.

A president would be wise to get to know his key generals and admirals and be actively involved in their selection. He also should look for his Marshall or Grant and invite him in on the thinking and decision making early in the process.

NINE

BODY COUNT

*Preoccupied with body count during the Vietnam War, fueled by Secretary
of Defense Robert McNamara's obsession with statistical indicators, General
Westmoreland pushed commanders to achieve the "crossover point" at which
more of the enemy were being killed than could be replaced by infiltration or
recruitment, essential to success in his strategy of fighting a war of attrition.*

Spencer C. Tucker, Editor
The Encyclopedia of the Vietnam War

HOW DO YOU KNOW WHEN YOU ARE WINNING A WAR?

There's the old-fashioned way. You beat your enemy in a decisive battle, seize terrain, march up to his capital, eject the government, and install
a new one more congenial to your interests. We're very familiar with fighting that kind of war. We know how to fight an enemy whose sources of
strength and vulnerabilities—centers of gravity—are similar to ours . . .
that are, in military language, "symmetrical" with ours, and are vulnerable
to destruction or disruption by weapons and systems we are familiar with.
But how do you know whether you're winning when you don't know how
many points you've scored, there's no scoreboard, and the enemy fights a
seemingly endless war anywhere and everywhere in the country? How do
you win against a shadowy enemy with no uniformed units willing to meet
you in war-deciding battle, no capital he needs to defend, and no particular
pieces of ground he needs to hold?

How do we fight an enemy that refuses to fight by our rules?

In Vietnam, Secretary McNamara's answer to these questions was body count.

The Vietnamese Marines constantly complained that our American obsession with body count was nuts. They knew from long experience that it made no sense as a measure of success or failure in battle. I agreed.

That truth really hit home one day in late November 1967, after we were heloed in to reinforce a Vietnamese army unit that had been severely mauled by a large Vietcong force caught moving into position near the coastal city of Qui Nhon for the soon-to-be-launched Tet Offensive. I was with our lead elements, who had been ordered to attack what we thought was a still largely intact VC regiment. We expected heavy fire, but as we advanced, the fire turned out to be sporadic. The VC were clearly withdrawing and fighting a delaying action. The very experienced and aggressive Vietnamese Marine commander I was with, Captain Kinh, wanted to move out fast to catch the retreating VC. But there was a catch. As we moved through the enemy's evacuated fighting positions, we found large mass graves—hastily dug pits with scores of bodies thrown in. I mentioned the graves in a sitrep (situation report). I radioed up the US chain of command, and orders soon came down from the US Corps headquarters for that region to stop and count bodies. Count bodies? That was insane. Insane not only because it was a stupid way to tell if you were winning or not. Even more insane because the battle had lasted several days, leaving hundreds of dead VC whose bodies had been quickly dumped in those barely covered pits. It was hot and they were decomposing; the stench was overwhelming. And even more insane because our troops were ready to move on; the enemy was reeling from continuous air and artillery strikes and on the run.

When I told Kinh about the orders I received from Corps headquarters, he gave me a hard look. Kinh was fifty-five years old. A tough old warrior who had seen combat in World War II, the Indochina War, and now the Vietnam War. He was a legend in the Vietnamese Marine Corps. His years of combat with nine war wounds and countless awards for bravery had taught him a lot about winning and losing. Body count was not one of his metrics.

Great, I thought. I happily passed Kinh's message back to the Corps headquarters, and got a lot of grief for it later. But what the hell, he had the right priorities. Hitting the enemy hard and liberating the devastated villages they held was more important than counting bodies.

All of us who fought in Vietnam eventually learned that body count was a disastrous way to determine success.

In 1974, film director Peter Davis made a documentary, *Hearts and Minds*, about the Vietnam War. During the making of the film, Davis interviewed General William Westmoreland, the US commander in Vietnam for most of the war. In the interview, Westmoreland made this comment: "The Oriental doesn't put the same high price on life as does a Westerner. Life is plentiful. Life is cheap in the Orient"—a shocking statement that personally appalls me. I saw many Vietnamese die. Their loved ones grieved with no less passion than American families or friends.

And yet I knew that wasn't the whole story. Westmoreland's generation had come through powerful experiences that had led many of them to accept this prejudice as true. They had witnessed the Japanese suicidal frontal attacks of World War II and the Chinese and North Korean mass human wave attacks in the Korean War. These actions could appear to result from an absence of feeling for the value of human life. Westmoreland doubtless assumed in Vietnam the same willingness to sacrifice lives he had experienced in earlier Asian conflicts; he must have understood that to mean we could kill our way to the tipping point that would turn the war. The enemy would throw bodies at us; we just needed to deplete the supply until they ran out of bodies.

I felt for General Westmoreland. He was a soldier formed in a different era and by different conflicts than the one he was tossed into.

During the early 1990s, when I was the deputy commander at Quantico, the Marine base that houses most of our professional schools, Westmoreland came to give a talk on lessons learned from Vietnam to our officers attending school there. The commanding general was away on a trip, so I hosted Westmoreland's visit. On the evening before his talk, he and I had dinner at a table in the back of a small restaurant. Most of the evening he was quiet and reflective; he didn't say much. We chatted about the war, and he asked about my service in it and about shared personal experiences. But then at one point his face clouded and he lowered his eyes. "You know, General (Vo Nguyen) Giap has asked to meet with me and talk about the war," he said quietly.

"Sir, you have to do it!" I immediately responded. I was thinking about all the valuable insights to be gained from that meeting and the historical importance of what could come out of it.

"I can't," he replied with deep regret. "The soldier in me wants to do it, but the publicity would open the still healing wounds of our veterans."

I understood what he was saying. The media would be blind to the true value of that meeting. It would be perceived as admitting guilt over losing a war and blaming those who had fought it—the 1970s and 80s revisited. And yet if he could have done it, we could have learned so much.

Just then I looked at him and wondered how Westmoreland would have experienced the Vietnam War if he had been, like me, a lieutenant and captain in the 60s, and if past experiences hadn't already shaped his views. He was a good soldier who knew combat in his bones. And he was anything but blind and insensitive. I was convinced he would have seen Vietnam the way I did. He would have seen it with the feelings that inspire the last line of his memoirs, *A Soldier Reports*: "As the soldier prays for peace he must be prepared to cope with the hardships of war and bear its scars."[1]

Body count wasn't the only flawed metric used in Vietnam.

Robert McNamara brought a highly technical and statistically oriented approach to judging progress on the Southeast Asian battlefield. His background in operational analysis, founded on his education and business experiences, didn't fit that war . . . or any war. The brilliant, Harvard-educated "Whiz Kids" that McNamara had gathered around him could not grasp the nature of the conflict we were in. Body count and the McNamara Wall—an attempt to seal off the DMZ (demilitarized zone) that separated the two Vietnams with high-tech detection systems—symbolized the failed attempts to objectively measure success and apply technology to an environment that could not be fundamentally affected by those approaches. It was a grunt's war.

Yet the idiocy never completely disappeared. Many years later during a press conference in Somalia, a reporter asked me how many bad guys we'd killed. I snapped back with Captain Kinh's reply, "We don't count bodies." I received criticism for that response, as some misinterpreted it as a callous remark (as though I'd meant that those who had died didn't matter).

My successor as CENTCOM commander, General Tommy Franks, got the same criticism from reporters during the Iraq War after he gave the same reply. The Vietnam generation of reporters would have understood immediately.

INDICATORS

In December 1992, it had become clear that there was no exit strategy for our mission in Somalia. The Pottery Barn principle had taken effect. We now owned it, and our mission was now in full "creep." We were now trying to stabilize Somalia.

Our initial direction had not included anything like that. We hadn't planned for that. Now we were doing it. Or, anyhow, we were taking initial steps on that road. That meant we needed to find ways to measure how we were doing in the chaotic environment we were up against.

The military has teams of "thinkers" whose job it is to ask and answer questions like these. Our service doctrine centers have scores of exceptionally bright officers who try mightily to figure out the best ways to fight. Without much guidance or direction from our political masters about what they want to accomplish, the military is often left with the job of divining objectives and end states. With that comes deciding how we are doing along the way.

We asked the Army's Training and Doctrine Command (TRADOC) and several other doctrine centers back in the US for their help about how to measure progress in low-intensity conflict and peacekeeping operations, as these missions were then called. Their response was cautious. Serious studies of environments like ours, as well as the lessons of Vietnam, had made them and other doctrine producers leery about offering absolute answers. They sent us draft sets of guidelines—"indicators," they called them. Don't think of them as definitive, they warned, but carefully consider them in the local context. Wise advice.

We also asked the Army–Air Force Center for Low Intensity Conflict for help and advice, and they sent us a detailed and voluminous study of indicators, with very complex matrices and analyses. Though these papers required a lot of thought and work, they got them to us with amazing speed, which we greatly appreciated. We needed answers badly.

The handbooks from TRADOC and the others called, among other things, for tracking arms reduction and violent acts, re-establishing local markets, and working to obtain the cooperation of the civilian population. We did all that, while remaining careful not to count any of it as an absolute measure of success, as they had warned. As time passed, the "indicators" seemed to reveal favorable progress, yet we had the feeling that progress was fragile and the underlying instability was still there.

I remembered Vietnam. You can put all kinds of points on your scoreboard that have no relation to the unstable conditions that actually exist. It's like counting first downs in a football game to measure progress toward victory. First downs don't matter much in the end if the scoreboard is not in your favor. Headquarters in Vietnam often had color-coded maps indicating progress toward victory when the violence I was experiencing in the field denied it. In Somalia after the Black Hawk Down incident, I saw the same delusion in the bunkered UN headquarters in Mogadishu. You can put all kinds of points on your scoreboard that have no relation to fighting that raged right outside in the city. Déjà vu.

Many indicators we were sent were helpful, but some were at best ambiguous. For example, it was always easy to buy AK-47s in the arms markets that popped up on Mogadishu streets. We tried to raid these moving markets in order to reduce the numbers of arms on the street; and Counter Intelligence Teams tracked the cost of AK-47s as a measure of the success of our arms confiscation programs. One day at a morning briefing, it was reported that the cost of an AK was up, and now equivalent to $100 US. "That's good," someone blurted out. "It means weapons are becoming more scarce and our programs are working." But someone else chimed in, "Couldn't it also mean that people are feeling more insecure and are willing to pay more?" I received a degree in economics in college: Was it supply or demand?

What was really going on out there in the Mogadishu market for AKs? What did it say about our programs? We were not sure. We were sure that no simplistic collection of statistical data alone would tell us. It would require a deep understanding of all the dynamics that were driving this environment, many of which were not readily apparent.

ALPHABET SOUP

Right after I retired in 2000, I was invited to participate as a senior mentor at the now-defunct Joint Forces Command (JFCOM, formed in 1999 and disestablished in 2011). Among its missions was to develop joint concepts and doctrine and to conduct joint experimentation. When I first arrived at JFCOM headquarters in Suffolk, Virginia, I was dazzled by the endless cubicles containing bright young officers along with civilian contractors, many of whom were retired officers, laboring away to produce supposedly cutting-edge concepts for fighting future wars. They delivered staggering quantities of PowerPoint briefs with mind-boggling acronyms and undecipherable terms. Much as DARPA (Defense Advanced Research Projects Agency) and other private and government labs work to produce superior technology, JFCOM aimed to produce superior thinking. Put the best brains to work, allow creative, out-of-the-box thinking, then test the results through a sophisticated gaming and experimentation process.

All this sounded exciting and challenging. To put the icing on the cake, the guy in charge of testing efforts at JFCOM was retired General Gary Luck, a brilliant operator and former commander of US Forces Korea. While I was on active duty, Luck was one of my finest mentors in the operational art. Also on board as a fellow senior mentor was an old and dear friend, retired Marine General Paul "Rip" Van Riper. I, and many others, regarded Rip as the foremost military thinker in our Corps.

As Rip and I listened to endless briefings of concepts being produced, we began to feel uneasy.

"It doesn't make sense," Rip said. "There's no underpinning, no foundation based on the sound principles and tenets of warfare learned over time. It's gobbledygook!"

Try as I might to a find useful nugget in the massive amount of stuff being churned out, nothing much offered itself. Rip, as usual, was right.

The alphabet soup of acronyms poured out—RDO, ONA, SoSA, and on and on. One highly touted concept was called effects based operations (EBO), a highly technical approach to assessing results based on specific desired effects that would lead to successfully accomplishing the mission. It had been born out of a targeting concept that measured specific technical effects like degree of damage from strikes conducted, and had evolved into a statistical approach to determining metrics for all aspects of operations. Simply put, you described your intent in terms of effects you wanted to achieve, then measured success by the technical achievement of those effects. Bombing power plants, destroying bridge spans, and disrupting communications facilities could all be measured precisely and calculated directly as a measure of progress toward victory. "McNamara returns," Rip muttered.

Network-centric warfare, rapid decisive operations, effects-based operations—these and other three-word terms that promised to improve all our approaches to military missions flowed freely from the computers of those tasked to produce brilliance. Rip and I composed a three-column list of meaningless words, randomly combined sets of three (centric decisive operations, network effects warfare, rapid oriented operations, and so on), and suggested to some of the brilliants that we were working on these cutting-edge concepts. There was always excited interest.

JFCOM put together a highly sophisticated and complex series of games called Millennium Challenge to test their emerging concepts. The crowning jewel was supposed to be Millennium Challenge 2002, which was to cost $250 million. A great deal of fanfare and press attention accompanied the exercise, which was advertised as free play, with no scripted actions. The concepts would be tested against a free-to-act, thinking "enemy."

They made one very big mistake. They asked General Van Riper to head the enemy force.

The game began, and Rip immediately administered catastrophic losses on the "Blue" (good guy) forces. Play was stopped so they could gather their wits. When play was restarted, Rip immediately slammed them again. Again play was stopped as the embarrassed JFCOM folks tried to understand what hit them. They decided to restart, but this time Rip's actions would be scripted and certain capabilities would be taken away from him. This was shocking. The game was set up and promoted as play against a real-world threat, so how can you test your capabilities if you remove real "enemy" capabilities and direct them how to act? Rip told the JFCOM folks he would agree to those conditions only if they did the honorable thing and changed the public statement that the game was free play. They refused and he stepped down from his position leading the Red forces.

The fallout afterward from press comments was immediate and damning. Most of the damning info that went to the media came from junior officers who were outraged by the sham they had just observed. Reverberations went all the way to the chairman of the Joint Chiefs of Staff, who attempted to sweep the mess under the rug. Everybody up the chain made excuses, obfuscated, and waffled. They felt they had good reason for covering up the Millennium Challenge mess. We were preparing to invade Iraq in the months ahead. Millennium Challenge was not only a $250 million war game that had gone bust, but the concepts developed and supposedly validated in this game were to be exported to CENTCOM and included in the "revolutionary" Shock and Awe approach that was about to be used in Iraq.

The effects-based operations concept did go to CENTCOM, and the planning for Iraq included it.

During that process, General Luck called to tell me that my successor, the CENTCOM commander General Tommy Franks, wanted me to visit his headquarters to advise them in the gaming and preparation for the attack. I hesitated, but agreed. Weeks went by, and no call came. Puzzled, I called General Luck. My participation had been blocked, he confessed. The reason was obvious—my criticism of the way we intended to conduct operations. This was confirmed when I called the deputy CENTCOM commander. "The highest level of the Pentagon doesn't want you here," he told me. I later learned in another conversation with General Luck that the JFCOM commander, the former vice chairman of the Joint Chiefs, had "banned" me from JFCOM as well. Luck was apologetic, and I sympathized with him; I knew he felt badly about what was going down. His practice had always been to invite Rip, me, and others he respected to games he was running, to voice our views—positive or negative. He knew that a devil's advocate approach was the best way to check new thinking and untested concepts. And I knew that even a great soldier like Gary could get stifled in a world dominated by political generals and admirals and arrogant civilian leaders who know nothing about the conduct of war.

Rip and I chatted about all this . . . and decided to go fishing to get our minds off how JFCOM had pushed us out when we failed to follow their idiotic rules. But we couldn't forget the disaster we feared lay ahead in Iraq.

"What do you think will happen?" Rip asked, casting a line into our favorite stream.

"They will find no WMD," I said. "The removal of the regime will be swift, less than three weeks. Then the real problems will begin, and the price for too few troops and no real planning for the aftermath will take its toll on our forces."

He nodded and sadly shook his head.

I criticized the Iraq War not only because it was unnecessary, but also because we were going about it the wrong way. The crazy Shock and Awe idea, along with JFCOM's half-baked, pseudo-scientific concepts and mechanical and statistical measures of success, greatly troubled me and many others. War is still an art supported by science, not the other way round.

In 2008, Marine General Jim Mattis, the new commander of JF-COM, issued this statement: "It is my view that EBO has been misapplied and overextended to the point that it actually hinders rather than helps joint operations. . . . After a thorough evaluation, it is my assessment that the ideas reflected in EBO, ONA, and SoSA have not delivered on their advertised benefits and that a clear understanding of these concepts has proven problematic and elusive for US and multinational personnel. . . . The underlying principles associated with EBO, ONA, and SoSA," he concluded, "are fundamentally flawed and must be removed from our lexicon, training, and operations."

As Rip and I were strolling the banks of our stream, I had one last thought. "If we get into a budget crunch," I told him back then, "JFCOM will be the first command to go."

It closed its doors in 2011.

GOOD-BYE, GOOD WARS

Ah for the good old days of the Good War! The old-fashioned and *simple* conventional war: defeat the enemy's military forces, remove the regime, and reconstruct a defeated and compliant population. Then you could look at a map in the operations center or look at the enemy attrition charts provided by the intel folks and know if you were winning or not. The conflicts we find ourselves in today are far more complicated. As the military is fond of saying, these conflicts are "asymmetrical"—enemy forces don't play by established rules or conventions, they are indistinguishable from the (non-combatant) civilians, geography is not important to them, and they cannot be defeated only by attrition.

During my visits to Iraq and Afghanistan after I retired, the briefings I attended in the operations centers left my head spinning. A slew of briefers, watching over a wide-ranging list of obscure programs, described them in mind-numbing detail—date palm harvests, opening up recreational swimming pools, museums now up and running, tracking government corruption, status of the electricity grid. Were they groping for metrics, or were they trying to thoroughly and completely understand where they were? As commanders and units came and went over the course of the two wars, each of them had to add metrics, change metrics, or ditch some. A lot of good men and women were involved and tens of millions of dollars were spent on these tracking and assessing efforts. Did they learn anything?

One example: low-level commanders were liberally spreading money around trying to buy cooperation. The action was well meant: Don't go through elaborate, time-consuming processes to aid people, pay claims, or improve infrastructure. Greater impact and support would come from immediate actions there and now by the troops who could most benefit from the immediate cooperation of the populace. Later, accountability questions came up. People were asking how and why these funds had been spent. Was the expense worth it? Could anybody measure the cost versus benefit? American taxpayers had little to show in the end for the liberal distribution of those hard-earned dollars.

The 2006 congressional elections proved devastating to the Bush administration. Both houses of Congress went overwhelmingly Democratic. It was obvious to Americans that the wars in Iraq and Afghanistan were turning into unending quagmires. This was all "predictable and predicted," Virginia senator Jim Webb, a highly decorated Marine Vietnam vet and critic of the wars, remarked.

Secretary of Defense Rumsfeld was sent packing. And in January 2007, President Bush announced in a speech that there would be a "New Way Forward" in our approach to the conduct of operations in the war zones.

Enter the "surge," the addition of 20,000 more soldiers and marines to the Iraq battlefield. It had finally dawned on our leaders in Washington, after years of fighting, that we needed more troops. Brilliant. But just adding troops wouldn't be enough. We needed a new approach, a new "doctrine." And we needed David Petraeus and his counterinsurgency (COIN) doctrine, whose aim was not just defeating the enemy but rebuilding society. Noble task. Since no stated, viable end state had come from the political leadership, nobody had to worry about when or whether we would reach our goals. It was a direction without a destination. This was a godsend.

But again, how do you know if you're winning? The doctrinal manual that was produced, Counterinsurgency (FM 3-24), became the rage in doctrine centers and think tanks. It laid out in detail so-called progress indicators—fourteen of them to be tracked and measured:

- Acts of violence
- Dislocated civilians
- Human movement and religious attendance
- Presence and activity of small and medium sized businesses
- Level of agricultural activity
- Presence or absence of associations
- Participation in elections
- Government services available
- Freedom of movement of people, goods, and communications
- Tax revenue
- Industry exports
- Employment/unemployment rates
- Availability of electricity
- Specific attacks on infrastructure

The manual described in exhaustive detail measures of effectiveness (MOEs) and measures of performance (MOPs). The definitions were very specific. A MOE assesses changes in system behavior, capability, or operational environment; it is tied to measuring the attainment of an end state, achievement of an objective, or creation of an effect. A MOP assesses friendly actions; it is tied to measuring task accomplishment.

All this sounds very prescriptive, but the manual was quick to add a disclaimer: "Numerical and statistical indicators have limits when measuring social environments," and adds, "the Vietnam body count metric as an example of how not to measure progress."

A lot of hard and creative work went into the COIN doctrine. But it was written for Americans and not for the host nation government and forces that, in the end, must understand it, take it on, execute it, and sustain it.

Its severest critics were on the battlefield. Commanders complained that they had too few troops to execute this new approach, that there weren't enough skilled people from other agencies to conduct the non-military tasks required, that they were expected to execute actions that couldn't be sustained, and that restrictive rules of engagement designed to prevent civilian casualties exposed troops to unacceptable vulnerability.

In my assessment trips to Iraq and Afghanistan, I saw excellent examples of progress on the ground, but these seemed totally dependent on the quality of the local US or allied commander. When he left, could it be sustained by his successor or the host nation commander who would inherit it? I wasn't confident that they could. Here and there, a police chief, governor, mayor, or military unit commander showed promise, but these were few and far between.

The political leadership soon realized that COIN wasn't the quick and cheap answer to their prayers.

Years earlier, during my first tour of duty with the Vietnamese Marines, we entered a small village in the Mekong Delta where the houses were very odd. I had not seen anything like them. When I asked the village chief about them, this is what he told me. "American aid workers came here several years ago to help us improve our economy. When they asked about how we made our living, we explained that our primary source of income was raising pigs for sale. So they established a program to help us produce more and better pigs. They built very nice pig sties. They were better than our homes, so we moved into them."

If we don't understand who we are dealing with, our well-intentioned actions will likely be misguided. Obviously, I thought at the time, the aid workers didn't understand psychologist Abraham Maslow's "Hierarchy of Needs Theory," as these Mekong villagers interpreted it.

Fast-forward forty years.

My son was a company commander with the marines when they moved into Marjah in southern Afghanistan. They were the first US troops to enter that Taliban-infested area, and it was a tough fight to clear it. Afterward, he asked one of the village chiefs if they'd had any previous contact with Americans.

The village chief answered that he had thought at first that our guys were Russians, (Soviet troops had invaded Afghanistan in 1979). But then he remembered Americans from 1952, when they'd come to put in an irrigation system—canals. He brightened. "Have you come back to fix the canals?" he asked.

Our ideas and the local expectations can easily be out of sync.

We have somehow come to the belief that elections spell democracy. The Bush administration rushed to hold elections in Iraq as soon as possible after our occupation was completed as a sign of progress and proof of success. When the first Iraqi elections were held, I listened to a radio broadcast from a polling place in Basra, in southern Iraq. A woman came in, screaming with joy. "This is the greatest day of my life," she yelled. "I must vote." She dipped her finger in the purple ink (used to indicate that one had voted so that one could not vote more than once), ran up to one of the polling monitors and repeated, "This is the greatest day of my life, God is great." Then she said, "Who do I vote for?" The shocked polling monitor explained that he was not permitted to tell her who to vote for. The best he could do was read to her the list of political parties. She said OK and waited anxiously for him to go down the list. Suddenly she said, "That's it. I'm voting for that party." When the monitor asked her why that party, she said, "Because it has Islam in its name!"

We, of course chalked this up as a victory for democracy.

A scene from one of my favorite movies, *Lost Command* (1966), starring Anthony Quinn, has stuck with me over the years. It is based on *The Centurions,* by Jean Lartéguy, a novel that was avidly read by our Vietnam generation. The movie, about French paratroopers, follows Quinn's character from the Indochina War to the Algerian War. In the final scene, we see a formation where a general is pinning battle streamers on the unit colors and presenting medals to individual soldiers to honor their battlefield successes and heroism. As the citations are being read, the camera rises up, pans outside the military compound, and descends to reveal a young Algerian boy painting anti-French and anti-colonial slogans on the wall of the compound. Fade to black.

UNIVERSAL VALUES LIKE HUMAN RIGHTS, SELF-determination, equality, and the freedoms are articulated in our Constitution. Unfortunately, not all societies have reached a point in their histories that allows them to achieve these. Some cultures will take frustratingly long to get there. We can and should help; but we should never believe that we can "shake and bake" a process that will get them there overnight or on the cheap. Elections do not equal democracy.

I have seen progress, or the lack of it, in the eyes of people in Vietnam, in Somalia, in Iraq, in Afghanistan, and elsewhere. I have heard it in the cooperation or defiance in the voices of the prisoners we took. It seems to me that measures to determine whether we are winning and losing in unconventional conflicts have to be far more subjective than objective, tailored to the given culture. In order to win, we must ensure that we support honest and capable leaders. That is the best way to succeed. To tolerate corruption and incompetence only prolongs the agony.

TEN

ENDINGS AND OUTCOMES

By God, we've kicked the Vietnam syndrome once and for all.

President George H. W. Bush, February 28, 1991

SOME OF OUR WARS AND INTERVENTIONS HAVE ended with the total defeat of the enemy—Germany and Japan in World War II. Some ended with the sides just separating and agreeing to disagree—Korea. Some ended with a US pullout and temporary support for our allies in the fight—Vietnam and Iraq. And some we just walked away from—Somalia and Beirut. There is no formula for the ideal ending, no guidance from military doctrine. Even the unconditional surrenders still left the United States with conditions, obligations, and commitments; and military actions on the battlefield do not necessarily influence the post-conflict outcomes. We eventually prevailed on the Iraq battlefield after a decade-long military intervention that was poorly run at the strategic level, but Iraq's corrupt and fragile governance, ethnic divisions, and chronic violence created a situation that is hardly the end state the Bush administration foresaw. Iraq remains fragile, teetering on the verge of civil war.

The ends of wars always require talking. And talking to the enemy is always tough. Even after victory it's difficult to put aside strong feelings and passions and work together to find a lasting status that both victor and vanquished can accept. Even dealing with allies' demands can be challenging, as it was with the Russians at the end of World War II as they gobbled up nations and territory and with our European allies seeking to reestablish and expand their colonial empires. Film clips from the Japanese surrender aboard the USS *Missouri* show the somber emotions on allied leaders' faces as they proceeded through the formalities with Japanese leaders for whom they obviously felt deep distain. Talking to the North Koreans, North Vietnamese and Vietcong, and now with the Taliban and Syrian regime, has been politically and emotionally difficult, even if it was and is necessary.

General Martin Dempsey, the chairman of the Joint Chiefs of Staff since 2011, recently hosted the head of the Vietnamese military for a dinner at his home at Fort Myers, Virginia. His emotions were torn, he said later, when he saw the North Vietnamese flag (now the flag of all Vietnam) flying over his quarters at Fort Myers. He had been at West Point when the war was raging; it had influenced his early days as a cadet and young officer. They were the enemy. Yet he knew we had to put those feelings aside and move on. When John McCain returned to Vietnam decades after the horrific treatment he received as a POW for five and a half years, he recognized the need to put his emotions aside and work to build a new relationship. You can bet that was hard to do.

Wars leave lasting wounds. Sometimes the wounds fester for centuries. Societies enmeshed in hostility—especially in centuries of hostility—have a hard time bringing themselves to negotiating tables.

Our nation has been blessed with the capacity to move on, put grudges aside, and let war wounds heal. That's not always easy to do. We certainly don't forget the bitter memories, the sacrifices, or the deaths—so many hopeful futures cut short. But we have learned that embracing ancient hatreds only corrupts a people's ability to move forward and create better conditions in the future.

Despite the difficulties inherent in the process, Americans traditionally engage in dialogue with enemies far better after a conflict ends than before. We are reluctant to try resolving differences with potential enemies before conflicts explode. Proposing dialogue is often seen as weakness in a leader;

great political heat can come from it. President Obama has faced considerable heat as he has searched for a nonmilitary approach to Iran, Syria, and Ukraine. President Nixon took a great political risk, and was hit by considerable criticism, when he went to the People's Republic of China in 1972.

The Obama administration is currently involved in five critical sets of negotiations. Our diplomats are working on Iran's nuclear issues, removal of Syria's chemical weapons capabilities, peace talks with the Assad regime and the Syrian opposition, the Israeli-Palestinian peace process, and talks with Russia and our allies over Russia's invasion and annexation of Crimea and its subsequent actions to destabilize Ukraine. The stakes are high in each of these areas, and the skills of the negotiators on all sides are crucial to success.

SWORDS VERSUS WORDS

If negotiations like these have any chance to succeed, our leaders—both civilian and military—must be committed to the process and must possess superb negotiation and mediation skills. You can lose or win at the bargaining table just as you can win or lose on the battlefield. Even the weight and involvement of our most senior leadership, however, may not guarantee success. Woodrow Wilson experienced the frustration and disappointment of losing the dream for a more stable and just world articulated in his famous Fourteen Points despite his personal long-term commitment to the negotiations in Paris at the end of World War I. The handpicked team who accompanied him—more than 150 negotiators—worked through painful sessions with our allies to deliver the victory at the bargaining table that our troops had earned on the bloody battlefields of France against our enemies. To Wilson's bitter disappointment, it was eventually lost in the halls of Congress.

Many years later, in 2000, Bill Clinton had a similar experience after his personal commitment to the Middle East peace process failed to produce a peace deal at Camp David between Israeli prime minister Ehud Barak and Palestinian Authority chairman Yasser Arafat. At decision time

Arafat balked, and Clinton came out of the meetings without the treaty he'd invested so much time and personal commitment to achieve.

Toward the end of my military career, I found myself involved in a number of mediations and negotiations, beginning in Europe in 1990, to resolve ongoing or looming conflicts or to open critical dialogues.

In the aftermath of the sudden and unexpected collapse of the Soviet Union, our political and military leaders wondered how the transition would play out. Would there be a smooth changeover to democracy? Would the Soviet military move to set back the clock? Would a hostile relationship between us continue, or worsen?

Our leadership launched a two-pronged effort to connect with the Soviet Union and Eastern European political and military leaders in an attempt to build positive relationships, assist in a smooth transition, and convey the message that "There are no military winners or losers. It is the people of the Soviet Republics and Eastern Bloc nations who have won" (in the words of General Jack Galvin, the commander of the US European Command and NATO's supreme allied commander Europe).

I joined a number of NATO generals in the military and political discussions, and later I joined a team headed by Ambassador Richard Armitage aimed at engaging the former Soviet Union in parallel with this military-to-military engagement. The military conferences were held in Moscow and Eastern European capitals, where an impressive lineup of senior-level participants gave every appearance of welcoming our attempts to establish a friendly connection, and proved to be surprisingly open about internal problems like alcoholism and brutal hazing in the barracks. Issues discussed ranged from future military-to-military relationships to how militaries function in democracies. Some NATO generals came from countries with unionized militaries, sparking heated arguments among the NATO contingent over the wisdom of unions in the military—dissension that delighted the Russian officers. The good feeling generated made me wonder why we and the Soviets had not attempted before their collapse tension-reducing actions like these at lower than heads-of-state summit levels.

The Russian military provided me with an aide, a cadet from the Propaganda Corps, to escort me and take care of translating speeches, conversations, and the endless Russian toasts. He had perfected his English by watching Arnold Schwarzenegger movies and spoke with a deep Austrian accent. I must have come across as the Terminator.

After the conferences, as a gesture of good faith, the European Command put together a series of humanitarian aid missions (Operation Provide Hope) that emptied Cold War stocks of medical, food, and other useful items that we had stored throughout Western Europe to support a potential hot war. We flew them to orphanages and charitable organizations in the former republics of the Soviet Union. I coordinated these efforts with Rich Armitage's team, working with government agencies on governance, economic, social, and other nonmilitary programs. Eventually my boss, General Galvin, sent me to work directly for Ambassador Armitage, and I accompanied him on shuttle trips throughout the region and back and forth from the State Department in Washington.

The military-to-military meetings left me profoundly moved; but the non-military meetings were a true education. Armitage was a brilliant negotiator and diplomat, and I was witnessing his skills firsthand. The issues discussed opened my eyes to the importance of the elements beyond the military that go into our relationships around the world. During this process Armitage and I became close friends; he ensured that I attended every meeting and was involved in every discussion. I put the lessons he provided in negotiating to good use in the years to come.

Although these early actions laid a superb foundation to build on, there was no real follow-up to Armitage's efforts . . . a major missed opportunity. The meetings between leaders dwindled away, and expectations that were built up never were truly realized.

SOON AFTERWARD, I FOUND MYSELF IN SOMALIA AS the director of operations for Operation Restore Hope and was now thrown into another facet of engagement—mediation.

Part of our task in Somalia was to pacify warring clans, which meant somehow calming their warlord leaders. Ambassador Bob Oakley, the US head of mission in Somalia, had a plan. He arranged a mind-numbing proliferation of talks and meetings with the warlords, and formed enough coordination committees to stagger Washington bureaucrats. Though I thought my operational duties would keep me from having to attend these meetings, both Oakley and my boss, Lieutenant General Robert B. Johnston, wanted me to be directly engaged. They both wisely wanted any agreements to be totally coordinated with our military operations. I gave it my best efforts, but nothing much seemed to come from them. One day, in frustration, I asked Bob Oakley what was the purpose of all our meetings and marginally meaningful agreements. "When they're talking," he said sagely, "they're not shooting." He was right. The violence and inter-clan and faction fighting were greatly reduced.

He had brilliantly netted the warlords into all sorts of meetings and committees—on security, judicial, police, and many other matters. Not only did we distract the warlords from violent activities, it gave us an opportunity to get to know them and their lieutenants. This paid off later. We were able to directly and personally resolve issues when misunderstandings could have exploded into violence; and it gave us insights into their organization and thinking that no amount of intelligence reporting could provide. I actually received tips from "new friends" that led to the prevention of planned attacks against incoming UN forces.

Another benefit to ongoing dialogue is the encouragement and hope it creates among the populace. Mogadishu became more and more alive again as word spread that the warring factions were actually talking. Crowds began to fill markets; traffic grew in the streets. Even the old respected police force began to appear on the street after long, fearful absence, to direct traffic and settle disputes.

In 1993, following the disastrous clashes between the militias of warlord General Mohammed Farah Hassan "Aidid" and the UN led to the infamous Black Hawk Down incident where nineteen US special operations troops were killed, the White House sent Oakley and me back to Somalia.

Soon after our arrival, the two of us were whisked off by Aidid gunmen to his hideout in North Mogadishu to arrange for a cease-fire, the release of the wounded American pilot held by Aidid, and the resumption of the engagement we had established with him during our initial operation. The agreement we reached reduced tensions; the US and UN withdrawal from Somalia eventually followed. Later, when I commanded the operation to protect the final UN withdrawal, I reconnected with key warlords, to include Aidid, to minimize hostile actions toward our forces. Aidid actually warned me about which warlords would oppose our withdrawal and where they would engage our forces.

This experience taught me the necessity of character and temperament, along with knowledge and experience, in a mediator. All the warlords admired Oakley. He knew them, and his previous diplomatic experiences in the third world had given him insights into their culture and psychology. They addressed him with respect, deferred to him, and listened to him carefully. After he left, his successors' achievements paled next to his.

IN 1999, WHILE I WAS CENTCOM COMMANDER, THE Clinton administration directed me to join the president's skilled national security advisor, Tony Lake, in talks with the Ethiopians and Eritreans (nations in my area of responsibility) to try to persuade them to abandon preparations for a senseless war that was about to break out over a border dispute in a remote and insignificant piece of territory. Although in the end mediation frustratingly did not prevent the war, working with Tony Lake furthered my education in negotiation and mediation.

Lake's plan was to present a military and diplomatic united front. Each of us pointed out from our particular perspective the advantages of peaceful resolution and the disadvantages of fighting—a lesson I took with me into future mediations: the military and the diplomatic sides should be equally represented at the table in any mediation.

Years before, when Eritrea had been a part of Ethiopia, the political and military leaders we were talking to had fought side by side in a twenty-five-year war against a repressive dictatorship. I knew the leaders of both sides well. It was sad to watch them fighting each other over a few rocks in the desert.

Months later, after they'd fought a senseless and bloody stalemated war, their dispute was resolved by arbitration. Both sides admitted that they should have worked harder at the peace table. They realized that our predictions of the consequences of fighting had been accurate both diplomatically and militarily.

LATER IN 1999, PRESIDENT CLINTON ASKED ME TO lead an effort to persuade the Pakistani government to withdraw from an advanced position they had secured on the line of control along their tense border with India. Their incursion had ratcheted up military exchanges of fire; and the situation threatened to escalate into a full-blown war between nuclear powers. The plan was to offer to Pakistani prime minister Sharif a meeting with President Clinton that would provide support and political cover for a withdrawal. Though Sharif initially refused to see me, the then head of the military, General Pervez Musharraf (a close friend of mine), intervened. Sharif and I met, and he reluctantly agreed to back off, averting the crisis. After the withdrawal began, Sharif and President Clinton met in Washington.

The Pakistanis knew the potential catastrophic outcome of prolonging the confrontation, but needed the intervention of the president of the United States to give cover to a cool-down on both sides. President Clinton needed assurances that a withdrawal was taking place before he could be seen to grant his personal intervention. Many lives were saved and a potentially catastrophic war was averted by some cool-headed diplomacy.

Another valuable lesson: third-party assistance can allow sides to make accommodations that they could not otherwise accept when they are faced off against each other. That can be especially so if the third party brings the prestige and power of a world leader like the president of the United States.

IN ADDITION TO SHOWING ME HOW SKILLED AND savvy mediators and negotiators can help prevent or end conflict, these experiences left me with a new understanding of the structural issues that have to be established or resolved.

Will it be a mediation with a third party engaged in developing the solutions, or facilitation with a third party observing and monitoring as the two protagonists resolving their issues, or will it be negotiation with a third party in a position to arbitrate? Will it be done on one or more levels where executive or senior-level mediators work at one level (policy) and working group sets at another level (detailed procedures to be implemented)? Where will the discussions be held so that security, neutrality, or international visibility considerations can be met? Who will be involved? What kind of agreement is possible? Will the process come in phases—necessary if the issues are too complex or require incremental resolution to build toward a final status. How will implementation be monitored and issues adjudicated? Even the shape of the table can become a point of contention, as it was during the Paris peace talks with the North Vietnamese and at the post–World War I conferences at Versailles in 1919.

These are only a few of the questions a mediator must ask and answer before he or she can get to work. Mediation is an art form; real pros understand the art.

AFTER I RETIRED, AN OPPORTUNITY CAME TO HEAD up the most significant and challenging mediation effort of our time.

In 2001, Secretary of State Colin Powell asked me to be the US envoy to the Middle East peace process working to settle the Israeli-Palestinian conflict. Though the complexity of the issues, the profound regional and international implications, and the failure of numerous well-known and highly skilled diplomats before me to get that elusive peace made it a challenging, daunting, and frustrating mission, I agreed to take it on. There weren't many people who were optimistic about the chances of success, but I had to try.

As I plunged into the many conflicting issues and the possibilities for resolution, I found myself engaged in another deep learning experience. I had to bring myself up to speed on complex final status issues like borders, refugees' right of return, the status of Jerusalem, control of water, and many others. Behind the positions taken by each side were millennia of history and deep religious roots. I knew that success would lie in the details. There had been many agreements in principle, but no workable plans to establish implementation on the ground.

Wisely, Secretary Powell instructed me to allow no more agreements in principle. We aimed to get that elusive workable implementation.

I spent long months meeting with Prime Minister Sharon and Chairman Arafat and their negotiations teams. We weathered vicious terrorist attacks by Hamas and other elements determined to derail the talks. And I saw many honorable people on both sides desperately working for peace. Although in the end we couldn't achieve what we set out to do, I came away with many thoughts about how we should move forward on this complex process.

As the split between the Israelis and Palestinians widened and grew more heated, I advised changes to the mediation structure and process, but that fell on deaf ears as frustration and anger in the wake of relentless terrorist attacks brought an end to the mediation efforts.

IN 2001, BACK HOME FROM THE ISRAELI-PALESTINIAN experience, I was asked by the State Department to assist the Henri Dunant Centre (HDC) in Geneva in a peace mediation process between the government of Indonesia and the Free Aceh Movement. (Aceh is a province of Indonesia on the extreme northwestern tip of Sumatra.) This was my first experience working with truly seasoned and professional peace mediators who did it for a living (diplomats may take on mediation, but it's usually only an adjunct to their other primary duties). The mediators at HDC were working on several efforts, including Aceh. Each process was handled differently based on the situation, parties involved, or nature of differences. Expert advice in historical disputes might be brought in, professional negotiators might be added to reinforce a side that was unsure of how to conduct such a process, and individuals were added who might build confidence on one side or another. The knowledge, experience, skill, and dedication of the HDC mediators hooked me on the potential of a robust mediation structure to resolve conflicts once it has been given the resources, backing, and commitment of the international community. I assisted with other efforts they had ongoing and eventually joined their board of directors. This experience had me working with rebel groups in their environment and governments in exile in their asylum countries. I zipped back and forth from the areas in conflict to mediation sessions in places like Geneva, Stockholm, and Paris.

In 2003 the United States Institute of Peace (USIP), a federally funded but independent organization, asked me to work with them to mediate a long-standing dispute between the government of the Philippines and the Moro Islamic Liberation Front (MILF). Some Moros[1] on the island of Mindanao had signed a peace agreement with the government, but the MILF had not. Philippine president Arroyo asked President Bush for mediation assistance, and he asked USIP to aid the ongoing process. I went to Mindanao and met with the MILF. We worked with both sides to help define and resolve the issues. Though we did not resolve all the differences dividing the parties, progress was made, and the process has continued with other participants involved directly in the mediation efforts.

Conflict resolution and peace mediation institutions have received growing support in recent years from governments in Norway, Sweden, Switzerland, and our own country; and universities all over the world are offering courses and programs in negotiation and mediation. The University of San Diego's Joan B. Kroc School of Peace Studies is an excellent example of commitment to research and study in this critical discipline. These institutions have truly "professionalized" negotiation arts—sharing insights, techniques, and processes.

I continued to work with universities and peace mediation organizations in Norway, the United Kingdom, and the United States, sharing experiences, aiding in research on issues involved in conflict resolution, and serving on boards that oversee their work and organizations.

Political leaders are often reluctant to work on diplomatic solutions to problems. It can be politically difficult to be seen talking to the enemy. It takes political courage, and there are potential traps and snares; they must be wary of placing trust where it isn't warranted. But even successful wars require some form of resolution at the end. Finding the best people for that job is not easy.

The skills necessary for successful mediation or negotiation are rare in elected officials, and not necessarily inherent in good diplomats. It takes an unusual personality to be effective in this business. Patience, an even temperament, creativity, cultural knowledge and sensitivity, and determination are among the desired traits in a mediator. The tradecraft has also become increasingly sophisticated and technical. I am convinced that we need to develop a corps of skilled mediation and negotiation professionals within our Foreign Service, and even in our military. Ending conflicts has become too complex to leave to ad hoc processes.

While giving this element of "soft" power much greater emphasis, we must continue to back it up with the "hard" power of credible military strength. In this still new century, we must learn how to blend the powers we so successfully developed in the twentieth century—military, economic, and governance—with the ones we need to work on: diplomacy, conflict resolution, and building international partnerships.

HOW WARS END, OR DON'T END

We tend to think of wars as having a beginning and an end; but sometimes the way one war ends sets the conditions for the next one, or for continued strife for decades to come. The lines drawn on a map during World War I in the Sykes-Picot Agreement by hungry colonial powers still shape conflicts in the Middle East. The aftermath of the help we gave the Afghans during the Soviet occupation of Afghanistan set the conditions that drew us into the conflict currently raging there. The split of Korea after World War II and the split of Vietnam after the French Indochina War resulted in the inevitable conflicts that followed.

The consequences of wars and military interventions are far-reaching, unpredictable, and long-term. Today's wars don't end with the cessation of open hostilities, the signing of treaties, and the troops arriving home to a tickertape parade. After we left Vietnam, Vietnam stayed with us for decades. In some ways it's still with us.

Euphoria followed Operation Restore Hope, our first incursion into Somalia. The mission had lasted seven trying months, far longer and harder than the outgoing Bush administration anticipated when they committed US forces in December 1992. When we left Somalia, we handed off the mission to the UN with an uneasy feeling. Yet as we left, the situation seemed to be under control, and the new Clinton administration was beaming.

As the last elements of our task force were getting ready to fly out of Mogadishu, the mission commander, Lieutenant General Bob Johnston, received a call to stop in Washington before proceeding to our unit's home base in California. The president had invited us to visit him at the White House to thank us, get a debrief, and appear for a major media event on the White House lawn. It was a grand occasion. General Johnston and I met with President Clinton, Vice President Gore, and the Joint Chiefs of Staff in the Oval Office. The president was full of questions and effusive with praise. He liked the idea of using US power for humanitarian purposes, as we had used it in Somalia. At one point, he turned to the chairman of the Joint Chiefs, General Colin Powell, "How many of these kinds of missions can we do at one time?" he asked.

General Powell's eyes went wide, and his carefully worded response was vague and packed with caveats. General Johnston and I smiled at each other. We knew how much angst the president's question had ignited. Powell and the other chiefs feared wholesale commitments to humanitarian or peacekeeping missions like Restore Hope all over the third world. Nobody could fault Clinton's motives, but making these missions work was another thing.

That moment in the Oval Office sent my thoughts back to Mogadishu just hours before as we were driving to the airport in our Humvees. General Johnston was quiet during the drive; he had lots on his mind. We had just turned the mission over to a UN force that didn't seem to understand what they were in for. Suddenly he spied two young boys on a street corner. "Stop!" he shouted to our driver, and then turned to us. "Give me your pens, pencils, and tablets." We pulled what we had out of our pockets and map cases and gave it to him. He got out of the Humvee and handed it over to the thankful, smiling kids. Afterward, he remained standing there looking around, deep in thought.

"What are you thinking about, sir?" I asked him.

He looked at me. "I give it thirty days and it will all come apart," he said quietly.

He didn't have much confidence in the UN mission replacing us. None of us did.

Thirty-one days later, new attacks launched the battle with the warlords that led to the Black Hawk Down disaster and our eventual withdrawal of all US troops from the UN operation. Within months, the euphoric anticipation of humanitarian missions all over the third world turned to a rush to get out of Somalia, the resignation of the secretary of defense, and an eventual refusal to intervene to stop the Rwandan genocide. The Somalia Syndrome.

Many have attributed the Obama administration's wary approach to the use of force in Syria to an Iraq Syndrome. Vietnam, Somalia, Iraq. They have become more than wars, they have become "syndromes"—a lasting legacy to remind us of the catastrophes well-meaning interventions can lead to.

HOLD THE HURRAHS AND THE TICKERTAPE

When Americans commit our military to a mission, we have in mind an image like the one that inspired us back in World War I when the American Expeditionary Force (AEF) sailed off to Europe. We still imagine that plucky doughboys, led by charismatic generals like Black Jack Pershing, will sail "over there," vanquish the bad guys, come home to tickertape parades down Fifth Avenue and Pennsylvania Avenue, and that will be the end of it. Clean, complete, no loose ends.

We want wars to be "good wars," where bright-faced GIs courageously save oppressed peoples from monstrously evil regimes.

When I testified before Senator Dick Lugar's Foreign Relations Committee shortly before the Iraq invasion, Lugar knew that I had reservations about the invasion and our plans to execute it. During the hearing, a senator on the committee asked me why I was so concerned. "Nothing could be worse than Saddam," he said. "Going in and removing Saddam's regime is all good."

"We no longer go in, fix a problem, and come home," I replied. "Sometimes the result is worse than the evil we try to cure. We helped the Afghans expel the Soviets from Afghanistan; and the Taliban eventually took over." Today we remain with long-term troop commitments in Europe, Japan, South Korea, and the Middle East, decades after the wars that brought us there ended. When my father came home after fighting in World War I, he came back to a country that was free of a long-term military presence in Europe.

During the Cold War, we gradually solidified our role as global guarantor of security for the free world. As we entered World War II, nobody imagined we would be taking on that role. But the threats and instability that followed, plus our unmatched military and economic power, made it inevitable. The Goldwater-Nichols Act of 1986 established the unified commands, making a direct line of command from the president to the secretary of defense to the combatant commanders. Six of the nine combatant commands are regional. We divided the world up into regions and put a command over each region: European, Pacific, Africa, Southern, Central, and Northern commands all have areas of responsibility assigned in the Unified Command Plan (UCP). No other nation has this global structure. The primary motivation was to effectively integrate our forces under a streamlined command and control system and to give our efforts a regional focus, but not everybody in the world saw this new structure as benign. In her book *The Mission*, *Washington Post* reporter Dana Priest compared it to the system the Romans used to govern their empire.[2] She called regional commanders like me "proconsuls," picking up the label my political advisor, a seasoned foreign service officer and former ambassador, had given us. To many people out there, dividing up the world into regional commands looked like a global empire in the making. But others welcomed it. It showed that the United States was committed to regional allies and to protecting weaker states faced with hegemonic regional powers who had eyes on their turf.

We fall into "temporary" commitments; but gradually over time the commitments somehow stick until they become "permanent," and we rarely ask why we continue to maintain them. We end up with a web of installations all over the world that makes our global presence appear little different from a global empire. A former NATO commander tried to justify bases in Europe established during the post–World War II occupation and maintained during the Cold War to meet potential Soviet aggression. "They are now great forward operating bases that we can use to launch operations to anywhere else in the world," he explained. From bases used for post–World War II occupation to bases to fend off the Soviets during the Cold War to forward operating bases "just in case": the gift that keeps on giving.

We are certainly not an empire of conquest, but we have become an empire of influence and weight. We're not the elephant in the room—we're the elephant everywhere in the world. When the Soviet Union collapsed, many of its former republics and many Eastern Bloc countries, once under its control, came knocking at our door to become our allies. NATO quickly grew from sixteen nations to twenty-eight. In the early 1970s, the British could no longer police the Persian Gulf. The United States took over. The Obama administration launched its new strategy of "pivoting to the Pacific" by positioning troops in Darwin in northern Australia. The sun never sets on a US combatant command!

Although this is surely not our intention, many people in the various regions understand that our military presence is the physical symbol of the benevolent American empire, and we are there to police the neighborhood. We have built an expectation of security and stability that will be based on our commitment and done on our dime.

When we opt out of that tacitly understood policing duty, confusion and resentment follow.

"This is General Zinni. He is our commander." On more than a few occasions during my time as commander of CENTCOM, top political and military officials from the region introduced me that way. It always caught my attention. They were of course perfectly aware that I didn't command their national forces; yet they were conveying an unwritten sense that the security of the region was in US hands. We came. We stayed. We now owned the responsibility.

Wars and interventions change borders, fracture and dislocate societies, break or form alliances, establish long-term commitments, and affect the will of our own people and leaders to use the military. The costs of military intervention endure well beyond the end of military action. Before we commit to military action, past experiences have to guide our understanding of the outcomes. We have to learn to recognize the signs of long-term negative consequences so we can mitigate or avoid the worst of them. . . . And we have to be able to find a way someday to "come home."

In 2012, I was asked to participate in a small group discussing future US national security strategy, during which I found myself in a friendly back-and-forth with a well-known and respected former national security advisor. I suggested that we review and question all of our accumulated commitments. "Erase the board," I said. By that I meant we needed to periodically validate our commitments. Times and circumstances change. Rationales for some of the commitments may no longer hold, or there may be other ways to support them. He went absolutely ballistic. He had participated in the decisions that had produced many of these commitments. They were in some ways *his*. He didn't want to give them up.

"Erase the board?" he shouted back at me, "We have commitments and obligations. You can't just leave!"

"Why not?" I asked. "When do these commitments and obligations run out? If they are still credible and warranted, then we should revalidate and keep them, but we shouldn't assume the circumstances and justifications that were valid decades ago still obtain." I was deliberately being provocative, but I felt we needed to challenge ourselves from time to time to keep our strategic thinking fresh. I could see he was getting angry and frustrated, so I didn't push him further. But I realized then that we had accumulated these commitments like old family treasures we get tired of, store in the attic, and forget. No one wants to throw them out; they were Grandma's favorites, but no one has a good reason to keep them around any longer.

It may be that our commitments are still valid. It may be that they are not. It may also be that they need to be restructured or can be met by a different, and maybe nonmilitary, application of our power.

In the past, nations like South Korea and Kuwait have ensured that America will join them in a conflict by arranging, with the US, for American troops to be stationed in their countries as a "trip-wire." Any attack on them attacks American forces. We manned the frontlines in Europe throughout the Cold War face-off with the Soviets, and the 7th Fleet stood between China and Taiwan. Alliances, treaties, and guarantees can convey the same commitment. In this era of long-range strike capabilities, our commitments can be assured without large numbers of boots on the ground. Pre-positioned equipment can provide the same level of commitment. Frequent exercises that demonstrate our ability to rapidly close in on a threatened region can also prove our commitment. Given the level of interdependence in today's world, economic, diplomatic, and informational levers can be better used to threaten, assure, or incentivize.

Some of these possibilities were in play while I was at CENTCOM in the late 1990s. The Air Force offered to pre-position high-tech ordnance in our theater. This would give us the ability to be more accurate and effective, and we would require fewer aircraft based in the region to meet a surprise attack. I approved the move. I believed in a minimal, but sufficient, military presence.

In 1998, Secretary of Defense Bill Cohen formally announced a commitment to defend every inch of Kuwait (we had previously thought we'd have to defend and delay and give ground before we could build up forces to counterattack a surprise Iraqi invasion). The Kuwaiti military had a new sense of energy and moved to establish multiple armor and mechanized brigades that would be highly trained and integrated with our forces. And in 1999 we released to them higher technology systems for their attack helicopters and other military assets. This built even greater confidence and did not require us to put more forces on the ground.

When the new heir to power in North Korea, Kim Jong-un, began to rattle his saber and threaten South Korea and Japan, Secretary of State John Kerry embarked on a major diplomatic effort to assure South Korea and Japan of our commitment. Kerry went to China, whose support is essential to North Korea, and persuaded them to lean on the North Koreans. The fiery North Korean rhetoric was reduced and fears were calmed.

We must exercise our full range of powers to achieve our goals, guard against an overmilitarized foreign policy, and ensure that expectations are in line with our current ability, needs, and willingness to act, and we must constantly reassess each of these. We should also realize that whatever we do today to meet an immediate need can have serious consequences in the future and may set the stage for far more costly problems than those we're attempting to solve in the current environment. Today's necessities can't be tomorrow's unquestioned assumptions.

ELEVEN

AMERICA AND
THE WORLD

If we have to use force, it is because we are America. We are the indispensable
nation. We stand tall. We see further into the future.

Madeleine Albright, secretary of state (1997–2001)

MADELEINE ALBRIGHT'S STATEMENT IGNITED CON-
troversy here and overseas. Overseas it was often seen as arrogant. Domestically it was often seen as casting us into that dreaded role of the world's
policeman.

Are we arrogant? Are we the world's policeman? What in fact are we?

We cannot begin to answer questions on strategy, commitments, and
military structure until we are clear about America's role in today's world
and how indispensable we can or cannot be . . . or should be.

According to recent polls and surveys, a majority of Americans favor a
return to isolationism. They want our country to disengage from the rest
of the world's messy problems. Although this is certainly understandable,
given our recent experiences with two long wars, a host of other seemingly
unsolvable overseas crises, an economy in trouble, and the pressing need
to get our own house in order, isolationism in today's world is unrealistic.
Politicians who sell pre–World War II isolationism as a panacea that will
magically transport us to a happier, simpler, less anxious life are either naive or blind to the world we are living in.

In the decades since the Cold War ended, a whole new set of forces has been shaping the world and America's place in it. Our planet has shrunk—or flattened, as columnist and author Thomas Friedman puts it. Everyone on the planet has become inextricably intertwined and interdependent. Our economic, environmental, and informational interests—and our security interests—are global. Our rapidly globalizing economic system defies separation from overseas markets, suppliers, investors, and partners. Greece's economy takes a knockout hit and the US stock market falters. The demand for energy resources has grown exponentially, and the sources and free flow of those resources have become a global security issue.

Power is no longer condensed into two centers—the United States and Soviet Union. It has been diffusing, spreading, and diluting. Our chief threats pop up all over the globe. Some of these threats have no armies, borders, or capitals. Terrorists, drug cartels, human traffickers, international criminal gangs—all do business on an international scale and on a borderless basis. The indefinable threat of "instability" is now a major concern. Well over one billion people in the Islamic world are transitioning, awakening, or rebelling in what has been called the Arab Spring. This population spreads from North Africa to the Philippines and from the southern provinces of Russia to central Africa. But significant numbers of that population and from other struggling societies are abandoning their homelands and migrating to other countries. The developed nations become magnets for diasporas and migrations from the third world, fleeing failing or incapable states and seeking opportunity . . . or mere survival. The turmoil of the transition is having global effects.

Hegemonic designs by regional threats like North Korea and Iran (and now even Russia) continue to be disruptive and challenging. There has been a troubling increase in the proliferation, or potential proliferation, of weapons of mass destruction—especially nuclear WMD. This is a turnaround from the more hopeful period immediately after the end of the Cold War when WMD-reduction agreements were made and nations such as Kazakhstan and Libya gave up their nuclear and chemical weapons.

Environmental degradation, climate change, increased urbanization, greater demand for food and water, population growth, and changing demographic structures generate problems with global implications. Our well-being and security are directly or indirectly affected by the instability this fast-changing global environment generates.

Our "house" can no longer be defined by our geographic borders. Too many seemingly local or remote issues or problems have global impact. They affect us. And they can hurt us—bad. You can choose to play defense and wait for problems to wash up on your shores, or you can deal with them at their origins. That course promises more international cooperation, early resolution, and less costly solutions.

We cannot avoid a global commitment. We can't avoid a global leadership role. Our National Security Strategy must begin with these premises.

STRATEGY

We face a serious dilemma, however: we cannot do it all. So we must choose wisely and set priorities.

Two troubling facts are clear. We tend to lead with one element of our power, our military, yet we have failed to develop necessary capacity within the other elements of power. Our military has become "repurposed" as peacekeeper, humanitarian responder, nation-builder, insurgency fighter, and disaster reliever. We throw this, our power punch, at every threatening situation that confronts us; and it is then too often stuck with non-military functions that other means could handle more effectively and efficiently. We even posture with our military when we know there is no military option, as in the Ukraine crisis. Our media—with scarcely a thought of alternatives—rush to military options at the first whiff of crisis and harp on those options after it is clear we are either a long way from a decision to use the military, or else the military option is not feasible.

The other agencies of government needed to resolve the crises are anemic by comparison with our military capabilities. Our foreign aid budget is pitiful, our State Department, USAID, and the other critically needed government agencies are underfunded, undermanned, and poorly structured for the tasks we need them to accomplish.

We mouth words about the importance of applying "whole of government" approaches and "smart power" and the need for a more robust set of capabilities in our other agencies, but we do nothing in a practical way to fix the imbalance.

Neither the military nor the other agencies can solve this problem themselves. It has to be solved in Washington by Congress and the president through legislation and executive leadership. True champions in our political leadership have to rise up and effect real change. We need legislation like the 1986 Goldwater-Nichols Act or the 1947 National Security Act to restructure and fund the development of the "soft" components of smart power. In the long run this will create a less costly and more effective way to handle the chronic crises that are sure to plague us.

OUR NATIONAL AND INTERNATIONAL SECURITY STRUCtures are still based on late 1940s and 50s designs and global situation. When we deal with the rest of the world, we still think and act as though it is a world of clearly divided and defined regions. That is old-think. The actual world is increasingly a world of borderless threats and a borderless network of connections.

Few nations can be defined today merely by their geographic borders. The global network of linking domains has redefined them—the critical tentacles that know no borders and without which nations cannot survive and thrive. Space, cyberspace, critical land and sea regions, sea lanes, and air routes tie the world together. Protection of, and access to, these domains are critical to our own and worldwide security. We must negotiate new protocols, agreements, treaties, and other arrangements in order to avoid conflicts and dangerous competition. Though for practical reasons we may have to work from time to time on a regional basis to get things done, our strategic goals must be mutual and global.

Since we realize we cannot go it alone, the next objective we should include in any security strategy is the building or strengthening of global and regional partnerships. The ones we have need updating and revamping. The United Nations and NATO clearly need reconstruction; the support and development of regional organizations in Africa and the Middle East are necessary to help stabilize these regions and respond to local crises. Meanwhile, old, outdated treaties and obligations must be updated, restructured, or scrapped if they are no longer relevant. Erase the board.

Global partnering isn't only about military cooperation and crisis response. Developed nations of the world must work together (and with NGOs) in four key areas for the benefit of the entire planet: economics, energy, environment, and education. Cooperation and investment in these areas as a path to stabilizing the global community lead directly to greater security and prosperity for all. Creating agreements and international partnerships in these areas should be goals in any future strategy.

Our government departments, agencies, and military commands produce hundreds of documents with the word "strategy" in their title. We need a clearinghouse for all these documents that ensures consistency, accuracy, and logic. The National Security Council (NSC) seems to be the appropriate agency for this task and should be structured and manned to accomplish it.

To sum up: our strategy should begin with an understanding of the world we live in, the role we play in this world, the balancing of our tools for exercising our influence and power, the setting of global goals, the building of more viable partnerships, and the insuring of consistency in our articulated strategy. But the most brilliantly crafted strategy is useless if it doesn't guide our decision making and resource allocation.

POLITICS

Advisory bodies like the NSC that aim to provide experience, judgment, unbiased views, and recommendations to our political leadership only rarely live up to those expectations. Their membership too often comes out of presidents' and other political leaders' preferences and styles. We need a better way to structure how we fill key appointed positions in our government. Political patronage must give way to experience and merit. Decisions on policy, funding, and other resource commitments need to be grounded in strategic importance rather than local political pork.

Our founding fathers, in their wisdom, wrote into the Constitution requirements of confirmation by the Senate of certain senior appointees. I'm sure they saw this as a check to ensure that competence and merit were duly considered; but the confirmation process has now evolved into either a rubber stamp or a political football. Some important appointments are not even subject to confirmation (though all military appointments are).

We must consider more than political back-scratching, political like-mindedness, or political revenge when we send the nomination of an ambassador, assistant secretary, or agency director to the Senate for approval. Hurricane Katrina should have taught us that patronage is costly when a crisis hits and you need experienced experts to manage it. After Katrina we got "heck of a job, Brownie" and a majority of FEMA leadership without real experience in disaster relief. The recent embarrassing testimonies of Obama administration ambassadorial nominees—clueless about their duties, responsibilities, and issues of concern in nations they were being assigned to—ought to anger all Americans. (Al Kamen of the *Washington Post* called these performances "cringe-inducing.") A political donation should not be a ticket to a posting as an ambassador representing our great country.

MILITARY

Though in the long-running debate since the end of Cold War over the kind of military we need, costs, threats, capabilities, and risks have all come into play, there are two larger considerations that should drive that decision.

First, we clearly need a "prudent force." By that I mean a collection of military capabilities that we must have today and for the foreseeable future to deter or deal with an existential threat from a major military competitor. A prudent force's core capabilities should include a nuclear deterrent, air and missile defense, robust intelligence organizations and collection, a heavy ground force component split between active and reserve forces, a streamlined command and control system, and air and sea dominance capabilities.

Second, we need a rapid crisis response force. This requires highly mobile and deployable air, ground, and sea strike forces (some of which would be forward-deployed in order to shorten response times), robust special operations forces, and high-tech intelligence-gathering and strike capabilities, such as unmanned aerial vehicles, sea- and air-launched missiles, and cyber capabilities.

The link in our military functions of providing, integrating, and employing our forces is weakest at the integration component. The successes in integrating strategic systems, transportation, and special operations need to be expanded to include logistics, command and control, intelligence, and civil-military integration. All the disparate capabilities from the military services and other agencies of government have to be effectively and efficiently integrated well before we show up at the scene of the action. We have learned this lesson time and time again. It was a principal driver of Goldwater-Nichols. We no longer have the time or resources to waste working out integration on the ground. The complexities and threats we may face won't allow it.

We need to think through where we position forward-based forces. Dumping forces in places like Western Europe, Australia, Okinawa, or Guam adds to quality of life problems for our troops, limits quality training opportunities, stresses relations with locals, and often leaves these forces strategically stranded away from the sea and air assets needed to get them to the scene of the action. What makes more sense today would be overseas investment in sea and land pre-positioning of equipment, rapid response exercises, proximity of forces to strategic lift assets, and coalition agreements. Also, investment in the facilities at the home bases of highly trained forces that can respond in this manner is a more logical approach than investing in overseas bases where local politics and infrastructure can limit training.

These recommendations would help fix military structure. But a more important element in reforming our military requires consideration of leadership lessons by those whose job is to decide or advise on the commitment of our military.

LEADERSHIP LESSONS

We can learn a great deal from our past military commitments, yet more often than not we reflect on them only in the immediate aftermath of the ones that are most troublesome; and their lessons are quickly forgotten or lost as the next group of elected political leaders comes marching into their Washington offices. The Weinberger and Powell doctrines were disregarded soon after publication. Here are some thoughts that those who would lead us into conflict should consider first:

- Do you know what you are doing? We see less and less
  military experience in our executive and legislative branches
  of government. Political leaders would be wise to self-educate
  and form advisory bodies that are free of politics and provide a
  broad range of advice on military matters. An open mind and an
  objective, open debate lead to the best decisions.
- Is the case for war or commitment of our military clear? The
  incident, threat, or crisis that will be the foundation for acting has
  to be real and credible. The reasons for choosing or not choosing
  nonmilitary options should be considered and articulated as well
  as the reason for opting for military force.
- Is the analysis leading to the decision to use force solid, thorough,
  and unbiased? There must be a "devil's advocate" approach to
  reaching conclusions. The analysis has to be questioned and
  challenged. The basis for conclusions should be discussed and
  validated in detail. Beware the temptation to "cherry-pick"
  intelligence or conclusions to support a preconceived notion,

position, or recommendation. All assumptions should be questioned and viewed as risks.

- Is the decision clear? The decision needs to be articulated in terms of specific political objectives. Vague or nonexistent objectives or end states lead to misunderstanding, mission creep, and directionless and costly actions. Resolution can only be determined if the objective is clearly understood by all involved and is clearly achievable.

- Is the strategy thought out, clearly articulated, and constantly monitored and updated? We tend to do a lousy job developing strategies and using them as a framework for directing and overseeing a mission. The strategy for a given commitment must be rooted in our grand strategy and the impact on that grand strategy continually assessed. It must be a whole-of-government strategy and not just a military strategy. Buy-in and commitment must come from all agencies of government involved and from any allies that join us.

- Is the narrative convincing? The American people want a clear, understandable reason for military action. Constant clarity of purpose is necessary from the bully pulpit.

- Is there confidence that the operational design to conduct the mission is in harmony with the strategy and objectives? Everyone involved—political and military leaders—must share responsibility at every stage. Total responsibility must not be handed off to the military.

- Do the forces chosen provide the best chance of success? Our objectives should be to end a commitment swiftly, decisively, and at minimum cost in treasure and casualties. Politics should be kept out of these decisions.

- How will progress be measured? Everyone wants to put a positive spin on the conduct of mission. An objectively measured criterion of success coupled with experienced and wise judgments should be established and understood by all. Reality and context must underpin any metrics methodology. An independent body composed of experienced experts with no political or personal connection to the mission should be used to evaluate the course of a commitment.

- How will the mission end? If we are not careful, the way conflicts are concluded can snatch defeat from victory. The end of one conflict can set the stage for another, as was the case in World War I and the first involvement of the US in Afghanistan during the Soviet occupation of that country. More critical attention to and evaluation of end states needs to be made.

- In the end, who is held accountable? When things go wrong, those responsible tend to get off easy with a quiet resignation or retirement. Or, perhaps they are ushered out the door with a Presidential Medal of Freedom.

EPILOGUE

SEVERAL YEARS AGO WHEN I TRAVELED AROUND Iraq and later Afghanistan for our commanders in those countries, I met solid senior military leaders committed to their missions, young troops and junior leaders giving their utmost on the ground, and diplomats, aid workers, and other nonmilitary personnel working long hours trying to rebuild traumatized societies. All of these highly dedicated people had inherited missions that had reached their end stages after taking long and twisted paths. What rationales had driven the missions they had inherited? No one I met in Iraq and Afghanistan could answer that question. They had taken over responsibility for actions that had been set in motion by a revolving-door series of predecessors who had left them the ashes of flawed strategies, operational programs, and tactics that were difficult or impossible to change or salvage. Years earlier I had witnessed the end stages of Vietnam and Somalia. Déjà vu.

How the hell did we get here?

Wars have raged in Vietnam, Afghanistan, Iraq . . . and maybe someday they will rage in Syria or Iran.

Back in the United States, political leaders in Washington fold their tents, quietly retire, and write revisionist memoirs, often for generous advances. New political leaders come into office, swear not to repeat past mistakes, and appoint into key positions their own inexperienced and unwilling-to-learn friends and cronies. The military services produce volumes of lessons learned, change tactics, rebuild their structures, add battle streamers to their colors, and prepare for the next looming threat and budget battle. The American people, who start out supporting our missions in foreign lands, lose all hope of successful outcomes there. The media move on to other stories. And our veterans, too many of them broken, are left to remember and honor their too often forgotten brothers and sisters.

In Iraq and Afghanistan, meanwhile, Iraqis and Afghans, like the Vietnamese and Somalis, are left to pick up the pieces and brace themselves for the next round of confused violence.

Later, a new crisis appears on the horizon and we begin the cycle all over again, having failed to learn the hard lessons that time and again have stared us in the face.

The good news is that a new generation of military leaders has experienced a decade-plus of exhausting wars and military commitments. I have observed them on the battlefield fighting strange enemies and rebuilding societies; in the classrooms challenging leaders' decisions and thinking about the future; in their units tackling tough leadership issues such as gender and sexual orientation integration, sexual assaults, suicides, and post-traumatic stress disorder. They are fast learners and dedicated to making the changes necessary to maintain the best military on the planet.

In the post–Vietnam period, despite the obstacles we faced, we rebuilt and transformed our military into a powerful and highly capable all-volunteer force. Today's generation of soldiers, sailors, flyers, and Marines is ready, willing, and able to take on the challenges of developing an intelligently structured twenty-first-century military and to intelligently and strategically analyze and implement our requirements in a confusing and complex world. Can their generational counterparts in our political leadership join with them in bringing about the change and transformation that is needed across our government? My advice to them is "think big." The greatest generation's most significant contribution may not have been how magnificently they fought World War II, but how magnificently they handled the postwar environment. This generation can do the same.

The talent and motivation are there. Let's hope a will to act follows.

NOTES

PREFACE

1. Robert M. Gates, *Duty: Memoirs of a Secretary at War* (New York: Knopf, 2014).

ONE: HOW THE HELL DID WE GET HERE?

1. Karl W. Eikenberry, "The Limits of Counterinsurgency Doctrine in Afghanistan," *Foreign Affairs,* September/October 2013.
2. Robert S. McNamara, *In Retrospect: The Tragedy and Lessons of Vietnam* (New York: Random House, 1995), Preface.

TWO: A DATE WHICH WILL LIVE IN INFAMY

1. Henry Kissinger, *Diplomacy* (New York: Simon & Schuster, 1994), p. 18.

THREE: KNOWNS AND UNKNOWNS

1. Defined as the product resulting from the collection, processing, integration, analysis, evaluation, and interpretation of available information concerning foreign countries or areas.
2. Alissa J. Rubin, "Retiring Envoy to Afghanistan Exhorts U.S. to Heed Its Past," *New York Times,* July 28, 2012, http://www.nytimes.com/2012/07/29/world/asia/ambassador-crocker-sees-fraught-foreign-landscape-ahead.html?pagewanted=all&_r=0.
3. Bob Woodward, *Bush at War* (New York: Simon & Schuster, 2003).
4. Robert M. Gates, *Duty: Memoirs of a Secretary at War* (New York: Random House, 2014).
5. Wesley K. Clark, *Waging Modern War: Bosnia, Kosovo, and the Future of Combat* (New York: Public Affairs, 2002).
6. Robert S. McNamara, *In Retrospect: The Tragedy and Lessons of Vietnam* (New York: Vintage Books, 1996).

FOUR: THE BUCK STOPS HERE

1. Colin Powell with Tony Koltz, *It Worked for Me: In Life and Leadership* (New York: Harper, 2012).

2. Since the mid-80s, under the Goldwater-Nichols Act, the president is required by law to submit a National Security Strategy to Congress to help guide their deliberations on funding appropriations.

FIVE: EUROPE FIRST

1. "Strategy," *Department of Defense Dictionary of Military and Associated Terms.* The DOD Dictionary is managed by the Joint Education and Doctrine Division, J-7, Joint Staff. All approved joint definitions, acronyms, and abbreviations are contained in Joint Publication 1-02, *DOD Dictionary of Military and Associated Terms,* November 8, 2010, as amended through March 15, 2014. http://www.dtic.mil /doctrine/new_pubs/jp1_02.pdf.
2. "Testy Relations: Why Barack Obama and Vladimir Putin Will Never Get Along," *The Economist,* February 1, 2014, http://www.economist.com/news/books-and -arts/21595393-why-barack-obama-and-vladimir-putin-will-never-get-along -testy-relations.

SIX: MY FELLOW AMERICANS

1. Frank Aukofer and William P. Lawrence, *America's Team: The Odd Couple: A Report on the Relationship Between the Media and the Military* (Nashville, Tenn.: The Freedom Forum First Amendment Center at Vanderbilt University, 1995).
2. Harold G. Moore and Joseph L. Galloway, *We Were Soldiers Once . . . And Young: Ia Drang—the Battle That Changed the War in Vietnam* (New York: Random House, 1992).

EIGHT: THE NEW BATTLEFIELD

1. H. R. McMaster, *Dereliction of Duty: Lyndon Johnson, Robert McNamara, the Joint Chiefs of Staff, and the Lies That Led to Vietnam* (New York: HarperCollins, 1997).
2. Thomas E. Ricks, *Fiasco: The American Military Adventure in Iraq* (New York: Penguin Press, 2006).
3. Thomas E. Ricks, *The Generals: American Military Command from World War II to Today* (New York: Penguin Press, 2012).

NINE: BODY COUNT

1. William C. Westmoreland, *A Soldier Reports* (Garden City, NY: Doubleday, 1976).

TEN: ENDINGS AND OUTCOMES

1. A Philippine ethnic group; their name is derived from "Moors."
2. Dana Priest, *The Mission: Waging War and Keeping Peace with America's Military* (New York: W. W. Norton, 2003).

INDEX